Soft Power

Soft Power

China's Emerging Strategy in International Politics

Edited by
Mingjiang Li

LEXINGTON BOOKS
A Division of
ROWMAN & LITTLEFIELD PUBLISHERS, INC.
Lanham • Boulder • New York • Toronto • Plymouth, UK

Published by Lexington Books
A division of Rowman & Littlefield Publishers, Inc.
A wholly owned subsidiary of The Rowman & Littlefield Publishing Group, Inc.
4501 Forbes Boulevard, Suite 200, Lanham, Maryland 20706
http://www.lexingtonbooks.com

Estover Road, Plymouth PL6 7PY, United Kingdom

First paperback edition 2011

British Library Cataloguing in Publication Information Available

Library of Congress Cataloging-in-Publication Data

The hardback edition of this book was previously cataloged by the Library of Congress as follows:

Soft power : China's emerging strategy in international politics / edited by Mingjiang Li.
p. cm.
Includes bibliographical references and index.
1. China—Foreign relations—21st century. 2. China—Politics and government—2002- 3. World politics—21st century. 4. Power (Social sciences)—China. I. Li, Mingjiang.
JZ1734.A5S65 2009
327.51—dc22 2009014916

ISBN: 978-0-7391-3377-4 (cloth : alk. paper)
ISBN: 978-0-7391-3378-1 (pbk. : alk. paper)
ISBN: 978-0-7391-3379-8 (electronic)

™ The paper used in this publication meets the minimum requirements of American National Standard for Information Sciences—Permanence of Paper for Printed Library Materials, ANSI/NISO Z39.48-1992.
Printed in the United States of America

Contents

Acknowledgments vii

1 Introduction: Soft Power: Nurture Not Nature 1
Mingjiang Li

PART I: CHINA'S SOFT POWER: THE DEBATES AT HOME AND ABROAD 19

2 Soft Power in Chinese Discourse: Popularity and Prospect 21
Mingjiang Li

3 The Discourse of China's Soft Power and Its Discontents 45
Yongjin Zhang

PART II: SOFT POWER IN CHINA'S RISING STRATEGY 61

4 The New Hard Realities: "Soft Power" and China in Transition 63
Yong Deng

5 The Practice of the Mean: China's Soft Power Cultivation 83
Jianfeng Chen

6 Education: The Intellectual Base of China's Soft Power 103
Xiaohe Cheng

7 China's Soft Power Dilemma: The Beijing Consensus Revisited 125
Zhongying Pang

8 China's Cultural Exports and its Growing Cultural Power in the World 143
Xiaogang Deng and Lening Zhang

PART III: SOFT POWER AND CHINA'S INTERNATIONAL POLITICS 163

9 China's Soft Power in Africa 165
Joshua Kurlantzick

10 China's Warming Relations with South Korea and Australia 185
Zhiqun Zhu

11 China's Soft Power and NeoLiberal Agenda in Southeast Asia 207
Ignatius Wibowo

12 China's Climate Diplomacy and Its Soft Power 225
Gang Chen

PART IV: CONCLUSION 245

13 The Prospect of China's Soft Power: How sustainable? 247
Suisheng Zhao

Index 267

List of Contributors 271

Acknowledgments

This volume came out of a conference entitled "The Rise of China and Its Soft Power" held in October 2007 in Singapore. The whole project would not have been possible without the generous financial support by the S. Rajaratnam School of International Studies (RSIS) at Nanyang Technological University, my home institution. The management team and administrative staff at the school provided invaluable support for the conference. Special thanks to Ambassador Barry Desker, Dean of RSIS, for his enthusiastic support and encouragement. I am indebted to the following colleagues and friends who have kindly shared their views with me and other contributors of the book: Su Hao, Guo Shuyong, Tang Shiping, Wang Zhengxu, Goh Nguen Wah, Hiro Katsumata, Joseph Liow, Liu Jianfei, John Donaldson, Harry Harding, Zhao Litao, Francis Lim, Arthur S. Ding, Wang Shanshan, and Nadège Orban. I am also grateful to the editorial team at Lexington–Rowman & Littlefield for their efficiency and wonderful work in producing the volume. I take responsibility of any flaws of the book.

Mingjiang Li
Singapore, March 2009

Chapter One

Soft Power: Nurture Not Nature

Mingjiang Li

Soft power has become a very popular concept in international affairs. Ever since Joseph Nye coined it in 1990 in his book *Bound to Lead*,[1] the term has frequently appeared in government policy papers, academic discussions, and the popular media. The intensity of the discussion of China's soft power has been particularly notable. The concept of soft power provides a unique perspective not only on China's current foreign and security policy but, more significantly, on the trajectory of China's rise in the long term. In this introductory chapter, I will briefly discuss the ongoing debate about China's soft power, critically review Nye's conceptualization of soft power, propose a "soft use of power" approach, and outline the structure of the book.

WORLDWIDE SPOTLIGHT ON CHINA'S SOFT POWER

In China, soft power has become one of the most frequently used phrases among political leaders, leading academics, and journalists. What is most striking is the importance that Chinese leaders unequivocally assign to soft power in China's international political strategy. Party Chief and President Hu Jintao, for instance, noted at the Central Foreign Affairs Leadership Group meeting on January 4, 2006 that the increase of China's international status and influence depends both on hard power, such as the economy, science and technology, and defense, as well as on soft power, such as culture.[2] Hu again highlighted soft power in his political report to the 17th Party Congress in October 2007, stressing the urgent need to build China's cultural soft power to meet domestic needs and increasing international challenges.[3]

In the international arena, China's soft power has also become a spotlight issue.[4] The 2007 World Economic Forum held in Dalian, a coastal city in

China's Liaoning Province, addressed the issue of China's soft power. The then Australian Labor Party leader Kevin Rudd presented Joshua Kurlantzick's book *Charm Offensive: How China's Soft Power is Transforming the World* to U.S. former President George W. Bush to remind him "why the U.S. has been losing influence."[5] The U.S. Congressional Research Service (CRS) conducted two comprehensive studies on China's soft power influence in Asia, Africa, and Latin America in the first half of 2008, which clearly shows the concerns of U.S. leaders over China's soft power.[6]

The widespread attention on China's soft power notwithstanding, views on Beijing's capability to "charm" the rest of the world and the implications of such a capability have been varied. The Chinese discourse on soft power has mainly focused on its sources and potential utility in Chinese foreign strategy. The mainstream assessment of the state of China's soft power by Chinese analysts is that soft power is still a weak link in China's pursuit for stronger comprehensive national power. It has lagged significantly behind the growth of the country's hard power. Many strategists maintain that China is still not sophisticated in incorporating soft power into its strategic planning.[7] However, other observers believe that the prospect of China's soft power looks more sanguine because China has faired quite well in the international competition for soft power, since it boasts abundant sources of soft power such as culture, traditional philosophy, etc.[8]

The international discourse, perhaps understandably, has largely focused on the strength and potential implications of China's soft power for the international system and for the United States in particular. On the one hand, some international observers seem not to be worried about China's soft power. It is believed that China's capability to influence the rest of the world through soft power is restrained by a lack of agreement on what constitutes Chinese culture and values.[9] Fareed Zakaria, for instance, claims that "China has used soft power only in the sense that it has exercised its power softly. It does this consciously to show that it is not a bully." And he confidently notes that the U.S. can easily out-charm China.[10] A study conducted in early 2008 reveals that China still "ranks well below" the United States in terms of soft power influence in East Asia,[11] where China was expected to have the strongest sway. Others have been more uneasy and anxious about China's soft power. Kurlantzick asserts that China's soft power "is transforming the world."[12] Many also mention that the growth of China's soft power has been achieved at the expense of the United States.[13] Others warn that the U.S.-China competition is "most fierce over soft power issues" that will determine the rules of the game for the global economy as it evolves in the next generation.[14] The Chinese model of development—the so-called "Beijing consensus" in which a liberal market economy exists under an authoritarian political system—and

China's no strings attached assistance programs to many developing nations have been singled out as the most challenging issues for the West.[15]

WHAT IS REALLY SOFT POWER?

Before addressing all these competing and conflicting views on China's soft power, a crucial question that ought to be asked is what soft power really is. To answer this question, a critical review of Nye's conceptualization of soft power is necessary because it is his approach that has guided existing analyses of soft power, including China's. Analyzing the drawbacks but adhering to the core propositions in Nye's theoretical framework, I argue that soft power does not exist in the nature of certain resources of power but rather it has to be nurtured through a soft use of power. It has to be intentionally cultivated through prudent use of all sources of power available in certain social relationships.

According to Nye, soft power is "the ability to get what you want through attraction rather than coercion or payments."[16] It is the ability to get desired outcomes because others want what you want.[17] In an early article, Nye says that the ability to affect what other countries want tends to be associated with intangible power resources such as culture, ideology, and institutions.[18] He reasserts later that the soft power of a country has three primary sources: its culture (in places where it is attractive to others), its political values (when it lives up to them at home and abroad), and its foreign policies (when they are seen as legitimate and having moral authority).[19] Nye mentions that soft power also includes the ability to shape international institutions and agendas,[20] which actually can be seen as part of his reference to legitimate foreign policies. In this definition, the traditional components of power, military, economic, and technological strength would be sources of hard power.

Nye makes a clear-cut distinction between how soft and hard power are used. Hard power is evident in the practices of threat, coercion, sanction, payment, and inducement, whereas soft power is demonstrated in attraction, persuasion, appeal, and co-optation. Soft power is preferable whenever possible: "When you can get others to admire your ideals and to want what you want, you do not have to spend as much on sticks and carrots to move them in your direction."[21]

Despite the prevalent use of the term soft power since the 1990s, the complex relationship between hard power and soft power still needs to be scrutinized and better understood.[22] Nye's approach to soft power does not provide clear-cut answers to some notable puzzles. For instance, where is the exact boundary between hard power and soft power? If Country A provides economic aid to Country B without explicitly or implicitly asking for any favor in return, is that soft power or hard power for Country A? Does soft power include a laundry list of anything other than material factors, such as the morality of the citizens, national image, national cohesion, domestic political stability, leadership, and innovation?[23] How do we know soft power is in play in any given instance? How do we measure soft power? More importantly, how do we know that soft power, as defined by the existing approach, translates into policy outcomes?

In addition to these questions, there are quite a few empirical as well as logical puzzles that cannot be explained by the resource-based approach to soft power. Nye specifies the criteria of soft power—attraction, persuasion, cooptation, and emulation—that few analysts would dispute. But logically it is unclear why culture, ideology, and values have to be sources of soft power. Such a conclusion is obviously based on the assumption that these sources of power are inherently attractive, persuasive, and appealing in nature. But in reality this may not always be the case. On one hand, these sources of soft power do not always produce attraction, persuasion, appeal, and emulation. Culture, ideology, values, and norms also often result in resentment, repulsion, hostility, and even conflict. On the other hand, hard power is not always used for coercion, threat, intimidation, and inducement. Hard power can also produce attraction, appeal, and amity in certain circumstances.

We may think that culture serves only to enhance good relations among states. But if a country pursues an aggressive cultural policy, it may effectively result in fear of cultural hegemony or cultural imperialism. Culture, which is often regarded as the bedrock of soft power, can actually be a catalyst for major conflicts. Critics of cultural soft power have a lot to say about the excessively sanguine view of American culture. As James Traub writes, "Nye argues that, whatever its flaws, our culture projects the core values of 'democracy, personal freedom, upward mobility and openness.' . . . but you could make at least as good a case that our coarse entertainment products have proved even more frighteningly hegemonic than our military."[24] Katzenstein and Keohane argue that American popular culture partially contributes to anti-Americanism in some parts of the world.[25] Another skeptic argues that in reality it is doubtful whether American cultural power increases the world's love for America: "It is still power, and it can still make enemies. Between Vietnam and Iraq, America's cultural presence has expanded into ubiquity, and so has the resentment of America's soft power."[26] If Samuel Huntington's thesis has any truth, "the fundamental source of conflict in this new world will not be primarily ideological or primarily economic. The great divisions among humankind and the dominating source of conflict will be cultural."[27] The Crusades are still vividly remembered by both fundamentalist and ordinary Muslims. In the days following the 9/11 attacks, President Bush's use of the word "crusade" with regard to terrorists created notable apprehensions in the Muslim world.

Excessive or inappropriate use of hard power can lead to the decline of a state's soft power. A good example of this is the war in Iraq. Nye has been relentlessly criticizing the American war in Iraq as weakening U.S. soft power:

> The four-week war in Iraq was a dazzling display of America's hard military power that removed a dangerous dictator, but it did not solve the problem of terrorism. It was also costly in terms of America's soft power to attract others. In the aftermath of the war, polling by the Pew Research Center showed a dramatic decline in the popularity of the United States even in countries like Spain and Italy whose governments had supported the war.[28]

The Iraq war is not an isolated case. There are many historical cases in which the illegitimate use of hard power reduces a state's attractiveness. As Nye notes, "The Soviet Union had considerable soft power in Europe after World War II but squandered it by invading Hungary and Czechoslovakia even when Soviet economic and military power continued to grow."[29] China during Mao's reign effectively turned many countries in Southeast Asia, which had been under China's cultural influence for centuries, into Beijing's adversaries because of China's support for various communist insurgencies in the region. The question, then, is how can military power, the main source of hard power, produce a result that has dramatic negative consequences on soft power?

The traditional sources of hard power can also be sources of soft power if, for instance, they are used for international peacekeeping activities or for humanitarian purposes such as disaster relief. The response to the U.S. rescue efforts in the 2004 Indian Ocean tsunami was very positive. In the wake of the tsunami, a report in the *New York Times* carried this comment:

> Where, in this taxonomy, do we put the images we saw in recent weeks of United States Navy helicopter pilots aboard the aircraft carrier Abraham Lincoln ferrying supplies to victims of the tsunami in the Indonesian province of Aceh? Is that hard power with a human face? Soft power in a flak jacket? Whatever it is, it produces an inherently attractive narrative. . . . And the use of our immense hard power for soft purposes has the additional benefit of humanizing the fierce image inevitably projected by that power: the same military that shocks and awes can also save and heal.[30]

There are several other loopholes in the existing approach that should be noted. It is perplexing why we should juxtapose culture, values, and foreign policy as if the first two are not part of foreign policy. In fact, culture and values are very much part of a country's foreign relations. Political values have played no small role in foreign politics. By placing culture, values, and policy on equal footing, Nye is able to assert that some sources of power are soft in nature and at the same time criticize the wrongdoings of state leaders for damaging soft power because of their foreign policy mistakes.

What is also missing in much of the existing discussion on soft power is the social context that either engenders or hampers the growth of soft power. For instance, many people agree that American liberal democracy, as an ideology, is a strong source of U.S. soft power because it is very appealing to many social-political elites throughout the world. Yet it can also be a damaging factor among those ruling elites who deem democracy a threat to their domestic political power. American movies are popular throughout the world, yet some societies find them repulsive on the grounds that they excessively advocate individual heroism, violence, and sexuality. Another example is the so-called Beijing consensus. Many argue that the Chinese model of development—i.e., political authoritarianism plus economic liberalism—as been so successful that it is appealing to many third-world countries and thus is a source of Chinese soft power. However, the Beijing consensus may be attractive to some countries, but its negative effect on China's relations with most Western powers cannot be ignored. Whether or not these factors constitute hard or soft power, therefore, depends on the specific social context. This renders the categorization of power sources into the dichotomy of hard power and soft power inappropriate.

A few Chinese scholars have realized the shortcomings in Nye's conceptualization. Zhu Feng, for instance, argues that soft power is all about whether the international community accepts a nation's policies and strategic choices and to what extent those choices accord with most nations' interests.[31] Another study by Chinese scholars argues that depending on the context, any source of power can be both hard and soft, and that China's soft power is best illustrated by the "China model": multilateralism, economic diplomacy, and a "good neighbor" policy.[32] These studies suggest that we need to be more careful in treating hard power and soft power separately on the basis of resources.

Nye actually takes note of the interactions between soft and hard power, saying that the two "sometimes reinforce and sometimes interfere with each other."[33] But no convincing explanation has been provided for why the two kinds of power reinforce and interfere with each other. Nye implicitly refers to the distinction between hard power and soft power as largely a difference in how a country uses its power resources. For instance, in *Bound to Lead*, he says: "This aspect of power—that is, getting others to want what you want—might be called indirect or cooptive power behavior. It is in contrast to the active command power behavior of getting others to do what you want."[34] He further writes:

> Power is like love, easy to feel but hard to define. A basic distinction is between behavioral power, the ability to obtain outcomes you want, and resource power, or the possession of the resources that are usually associated with the ability to get the outcomes you want. . . . Behavioral power, in turn, can be divided into hard and soft power. . . . Soft power, on the other hand, is the ability to get desired outcomes because others want what you want, rather than do what you make them do. It is the ability to achieve desired outcomes through attraction rather than coercion.[35]

A "SOFT USE OF POWER" APPROACH

It is the behavioral approach that we believe best captures the essence of soft power. If culture, ideology, and values can be used for coercion, and military and economic strength can be used for attraction and appeal, a better approach to soft power is how the resources of power are used rather than associating sources of power as soft or hard. In essence, soft power lies in the soft use of power to increase a state's attraction, persuasiveness, and appeal. If a nation state (or any other actor) makes good use of its resources of power through various domestic cultural, economic, and political programs to bring well-being to its own nationals, it will produce a lot of admiration from other countries. If a state uses its resources of power in a prudent, cautious, accommodating, and considerate approach in its relations with other states and plays a leading role in providing public goods to international society, it will surely win respect, amity, and positive reciprocity from other states. If a state has the ability to make proposals in multilateral institutions that the rest of the international community regards as legitimate, feasible, and beneficial, it gains soft power.

By seeing soft power with the lens of how a state uses its capability instead of focusing on the resources of power, we can then better understand how culture, values, and institutions can be brought into the discussion of soft power. Culture and values contain social principles or normative guidelines on how power should be exercised. If we broadly define culture as "the beliefs, values, and expressive symbols (including art and literature) that any group (including a whole society) holds in common, and which serve as ways of organizing experience and guiding the behavior of the members of that group,"[36] culture is indeed a potential source of soft power. But we should be aware that not all elements in a culture produce attraction and appeal. Some aspects in a culture may seem natural and appropriate in a certain society or to a certain social group but may be completely unacceptable to people in other societies. For instance, no one would believe that the practice of feet-binding for women in traditional Chinese culture would be a source of China's soft power. Likewise, the traditional Chinese cultural emphasis on social hierarchy generates suspicion among some international observers that China seeks a Sino-centric international order in East Asia. To gain soft power, a state only attempts to display the good part of its culture that the outside world believes is enjoyable or agreeable and hides those elements that may cause uneasiness or misgiving in other states. It is no accident that many Chinese analysts now talk about the Chinese cultural emphasis on "harmony" or "peace" as the sources of China's soft power because these values essentially touch on the core issue of how power should be used.

Likewise, international institutions also become an important area to gauge a state's soft power. International institutions and norms essentially deal with rules and principles of how power should be exercised in international affairs. Non-participation in international institutions would generate suspicion of a state's motives because the international community is not sure how that state is going to use its power. Participating in and abiding by commonly recognized rules and norms reassures the international community about a state's behavior. A state gains soft power if it can propose solutions to certain international problems and the solutions are regarded by other states as legitimate.

In general, to generate soft power, a state has to be considerate of the concerns and interests of other states. Any action or inaction by a state has to be perceived as legitimate or beneficial to other states. As Nye suggests:

> American leadership will be more enduring if we can convince our partners that we are sensitive to their concerns . . . if we squander our soft power through a combination of arrogance and indifference, we will increase our vulnerability, sell our values short, and hasten the erosion of our preeminence.[37]

It would be ideal if a state could use all its resources of power to attract, appeal, persuade, and co-opt all other states. But in reality, this is simply impossible because any state has its own self interests that often diverge from the interests of others. The second best scenario would be to be able to have soft power over a majority of states. If a state could use its resources of power in such a way that the vast majority of states in the international system regard as legitimate, justified, and beneficial for international public good, that state possesses a significant amount of soft power. As Nye says: "When a country's culture includes universal values and its policies promote values and interests that others share, it increases the probability of obtaining its desired outcomes because of the relationships of attraction and duty that it creates."[38]

The "soft use of power" approach also helps us understand why the discussion of soft power breaks the boundary between domestic and international politics. The domestic political values, institutions, and political system are important considerations for a state's soft power because all these things demonstrate how the ruling elite in that state uses power on its own people. Such use of power in the domestic context can resonate in the international arena because people outside see and observe how foreign rulers treat their own nationals and associate that practice with their dealings with the international community.

The most significant achievement of U.S. soft power—i.e., the soft use of power—is that most states in the world today do not regard the U.S. as an empire constantly looking for opportunities to conquer or subjugate the rest of the world. This explains why, in the post-Cold War era, other major powers have not pursued a policy of the traditional realist balance of power policy against U.S. supremacy. In the eyes of some analysts, other major powers are practicing a "soft balancing" strategy against the U.S.[39]

Likewise, the most significant achievement for China on soft power has been the ability to forestall the formation of a containment policy among other major powers, largely because of Beijing's fairly accommodating foreign policy. Despite the popularity of the "China threat" thesis in the 1990s, China has not been perceived as an imminent threat to various international institutions, the security of neighboring states, or the well being of people in the rest of the world. On the contrary, China's international image has improved quite substantially. In fact, a BBC World Service poll of 22 countries found that China is viewed as playing a significantly more positive role in world affairs than even the U.S. What is particularly noteworthy in the survey is the fact that even in neighboring Asian countries that have been historically suspicious of China, the general views are relatively benign.[40]

The growth of China's soft power can hardly be explained by the existing theoretical framework—the global profile of China's culture, ideology, values, and ability to shape international institutions simply has not increased enough. China was able to achieve that growth because of its foreign policy and how it exercised its power in international politics in the past decade.[41] This new pattern of Chinese foreign policy has been described by many scholars.[42] The predominant feature in all these descriptions is a new orientation in China's foreign policy in the past decade, which "is manifested in Beijing's actions in promoting confidence-building measures (CBMs), settling border disputes, practicing relative self-restraint, reassuring neighbours of China's benign intensions, and actively participating in regional economic, political and security dialogues and institutions."[43]

Existing studies that adhere to the resource-based approach to China's soft power tend to be more pessimistic or equivocal because they focus on China's culture and values.[44] Studies that focus on China's foreign policy behaviors tend to see the growth and influence of China's soft power.[45] We believe that the behavior-based approach is more appropriate and better explains why China's soft power has increased over the past decade. The key to understanding China's soft power is to examine how Chinese cultural traditions, political values, and domestic and international imperatives ultimately shape China's choice of strategy and policy in its relations with the rest of the world.

ABOUT THIS BOOK

Consisting of 13 chapters, this book seeks to present an in-depth examination of China's soft power potential, the perspectives among Chinese elites on soft power, China's practice of soft power, and the impacts and implications of China's emerging soft power strategy in world politics. This study is interdisciplinary in nature since the subject of soft power involves domestic politics, culture, history, social relations, and, of course, conventional approaches to international relations.

The following twelve chapters are grouped into four parts. The first part (chapters 1–2) discusses the discourse of soft power at home and abroad. The second part (chapters 3–10) analyzes the potential resources, strengths, and weaknesses of China's soft power from various perspectives, such as foreign policy strategy, political economy, culture, history, and education. The third part (chapters 11–12) contains specific case studies that highlight China's relations with South Korea, Australia, Southeast Asia, and Africa, and Beijing's diplomacy in international climate change negotiations. The concluding chapter summarizes the major points raised in the book and poses additional questions for further study.

In chapter 2, Mingjiang Li attempts to analyze the Chinese discourse on soft power and address the following major issues: How do the Chinese elite conceptualize soft power and understand the state of China's soft power? Why has there been such a strong interest in soft power in China in recent years? What role do the Chinese elite assign to soft power in China's international strategy in the twenty-first century? To answer these questions, the author thoroughly examines various official documents, prominent scholarly writings, and the most influential national-level media reports and analyses. This study reveals that Chinese views on soft power widely vary, with the mainstream believing that soft power is still a weak link in China's strategic planning but nevertheless should be an important component in China's future. In fact, both Chinese decision-makers and intellectuals have been searching for a soft power strategy to upgrade China's international status and deal with various issues in international politics. At the moment, soft power is partially perceived as a tool for defensive purposes in China's international politics and as a means to achieve various domestic goals. The chapter concludes that a grand Chinese soft power strategy is still in its emerging phase.

The next chapter, by Yongjin Zhang, explores the external discourse on China's soft power. The author notes that the recent hype about China's soft power has evoked excitement, fascination, fear, apprehension, and anxiety among scholarly communities and policy establishments alike. It is claimed that China has built up its soft power 'at the expense of the United States' and to have mounted a 'charm offensive' globally to transform the world in its own image. Is there any substance behind such claims? What is China's soft power? In which way is China accumulating its soft power? Why should there be such a rage about China's soft power at this particular time? In this chapter, Zhang addresses these questions through an analytical examination of what he regards as the recent 'external discourse' of China's soft power in English in an attempt to unravel major puzzles about China's growing power. While maintaining that it is a genuine puzzle how a recent pariah state in international society advocating and practicing a political system contrary to the prevailing liberal democratic values could have achieved such a power status in so short a period of time and the implications of this phenomenon for the emerging global order are significant, he also makes two main arguments. First, the hype about China's soft power is fallacious and is mired in conceptual misconstruction; and second the current discourse prevents us from engaging in a dispassionate assessment of China's changing global diplomacy, hence the search for a new global order.

Part II of the book provides a comprehensive examination of China's soft power potential as well as its efforts to increase its soft power from various perspectives. Chapter 4 by Yong Deng investigates how soft power is treated in the rhetoric and practice of China's international strategy in the post-Cold War era. The author contends that heavily influenced by Joseph Nye's definition, most of the works, even when looking at China, invariably stress the ability to generate genuine affection, strong identification, and willing followership from others. He argues that this approach is misguided. First and foremost, the United States is the established (if contested) hegemon in world politics, whereas post-Tiananmen China must struggle for international recognition in a world defined by that fundamental reality. Such status asymmetry means that the sources, means, and objectives of their soft power differ. Thus, the author argues, China's soft power is evident in its ability to simultaneously assure and influence others that its goal is to achieve great power status without relying on traditional power politics or war.

Viewed in this way, soft power becomes integral to China's strategy to elevate itself on the world stage. But in the first decade of the post-Cold War era, there was a striking gap between China's rhetorical silence and its practices of soft power. Indeed, in the 1990s, the Chinese elite largely viewed soft power as the privilege of the strong—namely, the West—while at the same time they considered their nation a victim of a subtle form of power politics. With greater confidence at the outset of the new century, however, soft power has become increasingly an explicit choice in China's foreign policy. The more deliberate current pursuit has manifested itself in promoting its traditional and cultural appeal, economic ties, partnership diplomacy, and multilateralism. Domestic problems of governance, stability, and regime security have threatened China's soft power. Nevertheless, soft power will likely continue to drive China's aspirations abroad. In chapter 5, Jianfeng Chen explores China's soft power from the Chinese cultural Doctrine of the Mean, essentially a traditional Chinese philosophy about how to use power and influence. The Mean is one of the core values in Chinese culture. The nature of the Mean is one of appropriately balanced relationships between man and man, man and society, man and nature and equilibrium relations among nations. Actualizing the Mean refers to being neutral and harmonizing black and white, Yin (feminine or negative principle in nature) and Yang (masculine or positive principle in nature), right and left, good and bad, them and us. According to the Doctrine of the Mean, the ideal is when all parties arrive at an equilibrium acceptable to all. In the context of international relations, the Mean refers to a world that embraces a unity of opposites rather than absolute peace or absolute chaos. Confucianism insists on treating other nations with kindness and morality and believes that tenderness is the antidote to cruelty. Equilibrated relations, therefore, can be maintained among nations by trading interests. The chapter concludes that China, in practice, should strive for the "middle way" and orientate itself as a defensive participant who aims not at changing the status quo or opposing the hegemonic power of the system, but rather at defensively managing both internal and external challenges and avoiding costly competition. Such an approach will sustain its modernization and the stability of the international system. If China genuinely practices the Mean, the author argues, it will wield much soft power and avoid the historical experience that new rising powers are typically born in bloodshed.

In the next chapter, Xiaohe Cheng emphasizes education and international educational exchange programs in cultivating China's soft power. He first gives a comprehensive review of the achievements of Chinese education. After a decades-long concerted effort, China has grabbed the title of world's number one producer of college graduates and has become a major learning destination for international students. The brain drain that China has chronically experienced has been steadily mitigated due to the increased return of Chinese graduates from abroad. The Chinese government is not satisfied with having the largest educational enterprise in the world. As it redresses the fallout of the "educational great leap forward," it sets about to transform China into the world's major educational powerhouse on two fronts: to continue to push dozens of Chinese universities into the ranks of the world's best and to carry a new mission to project China's soft power overseas by promoting Confucius Institutes across the world. However, the author notes several challenges in this regard. First, to generate soft power is not easy for China's higher education system: China is still attempting to catch up to Western countries. Its Western counterparts will not give up their superior position and will intensify their efforts to strengthen their competitiveness. The quality issue also continues to haunt Chinese universities. Finally, the lack of understanding of the Confucius Institutes among other countries' people acts against China's "going abroad" strategy. All of these challenges from within and without will make the path of China's transformation a long and tortuous one.

In chapter 7, Zhongying Pang addresses the controversial issue of the Chinese model of development, also known as the "Beijing consensus." Pang begins by asking this question: Is China's dazzling development becoming the nation's soft power? Rapid economic development driven by market reform has been the dominant theme of China in the past three decades. The country has acted as a key participant and facilitator in globalization. Logically, China's economic "success" is a sign or source of Chinese national strength and its soft power. Pang concedes that the Chinese experience has indeed inspired much analysis in the rest of the world of the possibility of applying some aspects of the Chinese path of modernization to under-developed countries. Many political leaders in the developing world are also looking at the Chinese experience with admiration. However, Pang points out that China's development has some serious signs of weakness too. Its current lure to the world may not be sustained if China fails to meet the challenges it faces. In the long run, the Chinese model may not be a source for Beijing's soft power as China itself evolves and the political economies of other developing countries undergo transformations that may be very different from the Chinese model. However, as China explores its new path toward "scientific development," it is likely to attract external interest in its model.

In the next chapter, Xiaogang Deng and Lening Zhang investigate Chinese cultural influence in the world. The authors contend that little attention has been paid to China's sustained efforts to exercise its cultural power. Culture is a very important potential source of soft power as nation states constantly attempt to display the good aspects of their cultures to build a better image. However, the current discussion of the cultural dimension of China's soft power has predominantly focused on the Confucius Institute and the growing popularity of learning the Chinese language. Few studies discuss China's overall efforts to become a major world cultural power. The common perception is that China has very limited power in this regard. Deng and Zhang argue that China's goal is more than becoming simply an economic superpower. As the significance of Chinese economic power continues to grow, China also wants to become a major world cultural power. Using various sources of data, the authors assess whether China is becoming a major world power in cultural production by examining its cultural trade and the promotion of its media in the world. They conclude that China may indeed have more cultural power than people ordinarily think.

Part III of the volume takes a detailed look at examples of China's practice of soft power. The approach is comprehensive and focuses on how China uses its power resources to produce attraction and persuasion in other parts of the world. Joshua Kurlantzick in chapter 9 examines China's soft power influence in Africa. He observes that in a relatively short period of time, China has developed close diplomatic and economic relations with a wide range of African nations. In fact, China's public image in Africa is currently far more positive than on any other continent. In part, this African "charm offensive" is due to Chinese soft power—in particular, training programs for African elites, effective diplomacy, and the appeal of China's model of development, which has sparked more interest in Africa than anywhere else. Kurlantzick argues that since China has less hard power in Africa than in Asia, its soft power on the continent is even more critical. Indeed, it has used its soft power to help produce favorable policy outcomes, including substantial new oil and gas deals. However, in the long term, China will need to broaden its appeal in Africa to include the "African street" if its soft power is to prove long lasting and effective.

In the next chapter, Zhiqun Zhu examines how China has been expanding its influence in the Republic of Korea (South Korea) and Australia since the mid-1990s. The author finds that relative to the United States, the Republic of Korea and Australia are not so concerned about China's rise. Relations between China and these two countries have been developing rapidly in the past decade or so. It is therefore interesting to explore why South Korea and Australia hold a more benign view of China than the United States does. The author argues that China's soft power diplomacy has become more sophisticated and comprehensive in recent years. Its strategies now include engaging in high-level visits, promoting economic interdependence, highlighting expected benefits from China's prosperity, expanding cultural and social exchanges, and presenting a peaceful and non-threatening new image around the world. The PRC's warming relations with South Korea and Australia must be understood in the context of China's growing power and its more sophisticated new diplomacy. According to Zhu, although there are still some "hard security" factors in China's relations with both South Korea and Australia, such as the North Korea issue, China's heavy-handed approach to history and Australia's lingering mistrust, China's soft power diplomacy has been largely successful in strengthening China's relations with both South Korea and Australia.

China's growing influence in Southeast Asia has been a frequently discussed issue in the past few years. Ignatius Wibowo, in chapter 11, pays close attention to this matter. He contends that China's influence in Southeast Asia (SEA) has long been clear, even in the period of Cold War, when China supported revolutionary movements in the region. After Mao Zedong's death in 1976 and as a consequence to the reform of 1978, China pursued a new and different strategy of development, and accordingly, foreign policy. Still embedded in anti-communist ideology, countries in Southeast Asia initially looked to China with suspicion, especially its growing economic, political, and military power. Wibowo claims that the Asian financial crisis in 1997 changed this perspective forever: afterwards, it was not only clear that China made a financial contribution to multiple countries, but also that China managed to come out of the crisis relatively unscathed. The disillusion with the effects of neo-liberal capitalism and democracy demanded by the International Monetary Fund (IMF) and World Bank, countries in SEA looks to China with admiration and respect, to the extent that they take China as model of development that combines free markets and illiberal polity. Except in Indonesia and the Philippines, the "Beijing Consensus" is gaining ground in SEA, and has become the prime source of China's soft power in the region. This influence has actually been increasing due to China's accommodating posture in regional affairs and the cultural products flowing, since 2000, from China to SEA.

As the latest scientific findings describe the connection between climate change and human activity with more accuracy, China, one of the world's largest emitters of greenhouse gases, is now under closer international scrutiny. The chapter by Gang Chen addresses China's soft power in international institutions by examining the case of its participation in international negotiations on climate change. The author argues that active participation in these negotiations and institutions has been an important part of China's diplomatic activities since early 1990s, which has effectively promoted China's international image and elevated its soft power. In contrast to the U.S. withdrawal from the Kyoto Protocol, China's previous active participation in international agreements on global warming has proved to be a diplomatic success, winning applause from both developing and developed countries. Facing more international and domestic pressure in post-Kyoto climate talks, China understands its image will be greatly damaged if it still refuses to accept any mandatory emission cuts and its own emissions continue to grow rapidly. China is therefore in a dilemma. On the one hand, it frets about soft power damage due to its environmental problems, but hopes to utilize international cooperation to solve them. On the other hand, it fears that emission abatement obligations may block its fast economic growth and hence ruin its hard power.

In the concluding chapter, Suisheng Zhao sums up the major arguments and revelations of this endeavor. He also raises several questions that future analysts of China's soft power may consider. The author looks at the long-term picture of China's soft power by examining China's worldviews. He argues that although China has moved quickly and made self-conscious efforts to cultivate soft power in order to promote its interests and expand its influence as a rising power, its approach to exercising soft power is flawed. This is largely because the pragmatic political values behind China's rapid economic growth are attractive mostly to authoritarian elites and China's world order is hardly compatible with evolving contemporary international norms. In spite of its initial success, China's current approach to soft power lacks contemporary moral appeals and is therefore hardly sustainable in the competition with the U.S. to inspire the vision of building a free and prosperous world.

NOTES

1. Joseph S. Nye, Jr., *Bound to Lead: The Changing Nature of American Power* (New York: Basic Books, Inc., 1990).

2. Ma Lisi, "Guanyu wo guo jiaqiang ruan shili jianshe de chubu sikao" [Preliminary thoughts on accelerating China's soft power building], *Dang de wenxian* [Literature of the Chinese Communist Party] 5 (2007): 35–38.

3. Hu Jintao, *Report to the 17th Party Congress*, October 15, 2007.

4. For instance, Joshua Kurlantzick, *Charm Offensive: How China's Soft Power is Transforming the World* (New Haven: Yale University Press, 2007); Bates Gill and Yanzhong Huang, "Sources and Limits of Chinese 'Soft Power'," *Survival* 48 no.2 (Summer 2006): 17–36; Gideon Rachman, "The Hard Evidence that China's Soft Power Policy is Working," *Financial Times*, February 20, 2007.

5. Peter Hartcher, "Rudd Offers a Cheeky Lesson in Soft Power," *Sydney Morning Herald*, September 7, 2007.

6. Congressional Research Service, "China's 'Soft Power' in Southeast Asia," January 2008; and "China's Foreign Policy and 'Soft Power' in South America, Asia, and Africa," April 2008.

7. Men Honghua, "Zhongguo ruan shili pinggu baogao" [Assessment and report on China's soft power], *Guoji guancha* [International Observations], part one, issue 2, (2007): 15–26; and part two, issue 3, (2007): 37–46.

8. Jiang Haiyan, "Hongyang zhonghua minzu de youxiu wenhua yu zengqiang wo guo de ruan shili" [Promoting the outstanding culture of the Chinese nation and strengthening China's soft power], *Journal of the Party School of the Central Committee of the CCP,* vol. 11, no. 1 (2007): 107–112.

9. Clarissa Oon, "The Art of Education," *Straits Times*, November 12, 2006.

10. Fareed Zakaria, "The U.S. Can Out-Charm China," *Newsweek*, December 12, 2005.

11. Christopher B. Whitney and David Shambaugh, "Soft Power in Asia: Results of a 2008 Multinational Survey of Public Opinion," The Chicago Council on Global Affairs in partnership with East Asian Institute, 2008.

12. Joshua Kurlantzick, *Charm Offensive: How China's Soft Power is Transforming the World* (New Haven: Yale University Press, 2007).

13. Michael Elliott, "China Takes on the World," *Time*, January 11, 2007; Joshua Kurlantzick, "China's Charm: Implications of Chinese Soft Power," *Policy Brief* 47 (June 2006), Carnegie Endowment for International Peace.

14. Joel Rosenthal, "China Goes Global: Implications for the United States," *The National Interest*, September/October 2006.

15. Robert Kagan, "League of Dictators?" *Washington Post*, April 30, 2006.

16. Joseph S. Nye, *Soft Power: The Means to Success in World Politics* (Cambridge, MA: Perseus Books Group, 2004), x.

17. Robert O. Keohane and Joseph S. Nye, "Power and Interdependence in the Information Age," *Foreign Affairs* 77, no. 5 (1998): 86.

18. Joseph S. Nye, "Soft Power," *Foreign Policy* 80 (Fall 1990): 153–71.

19. Nye, *Soft Power: The Means to Success in World Politics,* 11.

20. Joseph S. Nye, *Bound to Lead: The Changing Nature of American Power* (New York: Basic Books, Inc., 1990); Joseph S. Nye, "Soft Power," *Foreign Policy*, 1990.

21. Joseph S. Nye, *Soft Power: The Means to Success in World Politics,* x–xi.

22. Zhang Xiaoming, "Yue se fu nai de 'ruan quanli' sixiang fenxi" [An analysis of Joseph Nye's soft power concept], *Meiguo Yanjiu* [American Studies]1 (2005):20–36.

23. Li Jie, "Tisheng ruan shili dui shixian wo guo heping jueqi zhanlue de zuoyong" [The role of increasing soft power for the realization of China's peaceful rise], *Taipingyang xue bao* [Journal of Pacific Studies] 12 (2005): 64-71.

24. James Traub, "The New Hard-Soft Power," *New York Times*, January 30, 2005.

25. Peter J. Katzenstein and Robert O. Keohane, "Anti-Americanisms: Biases as Diverse as the Country Itself," *Policy Review* 139 (October & November 2006).

26. Josef Joffe, "The Perils of Soft Power," *New York Times*, May 14, 2006.

27. Samuel Huntington, "The Clash of Civilizations," *Foreign Affairs* 72 no.3 (Summer 1993): 22–28.

28. Joseph S. Nye, "Hard Power, Soft Power, and 'The War on Terrorism'," in David Held and Mathias Koenig-Archibugi, eds., *American Power in the Twenty-First Century* (Cambridge, UK: Polity Press, 2004).

29. Joseph S. Nye, "Hard Power, Soft power," *Boston Globe*, August 6, 1999.

30. James Traub, "The New Hard-Soft Power," *New York Times*, January 30, 2005.

31. Zhu Feng, "Zhongguo ying duo cezhong 'ruan shili' jueqi" [China should give priority to raising soft power], *Huanqiu shibao* [Global Times], April 30, 2007.

32. Zheng Yongnian and Zhang Chi, "Guoji zhengzhi zhong de ruan liliang yiji dui zhongguo ruan liliang de guancha" [Soft power in international politics and an observation of China's soft power], *Shijie jingji yu zhengzhi* [World Economics and Politics] 7 (2007): 6–12.

33. Nye, *Soft Power: The Means to Success in World Politics,* 25.

34. Nye, "*Bound to Lead,*" 31.

35. Joseph S. Nye, "Soft Sells—and Wins," *The Straits Times*, January 10, 1999.

36. Neil J. Smelser, *Sociology* (5th ed.) (City, New Jersey: Prentice-Hall, 1995), 20.

37. Joseph S. Nye Jr, *The Paradox of American Power: Why the World's Only Superpower Can't Go It Alone* (New York: Oxford University Press, 2002), xii, xvi.

38. Nye, *Soft Power: The Means to Success in World Politics*, 11.

39. T.V. Paul, "Soft Balancing in the Age of U.S. Primacy," *International Security* 30, no. 1 (Summer 2005): 46–71.

40. British Broadcasting Service, "22-Nation Poll Shows China Viewed Positively by Most Countries Including Its Asian Neighbours" Program on International Policy Attitudes, 2005, www.globescan.com/news_archives/bbcpoll3.html. (accessed September 2, 2008).

41. Joshua Kurlantzick, for instance, argues that China has become a potential rival to American soft power in Asia largely because of Beijing's public diplomacy, development assistance, participation in multilateral institutions, and pursuit of mutual interests. See Joshua Kurlantzick, "The Decline of American Soft Power," *Current History*, (December 2005).

42. David Shambaugh, "China Engages Asia: Reshaping the Regional Order," *International Security* 29, no. 3 (Winter 2004/2005); Avery Goldstein, "The Diplomatic Face of China's Grand Strategy: A Rising Power's Emerging Choice," *The China Quarterly* 168 (2001): 835–64; Evan Medeiros and M. Taylor Fravel, "China's New Dipomacy," *Foreign Affairs* 82, no. 6 (November/ December 2003); Rosemary Foot, "China's Regional Activism: Leadership, Leverage, and Protection," *Global Change, Peace & Security* 17, no. 2 (June 2005).

43. Li Mingjiang, "China's Proactive Engagement in Asia: Economics, Politics and Interactions," *RSIS Working Paper*, no. 134, (July 2007).

44. Bates Gill and Yanzhong Huang, "Chinese 'Soft Power'," 17–36.; Yanzhong Huang and Sheng Ding, "Dragon's Underbelly: An Analysis of China's Soft Power," *East Asia* 23, no.4 (Winter 2006): 22–44.

45. Joshua Kurlantzick, "China's Charm: Implications of Chinese Soft Power," *Policy Brief* 47 (June 2006), Carnegie Endowment for International Peace, and two Congressional Research Service reports on China's soft power published in January and April, 2008, respectively.

Part I

CHINA'S SOFT POWER: THE DEBATES AT HOME AND ABROAD

Chapter Two

Soft Power in Chinese Discourse: Popularity and Prospect

Mingjiang Li

Observers of Chinese politics and international relations could hardly have failed to notice the upsurge of references to the term "soft power" in China in recent years. The popularity of this concept among Chinese political leaders, scholars, journalists and pundits has been striking. Its prevalence in the Chinese media is by no means an insignificant issue. International political leaders and pundits have paid a lot of attention to the growth and practice of China's soft power and have unequivocally expressed their concerns over its implications. Although it is arguably one of the most important aspects of China's foreign strategy that has emerged in the new century, it is insufficiently understood by the outside world. For these reasons, a thorough examination of the term is warranted.

A good starting point for understanding the importance of soft power in China's international politics is how the concept is discussed among the Chinese elite. How do they understand and interpret the meaning of soft power? Why is there such a strong and growing interest in soft power in China? What role do the Chinese elite assign to soft power in China's international strategy in the new century, especially in the context of China's rise? This chapter will neither delve into the theoretical debate of what constitutes soft power nor focus on China's actual practice of soft power. The purpose here is simply to examine the overall understanding of soft power among Chinese intellectuals and the implications of this understanding for China's international strategy.

Methodologically, a conscious effort has been made in this chapter to focus on official documents endorsed by the top Chinese leadership, articles in prominent Chinese journals and the most influential national-level media

---

A largely similar version of this chapter appeared in the *Chinese Journal of International Politics*, vol. 2, 2008.

reports and analyses. The first part briefly discusses the popularity of soft power in China. The second section analyses Chinese views on soft power and the mainstream assessment of the state of China's soft power. The next section examines the motivations behind China's strong interest in soft power. The fourth part addresses major approaches that have been proposed in China to increase Chinese soft power. The concluding section sums up the main features of Chinese discourse about soft power and analyses its potential implications for China's international strategy.

Several conclusions emerge from this study. First, decision-makers and opinion leaders in China have given an enormous amount of attention to the fate of their nation's soft power. Second, Chinese discourse largely conforms to Joseph S. Nye's conceptual framework but is not strictly limited to the scope of that conceptualization. Third, unlike Nye's primary focus on the efficacy of soft power in achieving foreign policy goals, Chinese discourse frequently refers to a domestic context and evinces a mission for domestic purposes. Fourth, soft power, as expounded by Chinese analysts, is still a weak link in China's pursuit of comprehensive national power and largely perceived as a tool for defensive purposes, including cultivating a better image of China to the outside world, correcting foreign misperceptions of China, and fending off Western cultural and political inroads in China. On the basis of these analyses, I argue that a grand Chinese soft power strategy is still in its embryonic phase, despite the painstaking efforts by Chinese strategists to devise various proposals. The lack of assertiveness in China's soft power discourse reflects the fact that China has few political values to offer to a world still dominated by Western philosophies and reveals the reality that China itself is still undergoing a profound social, economic and political transition.

SOFT POWER: SURGING POPULARITY IN CHINA

Flipping through official Chinese government pronouncements, academic journals and popular newspapers, one frequently comes across the term "soft power". This is a clear indication that soft power has become a noticeable part of official and popular discourse on foreign policy and international politics.

Soft power is no longer an alien concept for top Chinese political leaders. The political report to the 16th Chinese Communist Party (CCP) Congress in 2002, for instance, points out that, "in today's world, culture intertwines with economics and politics, demonstrating a more prominent position and role in the competition for comprehensive national power."[1] The 13th collective study session of the Politburo of the 16th CCP Central Committee, which was held on May 28, 2004, focused on how to develop China's philosophy and social sciences. This study session took place two months after the CCP

Center publicized a document titled "Suggestions of the CCP Center on Further Developing and Boosting Philosophy and Social Sciences". Cheng Enfu, a professor at the Shanghai University of Finance and Economics, and also one of the two scholars who gave lectures at the session, commented that the study session clearly shows the importance that Chinese leaders attach to soft power.[2] Media commentary echoes Cheng's assessment, saying that the study session signifies the leadership's will to accelerate the growth of China's soft power from a strategic height.[3]

Party chief and President Hu Jintao made it clear at the Central Foreign Affairs Leadership Group meeting on January 4, 2006: "The increase in our nation's international status and influence will have to be demonstrated in hard power such as the economy, science and technology, and defence, as well as in soft power such as culture."[4] Other leaders have also frequently referred to soft power. At the fifth session of the Chinese People's Political Consultative Conference (CPPCC) Tenth National Committee in March 2007, Jia Qinglin, CPPCC Chairman and a member of the CCP Politburo Standing Committee, delivered a speech in which he elaborated on China's soft power. In July 2007, the CPPCC National Committee held a special session on "cultural construction as the main approach for national soft power building." At the meeting, Jia urged Chinese officials to "deeply understand the importance of national soft power with cultural construction as the main task" in order to both meet domestic demands and enhance China's competitiveness in the international arena.[5]

President Hu, at the Eighth National Congress of the China Federation of Literary and Art Circles, instructed that more attention be given to cultural development and upgrading of China's soft power, which, he said, are major practical issues.[6] Hu again highlighted soft power in his political report to the 17th Party Congress in October 2007, stressing the urgency of strenuously building China's cultural soft power to meet domestic needs and increasing international competition. Hu's call aroused a new round of interest in soft power throughout China. Local governments and various cultural communities held discussion sessions on China's cultural soft power. Soft power and culture became the headlines in many newspapers in the aftermath of the 17th Congress. A *People's Daily* commentary, for instance, proclaimed that China has to substantially increase its soft power in order to play an active role in international competition.[7]

Various Chinese organizations and research institutes have followed up with and contributed to the growing popularity of soft power by organizing conferences on the topic. The China Foreign Languages Bureau hosted a forum on "trans-cultural communications and soft power building" in Beijing in August 2006. In early 2007, the International Public Relations Research Center at Fudan University sponsored a forum among government officials and leading scholars on "national soft power construction and the development of China's public relations." The China Institute on Contemporary International Relations carried out a special study on soft power[8]. The Institute of Strategic Studies of the Central Party School also conducted a comprehensive study on soft power.[9]

According to one Chinese strategist, soft power and its relevance to China has become an important topic of discussion in Chinese strategic circles.[10] This observation is indeed substantiated by the number of papers that have appeared in Chinese journals and newspapers. The China National Knowledge Infrastructure (CNKI) database, currently the largest and most comprehensive database of Chinese journals and periodicals, can be used to run a simple search. Searching the three sections of CNKI's journals and periodicals—liberal arts/history/philosophy, politics/military affairs/law, and education/comprehensive social sciences—resulted in 485 papers with the term "soft power" in their titles from 1994 to 2007.[11] Using the same search method for the period 1994 to 2000, the system showed a record of 11 articles, whereas from 2001 to 2004, the total number was 58. From 2005 to 2007, there were 416 such articles. In 2006, the number of papers was 104 and in 2007, this number rose to 237. Expanding the search to the full text and not just the title resulted in 1,211 articles in the same three sections of the database from 1994 to 2007. From 1994 to 2000, there were 57; from 2001 to 2004, there were 212; from 2005 to 2007, there were 942 pieces. In 2006, there were 273 papers, and in 2007, the number was 518. Using the Chinese newspaper section of the CNKI, the search results shows a total of 509 articles with the term "soft power" as part of the titles from 2000 to 2008. Not all of these papers or newspaper articles are specifically relevant to China's foreign policy or international relations, but a vast majority analyse soft power in relation to China's international politics. The fact that the term has become so popular in many fields in China is an indication of the extent of interest in soft power among the Chinese interlocutors.

CHINESE DISCOURSE: SCOPE AND ASSESSMENT

In the decade since Nye coined the term soft power, Chinese writings almost exclusively focused on introducing and evaluating the concept itself. But in recent years, Chinese writings on this subject have become conspicuously comprehensive and sophisticated, covering a wide range of topics: critical reviews of Nye's conceptualization, soft power in China's peaceful rise and development, as well as Chinese choices and strategies in cultivating and using soft power in international politics.[12]

Chinese writers who write on soft power frequently make references to the Great Wall, the Peking Opera, pandas, martial arts, sports star Yao Ming and movie star Zhang Zhiyi. However, the mainstream Chinese understanding of soft power has largely followed the conceptual framework proposed by Nye. The vast majority of Chinese analysts are quite faithful to Nye's definition of soft power, that is, "the ability to get what you want through attraction rather than coercion or payments."[13] They have also largely followed the parameters identified by Nye: culture, political values and foreign policy.[14] Yet the discussion in China is wider in scope and sometimes emphasizes areas that Nye paid little attention to.

China's Soft Power Sources: Culture, Development and Foreign Policy

According to Chinese analysts, the first Chinese article on soft power was written by Wang Huning, who is now a member of the CCP Central Committee Secretariat.[15] In that article, published in 1993, Wang argues that culture is the main source of a state's soft power. Chinese analysts have since followed this central thesis. This is discernable in various speeches by Chinese leaders and numerous scholarly writings.[16] Traditional Chinese culture, in particular, is singled out as the most valuable source of Chinese soft power on the premise that it boasts an uninterrupted long history, a wide range of traditions, symbols and textual records. Many Chinese writings also point out the good values in traditional Chinese culture found in Confucianism, Taoism, Buddhism and other classical schools of thought, for instance, winning respect through virtues (*yi de fu ren*), benevolent governance (*wang dao*), peace and harmony (*he*), and harmony without suppressing differences (*he er bu tong*).

They argue that the traditional Chinese cultural values with "harmony" at the core are the basis of Chinese cultural appeal in an era of cultural diversification and globalization. In modern history, Western civilization, epitomized by science, individualism and materialism, pushed for industrialization but at the same time caused a lot of problems, including environmental degradation, confusion in social ethics, and international and regional conflicts. Traditional Chinese culture, which stresses "giving priority to human beings" (*yi ren wei ben*) and "harmony between nature and humankind" (*tian ren he yi*), may provide alternative approaches in addressing these problems, thus putting Chinese culture in a more advantageous position in the post-industrialization, information era.[17]

It is also argued that history nicely demonstrates the advantages of China's cultural soft power. The Chinese nation has a long history compared to other nations, of which cultural glory was a prominent feature. More importantly, its culture has influenced East Asia for millennia. The socio-economic success of East Asian "dragons" and, now, the success story of China's own economy are evidence of Chinese cultural merits. While China and East Asia are in ascendancy, the West has started a cultural reflection and readjustment, which provides China with a good opportunity to expand its cultural influence.[18]

The discussion of cultural soft power, however, often easily turns to notable Chinese discontent about losing competitiveness in the international trade of cultural products. According to this utilitarian view, the Chinese cultural sector has lagged far behind its Western counterparts in competing for business in the world. This school of thought cares about China's soft power but is mainly concerned about being marginalized by Western cultural business juggernauts, particularly the predominant position of the U.S. in the international trade of cultural products, including movies, popular music, television programs, fast food and fashion.[19] In addition to this minor diversion, there are also dissenting views on Chinese culture as the main source of China's soft power. Echoing the intellectual tradition of criticizing the many negative aspects in traditional culture ever since the May Fourth Movement, some Chinese scholars maintain that there is very little in traditional Chinese culture that China could offer to the outside world because there are too many "backward" aspects to it. One scholar notes that Chinese culture is actually more diverse now, and includes the Han Chinese culture, the cultures of other ethnic minorities, folk culture, Confucianism, Buddhism, Taoism and other folk beliefs. In modern times, traditional Chinese culture has also been infiltrated by Western culture. Moreover, traditional Chinese culture has been reshaped by the revolutionary experience of the CCP to a significant extent. Putting too high a premium on Chinese culture in the pursuit of soft power may be misleading, according to some writers.[20]

Chinese analysts occasionally mention the Chinese model of development as a source for the nation's soft power. A study conducted by a scholar at the Central Party School concludes that China's gradualist approach to reform and opening up has provided a new alternative to the classic modernization theory and "Washington Consensus" for under-developed countries.[21] The Chinese experience of development is occasionally brought up at various forums, indicating that it is indeed part of the consideration for China's soft power among the Chinese elite.[22] However, there is no consensus among analysts about the efficacy of the so-called "Beijing Consensus" in bringing soft power to their nation, as further discussion in this chapter will reveal.

A number of Chinese analysts also follow Nye's emphasis on foreign policy and institutions. Su Changhe argues that soft power is evident in a state's ability in international institution building, agenda setting, mobilization of coalitions and ability to fulfil commitments.[23] Another study suggests that China's soft power includes three aspects: cultural diplomacy, multilateral diplomacy and overseas assistance programs.[24] These analysts tend to emphasize the flexibility in Chinese foreign policy as a source of Chinese soft power.

Moving Beyond Nye's Conceptualization

Deviating from Nye's core positions, many Chinese analysts attach much importance to the mass media, arguing that capability and effectiveness in mass communications are also an important part of a state's soft power. Chinese analysts are impressed by the dominant role of the Western media. According to Chinese statistics: "Currently, the major four Western news agencies, Associated Press, United Press International, Reuters and Agence France-Presse, produce four-fifths of the total news stories in the world every day. The fifty top Western trans-national media corporations hold ninety percent of the world communication market. The United States alone controls seventy-five percent of TV programs in the world. In many developing nations, sixty to eighty percent of the content in TV programs comes from the U.S. Over half of the total show time in the world's theatres is taken by American movies, which account for only 6.7 percent of the total global movie production." Western dominance in media and mass communications has resulted in their "cultural hegemony" or "media imperialism."[25]

There are several studies that challenge or are critical of Nye's conceptualization.[26] One scholar, for instance, argues that the sources of soft power come from three dimensions: institutional power, identifying power and assimilating power. Institutional power refers to a state's ability to propose or build new international institutions or arrangements. Identifying power refers to a state's ability to influence other states through the latter's recognition of its leadership role. Finally, assimilating power refers to the attraction of a state's cultural values, ideology and social system.[27] Yan Xuetong believes that soft power lies in political power that is exclusively found in political institutions, norms and credibility, rather than in culture.[28] Zhu Feng argues that soft power has little to do with sources of power but is all about whether the international community accepts a nation's policies and strategic choices, as well as to what extent those choices accord with most nations' interests.[29]

Concerning the relation between hard power and soft power, some Chinese analysts seem to be more willing than Nye to emphasize the inseparability of hard power and soft power. They argue, for example: "Soft power and hard power are mutually complementary to each other. Soft power can facilitate the growth of hard power; whereas hard power can demonstrate and support the increase of soft power."[30] Another study is critical of Nye's dichotomy of hard power and soft power, arguing that, depending on the context, any source of power can be both hard and soft, and that China's soft power is best illustrated in the "China model," multilateralism, economic diplomacy and good-neighborly policy.[31] Another scholar identifies five key elements for soft power: culture, values, development model, international institutions and international image.[32] In addition to these different views, there seems to be a tendency among some Chinese scholars to focus on anything that would be helpful in boosting China's international influence, ranging from traditional Chinese medicine[33] to the story of China's economic success[34] to sports culture[35] to educational exchange programs.[36]

Another major difference with Nye's analysis is the notable domestic context that numerous Chinese analysts frequently refer to, e.g., national cohesion, domestic political institution building, social justice, social morality and educational quality. Yu Keping, a well-known political analyst in China, argues that education, the psychological and physical condition of the people, technological advancement, superiority of national culture, human resources and strategy, social cohesion and unity, and the sustainability of socio-economic development, are all parts of soft power.[37] The domestic context is also evident in the remarks of top Chinese leaders. Hu Jintao, for instance, propounded that cultural soft power has two main purposes. One is to enhance national cohesion and creativity, and to meet the demands of people's spiritual life. The other is to strengthen China's competitiveness in the competition for comprehensive national power in the international arena.[38] Official documents and writings by prominent scholars frequently mention the urgency to rebuild Chinese culture and develop new values to hold the rapidly changing society together and strengthen national cohesiveness.[39]

Soft Power: A Weak Link in China's Comprehensive Power

The dominant view among Chinese interlocutors on the current state of China's soft power is that China has made much headway and still has great potential, but its score on soft power has lagged behind its own hard power growth and the soft power of other major powers, particularly that of the U.S.[40] In fact, Chinese strategists describe the current state of China's soft power and its future development as worrisome. This is so because not only is China's current soft power still weak, the issue of converting China's increasing national power into constructive international influence is also still a weak link in China's strategic planning.[41] Some argue that the most important gap between China and the developed countries, particularly the U.S., is not about gross domestic product or military force, but about soft power. This is due to China's drawbacks in domestic institutions, weakness in research, its low level of education, the not-so-good national image, and the decline of national identity and social cohesion.[42] Others base their pessimistic view on the fact that China has very few global name brands and a significant deficit in the trade of cultural products, even though it is becoming the factory of the world. The deficit in cultural trade, in particular, is a clarion call for many Chinese officials and scholars. For instance, in 2004, China imported 4,068 kinds of books from the U.S. and exported only fourteen, imported 2,030 books from Britain and exported only sixteen, imported 694 from Japan and exported only twenty-two. In 2005, in the intellectual property rights trade with the U.S., the ratio of import and export was 4,000 : 24.[43]

This pessimistic orientation was echoed by participants in a forum hosted by the Fudan University International Public Relations Research Center on "national soft power construction and the development of China's public relations" in January 2007. Many participants at the forum mentioned that China has indeed made many inroads in soft power. Wang Guoqing, deputy director of the State Council Information Office, noted in his keynote speech that China has gained much soft power in recent years, as evidenced by the international attention given to China's development, the international attraction of China's development model, the ability to shape the course of international affairs in China's diplomacy and the affinity emanated by Chinese culture. But overall, he noted, China's soft power has been lagging behind. Participants at the forum acknowledged that the weakness of China's soft power is most evident in China's export of cultural products and the relatively weak influence of China's mass media in the international arena.[44]

With regards to the international impact of China's development model, there is notable disagreement on whether the Chinese experience is or should be a source of China's soft power. Some officials and scholars believe that the so-called "Beijing Consensus" has indeed demonstrated its attractiveness to many developing countries. Wang Guoqing, as noted above, lists the perception of China's development and China's development model as the two most important sources of China's soft power growth.[45] But many others are doubtful that the Chinese experience provides much soft power to China. Their scepticism is based on the fact that Chinese development is not complete yet; it is too early to conclude that there has been a unique Chinese model of socio-economic development.[46]

A minority of Chinese scholars hold more optimistic views of China's soft power. Those who are more sanguine tend to emphasize the country's potential, arguing that China has all the elements of soft power, including cultural power, language power, and intellectual power. The fact that China is sponsoring "Confucius Institutes" throughout the world attests to China's determination to expand its soft power.[47] One author says that in today's world, interdependence is intensifying, calling for ever-closer cooperation among nations. International cooperation will have to depend on certain equality, mutual trust and mutual benefit. This increasing urgency for international cooperation provides a valuable opportunity for the Chinese culture, which emphatically values "harmony." The Chinese cultural proclivity of stressing "harmony without suppressing differences" (*he er bu tong*) is likely to provide new thinking and a new approach to international relations, thus highlighting the comparative advantage of Chinese culture. In the eyes of these optimists, "harmony"-laden Chinese culture can then proffer some universal values to the outside world.[48]

SOFT POWER: A MEANS TO MULTIPLE ENDS

The preceding discussion has clearly demonstrated an intense desire and a strong sense of urgency in China to build and promote its soft power. Many analysts have argued that China should treat soft power at the level of state strategy.[49] This urgency largely springs from the Chinese assessment of soft power as being the weakest link in its rise in comparison to Western powers.[50] There are also other reasons why China is so enthusiastic about soft power. In a nutshell, soft power is envisioned as a means to multiple ends.

Soft Power: An Indicator of World Status

The most frequent argument is that soft power has to be part of "comprehensive power" that a major nation is expected to possess. It is commonly believed in Chinese strategic circles that soft power has become an important indicator of a state's international status and influence.[51] A great power has to have material or hard power as well as soft power in order to enjoy flexibility in international politics and maintain advantageous positions in international competition. In light of this, many Chinese analysts have argued that soft power is inseparable from China's rise.[52] A world power has to be one of the cultural centres of the world where ideas, values, social life and beliefs are attractive and appealing to people in other countries. "If a major power cannot provide some guiding moral or cultural ideals of universal value for the international society, its major power status is unlikely to be acknowledged by other states, and even its own development is hard to be sustained."[53] Soft power, in the view of many Chinese strategists, does not grow automatically from the influence of material hard power. Instead, it has to be intentionally cultivated and built up.

According to various Chinese scholars, building soft power that is commensurate with China's major power status and influence has become an urgent task in China's development strategy. The sense of urgency comes from these factors. First, China's hard power—economic, technological and military—has already experienced a dramatic increase but its soft power has lagged behind, creating an imbalance in its national comprehensive power structure. This imbalance is not good for China's aspiration of higher international status and greater international influence.[54] Others have made it more specific by saying that building soft power is conducive to the domestic programme of building a "harmonious society," a concept that the Hu-Wen leadership has proposed to tackle mounting domestic social challenges. For the purpose of maintaining domestic stability more attention should be paid to culture, national cohesion, morality and institutions. All these measures are aimed at maintaining social and political stability in China to create some sort of favourable internal conditions for China's peaceful rise. In addition to these specific tasks at the strategic level, the building up of soft power is also useful for exploring alternative pathways to sustainable growth.[55]

A Soft Shield for Self-Defence

The emerging Chinese soft-power strategy also relates to the "important period of strategic opportunity" that the Hu-Wen leadership has emphasized. At a meeting with Chinese diplomatic emissaries, President Hu Jintao noted that to better serve Chinese interests during this "important period of strategic opportunity," China needs to strive to ensure four "environments," namely, a peaceful and stable international environment, a neighbourly and friendly environment in the surrounding regions, a cooperative environment based on equality and mutual benefits, and an objective and friendly media environment. Chinese analysts believe that soft power is instrumental in helping China achieve these goals. The immediate goal is to dispel what they see as misperception or misunderstanding of the real China by outside commentators, to develop a better image of the Chinese regime in the world, and also to fend off excessive influence or penetration of foreign cultures into China, particularly those ideologies or beliefs that might be harmful to the legitimacy of the ruling party.

First and foremost, soft power is intended to shape a better perception of China by the outside world. It is primarily utilized to refute the "China threat" thesis, facilitate a better understanding of China's domestic socio-economic reality, and persuade the outside world to accept and support China's rise.[56] Externally, building soft power is good for China in order to maintain a stable and peaceful neighbourhood. It also helps to solve various problems between

China and other countries so that these problems do not exacerbate any tensions.[57] The international strategic environment also contributes to China's sense of urgency in developing its soft power. Unlike the American experience of developing hard economic and military power first, then soft power influence, China does not enjoy such a propitious international context. China has to develop its soft power simultaneously because without the kind of soft power to maintain a favourable international status, many forces in the world will prohibit or hamper China's development.[58]

According to Chinese scholars, upgrading the capacity of Chinese mass media outlets can also help the outside world better understand China.[59] This is due to the worry that with the increase of China's hard power and its impact on the international order, many outside observers are hyping China's economic competitiveness and increasing energy demand in the world and external apprehensions toward China's military power. Building soft power would be beneficial to mitigate such outside concerns. Chinese scholars are also aware that other major powers, in particular those that are critical of China's rise, may amplify its negative impact. Thus, developing soft power would help create a more favourable international political atmosphere for China's rise.[60] Many Chinese analysts also fear that Chinese voices have to be heard in the international discourse on soft power, as Western analyses of China's soft power may be inaccurate due to ideological, social and cultural differences and the inclination of Western scholars to focus on countermeasures to China's soft power.[61]

International Competition: Soft Power but Hard Reality

The long-term goal for China is to face up to the perceived competition for soft power among the major powers. Echoing many international strategists, Chinese analysts also acknowledge the trend that in today's world, the role of traditional means of power—e.g., military power—is relatively decreasing. The world is experiencing ever deepening globalization and, in this new era, stability, cooperation, multilateralism and democratization in international politics are on the rise. New rules and approaches in international competition have emerged. In addition to the traditional dimensions of military, economic and technological hard power, soft power, as represented by culture, political ideology, development model and capacity in international institution-building, should also be part of the national comprehensive power.[62] In the words of one Chinese analyst: "Apparently, the competition among nation-states appears to be a rivalry of hard power, but behind such rivalry is the competition between institutions, civilizations, and strategies, which are essentially the rivalry of soft power."[63] Zhu Feng argues that China has to transcend the conventional approach in international competition that focuses on hard power, and instead seek to win ideas and international influence to maintain a "soft counterbalance" instead of "hard counterbalance."[64]

Many Chinese analysts claim that the major powers are all stepping up efforts to build up their soft power, including European nations, the U.S., Japan, India and South Korea.[65] Western powers have always been actively propagating their political system, ideology (democracy) and culture.[66] The U.S. is believed to continue to pursue an aggressive soft power strategy to practice "cultural hegemonism," using its strong economic and political power and advantages in global information networks to promote its spiritual and cultural products, socio-political ideals and values.[67] Japan publicized a national strategic plan in 2005 that called for greater efforts to promote Japanese culture in the world. South Korea proposed back in 1998 that its cultural sector should be one of the main industries for its economy in the new century.[68] Chinese analysts frequently refer to South Korea as an example of successful practice in soft power. Many argue that if South Korea, largely influenced by traditional Chinese culture, could be successful in projecting its soft power, China has no reason not to be successful, because many of the cultural fundamentals evident in South Korean cultural products had their origins in Chinese culture.

Many among the Chinese elite worry that American cultural hegemony is dominating the world, including Chinese society. They worry that the younger generation of Chinese is excessively exposed to American cultural influence. The fear of the political elite is peaceful evolution, i.e., Western liberal political ideology gradually infiltrating Chinese society to weaken their legitimacy. For many scholars, Western cultural penetration will result in the waning of Chinese traditional culture and ultimately the weakening of Chinese identity.[69] In this sense, "beefing up cultural competitiveness is as important as building a strong military."[70]

In accordance with the popular perception that "the competition of cultural power is the core on soft power contention,"[71] in September 2006, the Chinese government released an official document entitled "The National Planning Guidelines for Cultural Development in the Eleventh Five-Year Period."[72] The document asserts that today's world culture is increasingly intertwined with economics, politics and technologies, all of which are important indicators of a nation's comprehensive power. To win the international competition in this complex environment, a state will not only need strong economic, technological and defence power but also strong cultural power. In fact, the guidelines stipulate that one of the goals of Chinese cultural development is to increase the influence of Chinese culture in the world so that it can match the nation's economic power and international status.

THE CHINESE APPROACH TO STRONGER SOFT POWER

This section discusses roadmaps to stronger soft power that have been proposed by Chinese intellectuals. It should be noted from the outset that most analysts share the view that China should still focus on hard power and develop soft power on the basis of economic, technological and military advancement. Many of them, however, have proposed new ideas about how China can further strengthen its soft power.

A Cultural Offensive: Reaching Out to the World

In line with the dominant perception that culture matters most, both official and scholarly prescriptions for the growth of China's soft power have focused on various strategies to work on the cultural front. The 2006 National Planning Guidelines for Cultural Development vows to push for a "go out" strategy to ratchet up the competitiveness and influence of Chinese cultural products and actively promote Chinese culture in the world. One of the major policies that the document proposes is to utilize various festival occasions to promote international understanding of Chinese culture, to actively participate in international decision making in order to increase China's discourse right, to cultivate international sales networks for Chinese cultural products, and to provide support to those major overseas-oriented cultural enterprises. Zhao Qizheng, the former director of the State Council Information Office, mentioned that China should regard reviving its culture and strengthening cultural communication with the outside world as an important task for the nation's destiny.[73]

In recent years, the Chinese government has done a lot to promote cultural exchanges with the outside world. These efforts include participation in the United Nations Education, Science and Cultural Organization's (UNESCO) Intergovernmental Conference on Cultural Policies for Development in 1998, the 1999 Paris China Culture Week, the 2000 U.S. Tour of Chinese Culture, the China Festival at the Asia-Pacific Week in 2001 in Berlin, the Chinese Year in France from October 2003 to July 2004, the Sixth Asian Arts Festival, the Chinese cultural tour in Africa, the "year of Russia" in China in 2006, and the "year of China" in Russia in 2007. It has been stressed that the Chinese diaspora throughout the world is also a good platform in promoting Chinese culture.[74]

Official reports stated that part of the responsibility to increase the influence of Chinese civilization in the world lies with scholars in philosophy, humanities and the social sciences. It is their mission to further discover and promote traditional Chinese cultural values with "harmony" at the core. As noted above, Chinese analysts claim that in modern history, Western civilization spearheaded industrialization but may not provide effective solutions to various current challenges, including environmental degradation, confusion in social ethics, and international and regional conflicts. Traditional Chinese culture, according to their views, stresses "giving priority to human beings" (*yi ren wei ben*) and will be more valuable in overcoming the Western obsession with the omnipotence of material, in resolving the increasingly growing spiritual crisis of humankind, reversing the worsening natural environment and reining in escalating international conflicts.[75]

Political Values and Institutions: Officials vs. Critics

The Chinese political elite and state-owned media continue to advocate adhering to traditional Marxist and socialist ideology in constructing a spiritual civilization.[76] According to official pronouncements, China needs to make more effort to construct a socialist core value system to enhance the cohesion of the Chinese nation. Constructing a socialist core value system should be the primary task in upgrading China's cultural soft power. Sinicized Marxism should continue to be upheld as the guiding ideology for the party and people. The common aspirations under socialism with Chinese characteristics should serve as the cohesive force. The spirit of patriotism and reform and innovation should be used to inspire the people.[77] Although Chinese decision-makers have realized the importance of culture in promoting Chinese soft power, they still have to regard Marxism as the primary political framework for China's cultural development.[78]

Many liberal-minded intellectuals, however, tend to look at the root impediment of China's soft power. Qian Chengdan, a history professor at Beijing University who lectured members of the CCP Politburo, argues that the rise of China and the increase of China's soft power will need more institution building in the various fields—economic, social, cultural, jurisdictional and political—to ensure the transition from the rule of men to the rule of law.[79] Another scholar argues that in addition to significant changes that need to be made to the Chinese model—for instance, making it more sustainable, open, free and harmonious—China has to ultimately become a constitutional state in order to make its experience have universal application to the developing states.[80]

Other scholars have explicitly opined that the challenge for the growth of China's soft power is to elucidate a set of values that would unite the Chinese population domestically and be convincing, appealing and attractive externally. The author proposes that China should promote these values to increase its soft power: peace, development, cooperation, democracy, justice and human rights.[81] Another scholar argues that Chinese values that may have universal appeal include economic development, stability and harmony. The task for China is to integrate, institutionalize and operationalize these values.[82]

Public Relations: Expanding the Influence of Chinese Media

According to some scholars, another reason why China still lags behind in soft power is that previous and current Chinese efforts have concentrated on traditional Chinese cultural legacies but the government has not done a good job in conducting international public relations, particularly in dealing with the Western media. As a result, the Western media have excessively focused on the negative reporting of China.[83] One reason for China's lack of soft power, according to some Chinese scholars, is insufficient financial input in the tools of communication.[84] The solution for this problem is two-fold. First, China must learn to develop more effective strategies to better deal with the Western media. Second, China needs to strengthen the capacity of its media in international communications.

CONCLUSIONS

In recent years, both Chinese officials and scholars have gone to great lengths to explore soft power and its implications for China's foreign affairs. The popularity of soft power in China perhaps reflects the widespread excitement of the Chinese people about the pending rise of their nation as well as their sensitivity to anything that may have an impact on China's ascendance. Following Nye's conceptual framework, Chinese officials and scholars have shed much light on the sources, potential, practice and objectives of soft power in the Chinese context.

A few things, however, are still unclear in the Chinese discourse on soft power. For instance, it is not clear how soft power can be translated into the attainment of specific foreign policy goals. This is particularly the case in their discussion of culture being the main source of soft power. There are very few concrete suggestions as to how the Chinese "harmonious" worldview could restructure the world order. Moreover, available Chinese studies are short of empirical reviews or specific case studies, such as how its foreign policy or participation in international institutions has had an impact on its soft power.

Another key point is that in much of Chinese discourse, one finds constant reference to the domestic context, whether it is culture, values or institutions. This domestic orientation clearly indicates that China itself is in a state of significant changes—cultural, economic, social and political. This state of flux indicates that many sources of Chinese soft power are also uncertain, pending the ultimate transformation of the Chinese state and society. The uncertainties are also reflected in the debate among Chinese scholars, although the vast majority of analysts share some common views. Furthermore, even the domestic political environment has some impact on the Chinese understanding of soft power. For instance, in the analysis of media influence as a source of soft power, very few Chinese analysts, at least among those who are engaged in the soft power discourse, realize that Western media outlets, powerful as they are in shaping world opinions, are not submissive tools of their governments. As a matter of fact, the Western media, most importantly the U.S. media, has played a crucial role in bringing down the international reputation of the U.S. government soon after the invasion of Iraq.

The official inclination to cling to the last ideological straws may have quite a significant negative impact on China's soft power. First, given the preference of the decision-makers, a lot of resources will continue to be allocated to research projects that are closer to the official ideology, the new Marxist project being a good example. Second, it gives the political and ideological watchdogs the power to censure works that they may deem unfit, for political reasons, sometimes wantonly and arbitrarily. Third, it discourages intellectual innovations. Perhaps most importantly, the official discourse is likely to facilitate the slow political reform process. Given the predominance of Western ideological and political ideals, political stagnation in China will continue to put it in a defensive position. Instead of shaping worldviews and setting agendas in world affairs, soft power, however the Chinese elite may define it, will have to be used for defensive purposes.

In light of all these factors, it is perhaps understandable why Chinese discourse on soft power also seems to demonstrate a lack of confidence and forcefulness. This is particularly evident when compared to the American discussion of soft power. Chinese analysts seem to downplay or neglect the function of soft power to aggressively influence others. Chinese authors rarely discuss political ideology or beliefs and their potential for China's soft power promotion. They are more or less inclined to base their arguments on relativity, frequently stressing the relative nature of culture and ideology, whereas the American analysis of soft power tends to be more absolute in advocating the universal nature of their ideology, socio-political system, beliefs and cultural tenets.[85]

More often than not, official Chinese voices have steadfastly emphasized the importance of respecting the cultural, social, political and ideological diversity in the world. This emphasis on diversity is clearly a counter-measure to Western insistence on promoting its universal ideational influence in the world, including in China, which would pose a grave challenge to the ruling position of the CCP. The lack of confidence is also a reflection of the fact that the Chinese socio-political system is not in conformity with the global political discourse and atmosphere in which political openness and pluralism are the dominant norms. Another factor in Chinese reluctance to aggressively advocate soft power has to do with their caution that such a loud voice might be interpreted by the West as some sort of Chinese grand strategy to challenge the West. Beijing is fearful that some Western observers could use any fanfare on soft power as part of their evidence to support a "China threat" thesis.[86]

China has indeed done a lot to promote its soft power. These efforts include various large-scale cultural activities in other countries, putting in a large amount of financial resources to cultivate a better image of China, promoting the capacity of its mass media in international communications, and sponsoring Confucius Institutes throughout the world. Despite all these efforts, Chinese intellectuals seem to be uncertain about the ultimate fate of China's soft power. Numerous writings by Chinese analysts do suggest the validity of the thesis: "Soft power remains Beijing's underbelly and China still has a long way to go to become a true global leader."[87]

NOTES

1. Jiang Zeming, "Political Report to the 16th CCP Congress," November 8, 2002.

2. *Wen Hui Bao* [Wen Hui newspaper], "*Yi ruan shili tisheng guojia zhonghe jinzhengli*" [Use soft power to upgrade national comprehensive competitiveness], June 21, 2004.

3. Yang Taoyuan, "*Tisheng zhongguo ruan shili: jiedu zhongyang zhengzhiju di shi san ci jiti xuexi*" [Upgrading China's soft power: An explanation of the 13th collective study session of the CCP CC Politburo], *Liaowang xinwen zhoukan* [*Outlook News Weekly*] issue 23, June 7, 2004.

4. Ma Lisi, "*Guanyu wo guo jiaqiang ruan shili jianshe de chubu sikao*" [Preliminary thoughts on accelerating China's soft power building], *Dang de wenxian* [*Literature of Chinese Communist Party*], no. 7, 2007, pp. 35–38.

5. Pan Yue, "*Quan guo zhengxie zhaokai zhuanti xieshanghui*" [CPPCC National Committee convenes a special consultation meeting], *People's Daily*, July 25, 2007; Excerpt from Jia's speech at the CPPCC National Committee special session on July 24 *Dang Jian* [*Party Building*], issue 9 (2007): 6.

6. *Guangming Daily* commentary, "*Nuli tigao guojia ruan shili*" [Strive to raise national soft power], November 17, 2006.

7. *People's Daily*, "*Tigao guojia wenhua ruan shili*" [Upgrading national cultural soft power], December 29, 2007.

8. See Study Group on soft power at CICIR, "*Ruan shili guoji jiejian*" [International lessons about soft power], *Outlook Weekly* 11, March 12, 2007.

9. Men Honghua, "*Zhongguo ruan shili pinggu baogao*" [Assessment and report of China's soft power], *Guoji guancha* [*International Observations*] 1:2 (2007): 15–26.; 2:3 (2007): 37–46.

10. Men Honghua, "*Zhongguo ruan shili pinggu baogao*" [Assessment and report of China's soft power], 15.

11. The Chinese translation of soft power has four versions: *ruan shili*, *ruan liliang*, *ruan guoli* and *ruan quanli*. *Ruan shili* is becoming more popular than the other three. For the searches, I entered all four terms and used the "or" function.

12. For a comprehensive review of Chinese discourse on soft power, see Liu Qing and Wang Litao, "*Jin nian guonei ruan liliang lilun yanjiu zongshu*" [A review of Chinese studies on soft power theory in recent years], *Journal of Jiangnan Social University* 2:9 (2007).

13. Joseph S. Nye, *Soft Power: The Means to Success in World Politics* (Cambridge, MA: Perseus Books Group, 2004), x.

14. Nye, *Soft Power: The Means to Success in World Politics,* 11.

15. Wang Huning, "*Zuowei guojia shili de wenhua: Ruan quanli*" [Culture as national power: Soft power], *Journal of Fudan University* 3 (1993).

16. For instance, Luo Jianbo, "*Zhongguo jueqi de duiwai wenhua zhanlue*" [external cultural strategy in China's rise], *Journal of the Party School of the Central Committee of the CCP* 10, no. 3, (June 2006): 97–100.

17. Jiang Haiyan, "*Hongyang zhonghua minzu de youxiu wenhua yu zengqiang wo guo de ruan shili*" [Promoting the outstanding culture of the Chinese nation and strengthening China's soft power], *Journal of the Party School of the Central Committee of the CCP* 11, no. 1 (2007): pp. 107–112; Li Haijuan, "*'Ruan quanli' jingzheng beijing xia de wenhua zhanlue*" [Cultural strategy in the context of soft power competition], *Mao Zedong Deng Xiaoping liluan yanjiu* [Mao Zedong thought and Deng Xiaoping theory studies]12, (2004): 49–54.

18. Men Honghua, "*Zhongguo ruan shili pinggu baogao*" [Assessment and report of China's soft power].

19. Ni Xun, "*Quanguo zhengxie weiyuan tan zengqiang wenhua ruan shili de zhuoyandian*" [CPPCC National Committee members discuss how to strengthen cultural soft power], *Guangming Daily*, January 3, 2008.

20. Yu Xintian, "*Ruan liliang duanxiang*" [Some reflections on soft power], *Foreign Affairs Review*, no. 97 (2007), pp. 35–36.

21. Men Honghua, "*Zhongguo ruan shili pinggu baogao*" [Assessment and report of China's soft power].

22. Feng Jian and Qian Haihong, "*Gonggong guanxi shiye xia de zhongguo ruan shili jiangou*" [China's soft power construction in the perspective of public relations], *Journalism Quarterly* 92: 2 (2007), pp. 75–76.

23. Su Changhe, "*Zhongguo de ruan quanli— yi guoji zhidu yu zhongguo de guanxi wei li*" [China's soft power—an example in the relationship between China

and international institutions], *Guoji guancha* [*International Observations*] 2 (2007), pp. 27–35.

24. Zhao Lei, "*Zhongguo ruan shili tisheng yin ren guanzhu*" [Increase of China's soft power raises attention], *Zhongguo dang zheng ganbu luntan* [Forum of Chinese party and government officials], 1 (2007), pp. 45–46.

25. Yao Xu, "*Gonggong guanxi de chuanbo shouduan yu zhongguo ruan shili jiangou*" [Communication methods of public relations and China's soft power building], *Xinwen qianshao* [*News Frontline*] 93: 7 (2007), pp. 93–94.

26. For instance, Ji Ling and Chen Shiping, "*Guoji zhengzhi de bianqian yu ruan quanli lilun*" [Changes in international politics and the soft power theory], *Foreign Affairs Review* 96, (2007), pp. 97–105; Fang Changping, "*Zhong mei ruan shili bijiao ji qi dui zhongguo de qishi*" [A comparison of soft power between China and the U.S. and its implications for China], *Shijie jingji yu zhengzhi* [*World Economics and Politics*] 7 (2007), pp. 21–27; Su Changhe, "*Zhongguo de ruan quanli—yi guoji zhidu yu zhongguo de guanxi wei li*" [China's soft power—an example in the relationship between China and international institutions].

27. Gong Tieying, "*Lun ruan quanli de weidu*" [On the dimensions of soft power], *Shijie jingji yu zhengzhi* [*World Economics and Politics*] 9 (2007), pp. 16–22.

28. Yan Xuetong, "*Ruanshili de hexin shi zhengzhi shili*" [The core of soft power is political power], *Huanqiu shibao* [*Global Times*], May 22, 2007.

29. Zhu Feng, "*Zhongguo ying duo cezhong 'ruan shili' jueqi*"[China should give priority to soft power rise], *Huanqiu shibao* [*Global Times*], April 30, 2007.

30. Zhu Majie and Yu Xintian, "*Ruan guoli jianshe: bu rong hu shi de wu xing yingxiang*" [Soft power construction: Invisible influence not to be ignored], *Proceedings of Annual Meeting of Shanghai Social Sciences Circle*, 2004.

31. Zheng Yongnian and Zhang Chi, "*Guoji zhengzhi zhong de ruan liliang yiji dui zhongguo ruan liliang de guancha*" [Soft power in international politics and an observation of China's soft power], *Shijie jingji yu zhengzhi* [*World Economics and Politics*] 7 (2007), 133–138.

32. Men Honghua, "*Zhongguo ruan shili pinggu baogao*" [Assessment and report of China's soft power].

33. Zhao Haibin, "*Yi zhongyiyao chuantong wenhua tisheng zhongguo ruan shili*" [Use traditional Chinese medical culture to upgrade China's soft power], *Journal of Yunnan College of Traditional Chinese Medicine* 1: 30 (2007), pp. 4–9.

34. Zhao Shusen, "*Jingji shijiao xia de ruan quanli yu zhongguo de heping fazhan*" [Soft power in economic perspective and China's peaceful development], *Ya fei zong heng* [*All-round Asia-Africa*] 5 (2007), pp. 53–59.

35. Cheng Bin et al., "*Tiyu wenhua chuanbo yu tisheng guojia ruan shili*" [Communications of sports culture and the increase of China's soft power], *Collection of excerpts of papers presented at the 8th national sports science conference*, 2007.

36. Qian Zhengshun, "*Jiaoyu waijiao zai guojia ruan shili waijiao zhong da you ke wei*" [Educational diplomacy to play a big role in China's soft power diplomacy], *Journal of National Academy of Education and Administration* 2 (2007), pp. 33–35.

37. Yu Keping, "*Zhongguo moshi: jingyan yu jianjie*" [The China model: Experience and lessons], in *Zhongguo moshi yu beijing gongshi—chaoyue huashengdun*

gongshi [The Chinese model and Beijing consensus—beyond the Washington consensus], ed. Yu Keping (Beijing: Social Sciences Press, 2006), 19.

38. Hu Jintao, *Report at the CCP 17th Congress*, October 15, 2007.

39. Wang Zuoshu, *Goujian shehuizhuyi hexie shehui de ruan shili* [Building soft power for a socialist harmonious society], (Beijing: People's Press, 2007).

40. Zhan Yijia, "*Zhongguo shi ruan shili daguo ma*?" [Is China a nation with strong soft power?], *Shijie Zhishi* [*World Knowledge*] 20 (2006): 5.; Deng Xiaochao, "*Qiao ran jueqi de zhongguo ruan shili*" [Chinese soft power quietly growing], *Ascent* 24, no. 6 (2005): 89–93.; *Liberation Daily*, "*Touxi zhongguo 'ruan shili'*" [Analysing China's soft power], October 3, 2005.

41. Men Honghua, "*Zhongguo ruan shili pinggu baogao*" [Assessment and report of China's soft power].

42. Huang Renwei, "*Ruan liliang yu guojia anquan*" [Soft power and national security], *Xuexi yue kan* [*Study Monthly*] 202: 1 (2003), pp. 23–28.

43. Li Lei, "*Dazao zhongguo ruan shili*" [Moulding China's soft power], *Shangye wenhua* [*Business Culture*], (November 2006): 86–88.

44. Feng Jian, "*Gonggong guanxi shiye xia de zhongguo ruan shili jiangou*" [China's soft power construction in the perspective of public relations].

45. Ibid.

46. Zhang Jianjing, "*'Beijing gongshi' yu zhongguo ruanshili de tisheng*" [The "Beijing Consensus" and the increase of China's soft power], *Dangdai shijie yu shehuizhuyi* [*Contemporary World and Socialism*] 4 (2004), pp. 10–14.

47. Pang Zhongying, "*Kongzi sixiang de 'chukou' he ruan liliang de shiyong*" [The export of Confucianism and use of soft power], *Shijie Zhishi* [*World Knowledge*] 17 (2006): 67.

48. Yu Yunquan, "*Zhongguo wenhua ruan shili jianshe ren zhong dao yuan*" [China's cultural soft power construction has a long way to go], *Dui wai da chuanbo* [*External Communications*] 1 (2007), pp. 44–46.

49. Zhao Changmao, "*Zhongguo xuyao ruan shili*" [China needs soft power], *Liaowang xinwen zhoukan* [*Outlook News Weekly*], June 7, 2004.

50. Huang Renwei, *Zhongguo jueqi de shijian he kongjian* [Time and space of China's rise], (Shang Hai: Shanghai Social Sciences Press, 2002).

51. Men Honghua, "*Zhongguo ruan shili pinggu baogao*" [Assessment and report of China's soft power].

52. Li Jie, "*Tisheng ruan shili dui shixian wo guo heping jueqi zhanlue de zuoyong*" [The role of increasing soft power for the realization of China's peaceful rise], *Taipingyang xue bao* [*Journal of Pacific Studies*] 12 (2005): 64–71.; Huang Jing and Yue Zhanju, "*Ruan shili jianshe yu zhongguo de heping fazhan daolu*" [Building soft power and China's peaceful development road], *Dangdai shijie yu shehui zhuyi* [*Contemporary World and Socialism*] 5 (2006): 103–7.

53. Luo Jianbo, "*Zhongguo jueqi de duiwai wenhua zhanlue*" [External cultural strategy in China's rise].

54. Wang Jianjun, "*Ruan shili sheng wei*" [Soft power given more attention], *Liao wang* [*Outlook Weekly*] 11, March 12, 2007.

55. Men Honghua, "*Zhongguo ruan shili pinggu baogao*" [Assessment and report of China's soft power].

56. Fang Changping, "*Zhong mei ruan shili bijiao ji qi dui zhongguo de qishi*" [A comparison of soft power between China and the U.S. and its implications for China].

57. Song Xiaofeng, "*Shi xi zhongguo heping jueqi zhong de ruan quanli yinsu*" [A preliminary analysis of the soft power factor in China's peaceful rise], *Journal of Guangdong Institute of Public Administration* 17, no.13 (June 2005): 46–50.

58. Zhang Jianjing, "*Beijing gongshi yu zhongguo ruan shili de tisheng*" [The Beijing consensus and the increase of China's soft power].

59. Liu Sen, "*Xiang shijie shuoming zhongguo, guanjian kao tisheng ruanshili*" [Upgrading soft power is key in explaining China to the outside world], *Liberation Daily*, November 3, 2007.

60. Wang Jianjun, "*Ruan shili sheng wei*" [Soft power given more attention], *Liao wang* [*Outlook Weekly*] 11, March 12, 2007.

61. Fang Changping, "*Zhong mei ruan shili bijiao ji qi dui zhongguo de qishi*" [A comparison of soft power between China and the U.S. and its implications for China].

62. Huang Jing and Yue Zhanju, "*Ruan shili jianshe yu zhongguo de heping fazhan daolu*" [Building soft power and China's peaceful development road].

63. Zhang Jianjing, "*Beijing gongshi yu zhongguo ruan shili de tisheng*" [The Beijing consensus and the increase of China's soft power].

64. Zhu Feng, "*Zhongguo ying duo cezhong 'ruan shili' jueqi*" [China should give priority to soft power rise].

65. See Study Group on soft power at CICIR, "*Ruan shili guoji jiejian*" [International lessons about soft power], *Liao wang* [*Outlook Weekly*] 11, March 12, 2007.

66. Yu Xibin, "*Ruan shili liluan de neihan, chansheng beijing ji yunyong*" [Content, background and application of the soft power theory], *Dangdai shijie* [*Contemporary World*] 9 (2006): 33–5.

67. Zhao Yi, "*Ruan shili: daguo zheng xiong de jue li chang*" [Soft power: The arena of major power rivalry], *China Society Periodical* 12 (2005): 55–7.

68. Li Jie, "*Ruan shili jianshe yu zhongguo de heping fazhan*" [Soft power construction and China's peaceful development], *Guoji wenti yanjiu* [*International Studies*] 1 (2007), pp. 19–24.

69. He Ying et al., "*Qian xi guojia 'ruan quanli' lilun*" [Notes on national soft power theory], *Journal of University of International Relations*, no 12 (2005): 5–8.

70. Huang Renwei, "*Ruan liliang yu guojia anquan*" [Soft power and national security].

71. Li Haijuan, "*'Ruan quanli' jingzheng beijing xia de wenhua zhanlue*" [Cultural strategy in the context of soft power competition].

72. *Xinhua News Agency*, "Full Text of the National Planning Guidelines for Cultural Development in the Eleventh Five-Year Period," September 13, 2006.

73. Shen Suru, "*Kaizhan 'ruan shili' yu dui wai chuanbo de yanjiu*" [Conduct research on soft power and external communications], *Dui wai da chuanbo* [*Grand External Communications*] 7 (2006): 24–8.

74. Lin Guoxia, "*Zhongguo ruan shili xianzhuang fenxi*" [An analysis of the state of China's soft power], *Dang dai shijie* [*Contemporary World*] 3 (2007), pp. 24–28.

75. Jiang Haiyan, "*Hongyang zhonghua minzu de youxiu wenhua yu zengqiang wo guo de ruan shili*" [Promoting the outstanding culture of the Chinese nation and strengthening China's soft power].

76. Shen Jiru, "*Bu neng hushi zengqiang wo guo de 'ruan shili'*" [The enhancement of China's soft power should not be neglected], *Liaowang xinwen zhoukan* [*Outlook News Weekly*] 41 (11 October 1999): 12–13.

77. *People's Daily*, "*Tigao guojia wenhua ruan shili*" [Upgrading national cultural soft power].

78. *Xinhua News Agency*, "Full Text of the National Planning Guidelines for Cultural Development in the Eleventh Five-Year Period," September 13, 2006.

79. Wang Haijing and Qian Chengdan, "*Zhidu jianshe chengqi ruan shili*" [Institutions to Support Soft Power] *Liao Wang* [*Outlook Weekly* 11, March 12, 2007.

80. Zhang Jianjing, "*'Beijing gongshi' yu zhongguo ruanshili de tisheng*" [The "Beijing Consensus" and the increase of China's soft power].

81. Zhu Majie and Yu Xintian, "*Ruan guoli jianshe: bu rong hu shi de wu xing yingxiang*" [Soft power construction: invisible influence not to be ignored].

82. Chen Yugang, "*Shi lun quanqiuhua beijing xia zhongguo ruan shili de goujian*" [Thoughts on the construction of China's soft power in the context of globalization], *Guoji guancha* [*International Observations*] 2 (2007), pp. 36–59.

83. Wu Xu, "*Zhongguo ruan shili bun eng chi laoben*" [China's soft power cannot depend on traditions only], *Shiji xing* [*Century*] 6 (2007), pp. 47–48.

84. Shen Suru, "*Kaizhan 'ruan shili' yu dui wai chuanbo de yanjiu*" [Conduct research on soft power and external communications].

85. Fang Changping, "*Zhong mei ruan shili bijiao ji qi dui zhongguo de qishi*" [A comparison of soft power between China and the U.S. and its implications for China].

86. Yu Yunquan, "*Zhongguo wenhua ruan shili jianshe ren zhong dao yuan*" [China's cultural soft power construction has a long way to go].

87. Yanzhong Huang and Sheng Ding, "Dragon's Underbelly: An Analysis of China's Soft Power," *East Asia* 23, no. 4 (Winter 2006): pp. 22–44.

Chapter Three

The Discourse of China's Soft Power and Its Discontents

Yongjin Zhang

> A spectre is haunting the world—the spectre of the rise of (Communist) China. All the discourses about China around the world have entered into one spiral hype about this spectre: in print and other media, in academic discussions and policy briefings, in published books and articles, and all over the virtual space of Internet.

This light-hearted adaptation of the opening paragraph of the *Communist Manifesto* is in fact a rather accurate description of the continued fascination and obsessions about the recent transformation of China. Pei Minxin, writing in *Foreign Policy*, made a mischievously rueful comment. "The only thing rising faster than China," in his words, "is the hype about China."[1] If the rise of China is the topic of political moment, the latest hype about the rise of China is about China's soft power. Critics and enthusiasts of China alike are entranced and bewildered by the rapid increase of Chinese influence and assertiveness in global and regional economic development and political affairs. China is said to have mounted a "charm offensive" worldwide and to have made good use of "soft seduction" in its foreign policy. It is claimed that Chinese soft power is "transforming the world." Further, it is suggested that Beijing has implemented a masterful plan as part of its grand strategy in the last few years to project China's soft power, taking advantage of the U.S. preoccupation with the global war on terror, particularly in Iraq and Afghanistan. China has, in other words, built up its soft power "at the expense of the United States."[2] Not surprisingly, such novel rage about China's soft power has evoked excitement, fascination, fear, apprehension and anxiety.

Parallel to such hype and rage about China's soft power are, however, concerns about the "clash of Titans"—China and the United States.[3] It is worth noting that whether China is a status quo or a revisionist power is an ongoing debate;[4] and that China was a pariah state in the society of states, whose legitimacy has only been reluctantly and grudgingly accepted by the current international system not long ago. The public call for China to become "a responsible stakeholder of the international system" remains a prospect unfulfilled.[5]

Why should there be such a rage about China's soft power at this particular moment? Are there any substance in the claims about soft power that China is said to increasingly possess and command? How to understand the projection and purpose of such power? What is the political logic behind this raging discourse?

In this chapter, I address these questions through an analytical examination of the recent *external* discourse of China's soft power. I have chosen to concentrate on this discourse that looks at China's soft power from the outside-in perspective principally for two explicit reasons. One is that the discourse of soft power per se is originated outside China, and more precisely in the United States. In addition, much hype about China's soft power comes from academics, policy analysts and journalists based in the United States. The other is that this *external* discourse is a much richer one, better conceptualised and much more focused. It is this *external* discourse that has provided inspirations for the internal discourse. In contrast, the discourse of soft power inside China, if any, seems much more fragmented and reactive with less analytical rigor. It is, in my view, derivative from, thus secondary to, the *external* one.[6]

SOFT POWER: CONCEPTUAL AMBIGUITIES

The discourse of soft power was single-handedly started in 1990 by Joseph Nye. It is widely acknowledged that Nye's initial purpose for inventing the concept of "soft power" is to counter the prevailing pessimism about the decline of American power at the end of the Cold War with the disappearance of a defining Soviet threat. In *Bound to Lead*, Nye asked a seemingly mundane question: 'how is power changing in modern international politics?'[7] In the post-Cold War global order, Nye argued, the changing face of power was most clearly seen in the rising importance of what he called "co-optive or soft power"—"getting others to want what you want."[8] Given the U.S. command of soft power resources—cultural and ideological attraction and rules and norms of international institutions, Nye came to the conclusion that contrary to conventional wisdom, the United States has both traditional hard power and new soft power resources to meet the challenges of shaping the post-Cold War global order if it is willing to take the global leadership.[9]

The innovative nature of the concept of soft power is indisputable. It has affected our way of talking and thinking about global politics in very significant ways. Over the last two decades, the debates about soft power have been firmly entrenched in academic and foreign policy discourses globally and have inspired a wide range of diplomatic practices and foreign policy initiatives. Whether at Pentagon in Washington or at the Kennedy School of Government of Harvard, Nye has been an active participant in the discourse. Through his writings published in *Foreign Affairs* and *Foreign Policy* and numerous op-ed pieces in such media outlets as *The Wall Street Journal* and *Boston Globe*, Nye has sought to sharpen up the conceptualisation of soft power, and to refine its definition. In *Soft Power: The Means to Success in World Politics*, published in 2004 after the Iraq War, Nye provided a most systematic and incisive account of how soft power functions in contemporary global politics.[10]

Four key analytical questions in Nye's conceptualisation of soft power are of particular interest here. First and most fundamentally, what is or is not soft power? Nye initially conceptualised soft power "in contrast with command power of *ordering* others to do what it wants." Soft power occurs, in Nye words, "when one country gets other countries to want what it wants." Further, the exercise of soft power involves setting the agenda and structuring the situations in world politics "as to get others to change in particular cases."[11] Fourteen years later, Nye articulated his conceptualisation of this "second face of power" more subtly.

> A country may obtain the outcomes it wants in world politics because other countries—admiring its values, emulating its example, aspiring to its level of prosperity and openness—want to follow it. In this sense, it is also important to set the agenda and attract others in world politics, and not only to force them to change by threatening military force or economic sanctions. This soft power—getting others to want the outcomes that you want—co-opts people rather than coerces them.[12]

Nye specifically ruled out economic payoffs or inducements—the so-called carrots—as constitutive of soft power.

Nye's conceptualisations of soft power above are clearly problematic because they are invariably ambiguous. They only specify vaguely some resources of soft power. They do not tell in which way resources of soft power can be converted into power that influences the actual behaviour and produces favourable outcomes. They could not set the context in which power is exercised. This problem of ambiguity has been magnified as the concept enters popular and public discourse in the United States and around the world. As it becomes widely used in journalism, policy analysis and academic discourse, any residual conceptual clarity and nuances that Nye has tried to build into the concept tend to get lost. In which way is culture soft power? Why is economic strength more often regarded as hard power than soft power? Under what circumstances do military resources produce soft power? Is soft power more humane than hard power? How is the generic concept of soft power, originated largely from the experience of the United States, applicable in different contexts? These questions fundamental to the conceptualisation of soft power are among those Nye has tried to address most recently in order to counter the claims that soft power is too elastic and remains elusive as a useful concept in understanding power in contemporary global politics.[13] As Nye publicly acknowledged, it is his concerns about how soft power had been misused, misunderstood and even trivialized in the public discourse that prompted him to elaborate more systematically the concept in his 2004 book.[14]

Second and closely related to the above conceptual ambiguity is the confusion about the resources of soft power. The paradox is that Nye seems to have suggested clearly and consistently what main resources of soft power are. The soft power of a country "rests primarily on three resources: its culture (in places where it is attractive to others), its political values (when it lives up to them at home and abroad), and its foreign policies (when they are seen as legitimate and having moral authority)."[15] Elsewhere, Nye has written that the sources of soft power are "attraction" of ideas, the ability in shaping international norms consistent with the societal norms, and leadership in the Information Age.[16]

The confusion seems to have come from several directions. In the first place, attraction—the key word that underlies the conceptualisation of soft power—is very often implicitly assumed and rarely debated.[17] More problematically, it is value laden. The critical question is attraction to whom and for what purpose? And how does attraction happen? Hollywood and Bollywood may be attractive to certain sectors of the population, but repulsive to others. Ditto with Christian fundamentalism and Islamic fundamentalism. Democratic values may or may not appeal to the ruling elite of a state. Further, is there anything non-American that is inherently attractive to the Americans who, in Stanley Hoffmann's words, believe in "their own ideological supremacy?"[18] Second, culture can be such an all-embracing concept that it is susceptible to abuse. In what sense does the Japanese pop culture constitute the soft power of Japan? Does a Nobel Prize winner add any attraction, and therefore, soft power, to a nation and a state? Does Chinese or French cuisine constitute their respective soft power? Third, there is the problem of perspective. For those who exercise power, culture, political values and foreign policies may constitute sources of soft power. For those at the receiving end of such soft power, the differentiation between hard and soft power is only academic. To what extent is it possible for a state to have soft power without hard power? Can non-traditional powers claim any soft power? Who can claim any soft power vis-à-vis the United States?

This leads to our third question. Who has soft power? In Nye's scheme of arguments, in the twenty-first century only the United States, and to a certain extent, liberal democracies with a developed economy, could possibly possess the sources of and potential for soft power. More importantly, only these countries have the means, capacity and willingness to convert successfully such resources into real and sustained soft power that makes difference in global politics. Robert Kagan's celebrated characterisation that "Americans are from Mars and Europeans are from Venus"[19] seems to suggest that Europe is strong in soft power. But even Nye finds it difficult to identify exactly where Europe's soft power comes from. Nye's long list of European sources of soft power includes European countries' ranking in winning Nobel Prizes, music sales, book sales and internet website hosts, number of tourists, high life expectancy, attraction for political asylum applications and soccer, in addition to Europe's promotion of democracy and human rights and its high spending on public diplomacy.[20] Europeans are less convinced.[21] Even more contentious is the question of Japan's soft power.[22]

Nye has otherwise suggested that a wide range of non-state actors, from NGOs to virtual communities and networks created by the information technology revolution, can and do possess and exercise soft power. "Many of these organisations," he writes, "will have soft power of their own as they attract citizens into coalitions that cut across national boundaries."[23] Nye did mention the Soviet Union as possessing certain soft power in the Cold War period for historical and ideological reasons, but quickly dismissed it as 'never a serious competitor with the United States in soft power during the Cold War' because of "a closed system, lack of attractive popular culture and heavy handed foreign policies."[24]

Finally, there is the question of the use and purpose of soft power. On a broader scale, Nye argues that success in world politics increasingly depends on the exercise of soft power, or of smart power. Imaginative leadership and strategic vision are indispensable in effectively realising and exercising soft/smart power. Agenda setting in multilateral international institutions is a prime example of the exercise of such power. In this sense, soft power is a means to an end. In the context of the global war on terrorism, Nye has emphasized the special importance of public diplomacy—as part of American soft power—in legitimizing American policies and the American exercise of hard power in this war and in winning the hearts and minds of the Iraqi people. "In the information age," he argues, "the success is not only the result of whose arms wins but also whose story wins."[25] When politics becomes part of a competition for attractiveness, legitimacy and credibility, it is important "to be believed."[26]

Such framing of the exercise and purpose of soft power seems to have less to do with the inherent moral authority of American foreign policy. Rather, as contributors to *The Soft Power of War* demonstrate, public diplomacy of the United States has been concerned to "produce influential knowledge about the war and shape the ethical and political premises upon which the legitimacy of the Iraq war and the 'vision' of the emergent world order rests." Soft power is therefore used for the purpose of "narrating the world in coherent and persuasive stories." As the power of argument and belief, it has played a key role in "shifting global public opinion from a position of disapproving a war unauthorised by the UN to supporting the war in the name of global security."[27]

THE DISCOURSE OF CHINA'S SOFT POWER: CONCEPTUAL TWISTS

These conceptual ambiguities and confusions concerning soft power and contentions related to problematic exercise by state actors of such power in specific circumstances have naturally found their ways into the discourse about China's soft power. There are additional conceptual twists. Judging by Nye's standard account, China could hardly claim any soft power resources. The current Chinese political system could not be more different from that of the United States. China always has an "abysmal ranking" in the Freedom House's survey, even among the least free countries in the world.[28] Beijing openly rejects the "Western" liberal democratic values and the Chinese state has often been seen as the perpetrator of human rights abuses in domestic settings. It is difficult to see any political values and ideological beliefs that Beijing either preaches or practices to be universally appealing and attractive. In contrast to the European Union, Chinese policies on and approaches to global problems, ranging from climate change and environmental protection to pandemics and infectious diseases, lack moral authority. If traditional Chinese culture still holds its attraction in East Asia, contemporary China's cultural appeal is extremely limited. Unlike Japan, China cannot even claim to have produced a popular culture that is in any way attractive and competitive in East Asia. China's economic success story is often said to be built on perspirations, not inspirations or innovation.

It is not surprising, therefore, that even in his 2004 book, Nye spent less time discussing China's soft power than he did on that of the former Soviet Union. He did give four examples to illustrate China's nascent soft power.

Two of them, however, can be dismissed almost instantly. The example of Gao Xinjian winning the Nobel Prize for literature because Beijing had virtually disavowed Gao; and the example of the box-office success of *Crouching Tiger, Hidden Dragon* cannot be counted because it is a Hollywood production and the Director, Ang Lee, is from Taiwan.[29] Nye was quick to note that "in the United States, the attraction of an authoritarian China is limited by the concern that it could become a threat sometime in the future."[30]

Nye's change of mind seems to have occurred in late 2005. In an op-ed piece in the *Wall Street Journal*, he provided a more inclusive list of indicators of the rise of China's soft power. This includes tripling of foreign students enrolment in Chinese universities in a past decade, increasing number of foreign tourists to China, public diplomacy initiatives ranging from the establishment of Confucius Institutes to the increasing activities of China Radio International, China's participation in multilateral institutions such as the World Trade Organisation to the Shanghai Cooperation Organisation, and the broad appeal of the so-called "Beijing Consensus."[31]

By then, the discourse of China's soft power had taken on its own life.[32] It was claimed in *International Herald Tribune* back in 2004 that China was becoming a "cultural magnet" for many people in Asia.[33] *New York Times* asserted, also in 2004, that "China moves to eclipse the U.S. appeal in South Asia."[34] Robert Sutter noted in his 2005 book on *China's Rise in Asia: Promise or Perils?* more specifically that China's soft power in Southeast Asia

> is said to have resulted in and reflected by the rising prominence of ethnic Chinese communities in several Southeast Asian states, including Malaysia and Thailand. . . . Meanwhile, there was an upsurge of travel and migration of Chinese nationals to Southeast Asia as tourists, students and business people that was said to be welcomed by many in Southeast Asia, a further indication of the attractiveness of China and China's soft power to the people and officials of Southeast Asia.[35]

The establishment of the Confucius Institute worldwide has been scrutinized as one of Beijing's attempts to build up China's soft power through its new and coordinated public diplomacy.[36] Confucius Institutes are said to have a political agenda: "to present a kinder and gentler image of China to the outside world" and "to serve to advance China's foreign policy goal of marginalising Taiwan's international influence."[37] Together with the increased financial and human capital investment in such international broadcasters as China Radio International and CCTV 9, China is believed to engage in public diplomacy strategically in order to build up its soft power.

On the economic front, while Beijing remained ambivalent about a number of claims associated with the so-called "Beijing Consensus," China's success in promoting rapid economic growth seemed to have much wider appeal among developing countries.[38] Interestingly, it is the sources outside China that make more radical claims in relations to the attraction of the China experience in this regard. For example, Mark Leonard claims that the alternative development model presented by Beijing represents "the biggest ideological threat the West has felt since the end of the Cold War."[39] China's model of development, labelled as that of state-ordered economic liberalisation with minimal political liberalisation, is said to have significant appeal.[40] Rapid economic development of China, it was claimed, "is leading to a rethinking of both development economics and the relationship between economic and political freedoms."[41] China's aggressive economic diplomacy—trade, aid and investment—toward the global South, particularly Africa, which has often been criticized as "mercantilist" and "exploitative" and which is aimed at satisfying China's vivacious appetite for energy and other natural resources, is now seen as an indispensable part of China's soft power.

China is also seen as having exercised its soft power "with consummate skill" in global politics.[42] It is particularly successful in courting its neighbours in Southeast Asia with good neighbourly relations policies. China's active participation in the international peacekeeping under the UN auspices and its embracing of multilateralism in a wide range of global institutions and its active involvement in regional organisations such as the ASEAN Regional Forum (ARF) and Shanghai Cooperation Organisation (SCO) are also seen as enhancing China's soft power, as they afford legitimacy and moral authority to Chinese foreign policy. So are China's adopting global norms, and rules in the context of the WTO and beyond. The most recent advocacy of a harmonious world in China's global diplomacy harks back to traditional Chinese culture, which is regarded as another attempt to wield China's soft power.[43]

It is clear that this is a discourse of soft power with conceptual twists. It has slid over the main analytical and conceptual criteria of soft power carefully constructed by Nye over more than a decade. In this discourse, it is not political values that China articulates or the moral authority that Chinese foreign policies command that constitute China's soft power. The authoritarian nature of the regime has become less significant in considering issues related to either the trust of Chinese power or the credibility of China's public diplomacy. By smuggling in economic and diplomatic coercion into the equation of China's soft power, it has brutally dismantled the subtle differentiations between soft and hard power that Nye has tried so hard to make.

No other work can better illustrate this than Joshua Kurlantzick's *Charm Offensive: How China's Soft Power Is Transforming the World*. His catalogue of China's charming power includes a wide range of instruments (which he calls 'tools') that are more conventionally referred to as "cultural diplomacy" or "economic diplomacy." His discussions concern many initiatives of Chinese foreign policy that make China popular. Almost everything that China touches, ranging from China's unanticipated approach to the Asian financial crisis in 1997 and ethnic Chinese Diaspora in Southeast Asia to China's more recent forays into Africa and Latin America, Kurlantzick suggests, not only reflects but also augments China's soft power. Conspicuously absent are discussions of the question of the legitimacy and moral authority of Chinese power and universal appeal of Chinese ideas, cultural, economic and political. There are few convincing examples of how China has used its soft power to co-opt others to change their foreign policy behaviour to be in line with what China prefers in global politics.[44]

> Perhaps in his self-defence, Kurlantzick noted bluntly,
>
> But soft power has changed. In the context of China, both the Chinese government and many nations influenced by China enunciate a broader idea of soft power than did Nye. For the Chinese, soft power means anything outside of the military and security realm, including not only popular culture and public diplomacy but also more coercive economic and diplomatic levers like aid and investment and participation in multilateral organisations—Nye's carrots and sticks.[45]

If Kurlantzick is right, he has left unexplained a big puzzle: namely why should the discourse of China's soft power outside China have adopted the conceptualisation and ideas of soft power espoused by the Chinese government?

It would not be an exaggeration to say that here what remains of "soft power" as Nye has conceived it is just a conceptual shell without the original soul in it. *Charm Offensive* reads more like a "soft" application of China's newly found power, soft, hard and smart, or any combination of them. Put it differently, and more accurately perhaps, China has adopted a new approach to traditional statecraft. What is left for the discourse of China's soft power is, therefore, no more than a different way of talking about China's global diplomacy.

DOES CHINA'S SOFT POWER MATTER?

Even if the broader conceptualisation of soft power as enunciated by Kurlantzick can be causally linked to Chinese foreign policy initiatives, and even if China's soft power is for real and rising and China is becoming a super soft power, two analytical questions need to be addressed. Does China's soft power matter? If so, in what sense does it matter?

To answer these two questions, first, consider the exercise of soft power in terms of agenda-setting. Has China's soft power enabled it to set any agenda for global or regional institutions "as to get others to change in particular cases?" As has been widely observed and acknowledged, China's tentative participation in the 1980s in such global economic institutions such as the International Monetary Fund (IMF) and the World Bank has led to its full embrace of multilateralism and more recently in its full membership in the World Trade Organisation (WTO). It is true that in contrast to prevailing scepticism about the ASEAN Regional Forum (ARF) over ten years ago, China has sought successfully its regional integration with Southeast Asia through a number of regional mechanisms, from ASEAN Plus One to ASEAN Plus Three to the East Asia Summit (EAS). It is also true that China is pivotal in mediating between recalcitrant parties in the Six Party Talks and in the conception and operation of the Shanghai Cooperation Organisation (SCO).

The crux of the matter here is, however, that it is still hard to argue that China has played any decisive role in setting any agenda for these international organisations and negotiations. The evidence to the contrary, on the other hand, is overwhelming. As one of the Permanent Five at the Security Council of the United Nations, China in general follows rather than takes any leadership on global issues. At such regional organisations as APEC, China seems to be comfortable simply accepting the agenda set by others rather than trying to assert its own agenda. In the case of the East Asia Summit launched in December 2005, the inclusion of Australia, India and New Zealand was certainly not on China's agenda and was very much against China's wish. Yet, China accepted it.

Second, it is the question of co-optive behaviour. It is generally acknowledged that China's international behaviour has changed significantly in the last two decades. It is "more integrated into, and more cooperative within, regional and global political and economic systems than ever in its history."[46] China has become more cooperative, for example, in dealing with regional and global security issues. Its cooperation is crucial for moving forward the process of the de-nuclearisation of the Korean Peninsula forward through the Six Party Talks and it is generally supportive of and cooperative in the global war on terror. It is also noted to be readily accommodating in negotiations leading to the resolution of a number of stubborn territorial disputes with its neighbours. China's compliance to global norms embodied in the WTO has improved by leaps and bounds since it became a full member in 2001. Indeed, according to Johnston, in terms of five major international normative regimes, namely sovereignty, free trade, non-proliferation and arms control, national self-determination and human rights, "China appears to be conforming more with an extant international community, such as it is, than it has in the past."[47]

One may question whether such behaviour represents normative changes in Chinese foreign policy. It can be argued that China's changing international behaviour is driven by the consideration of its national interest. For our purposes here, the normative and instrumental arguments are not important. What is important is the fact that it is not China's soft power that co-opts others and changes others' behaviour. Rather, it is China that has been subject to the co-optive power of those dominant in the international community and global governance, as its behaviour has become increasingly convergent with accepted international norms and rules. Viewed in this perspective, it is not China that is transforming the world. Rather, it is the world that has changed China!

Changes in China's international behaviour are closely related to China's changing image in global international society. This is the third point to consider. It is true that China started an "image project" back in the late 1990s when Beijing was particularly concerned about a series of claims about the so-called "China threat." But the world seemed to be genuinely surprised when two polls conducted respectively by the Lowy Institute for International Policy and the BBC World Service, both in 2005, revealed an increasingly positive image of China. Indeed, China's influence on the world is seen as more positive by more people than that of the United States.[48] The popularity of China in the developing world is particularly striking. Kurlantzick notes, for example, the positive image of China in the media of Thailand in sharp contrast to a decade before.[49] He also notes the broad appeal of China's model of state-directed growth and poverty reduction to developing countries in Africa and Latin America, which helps depict China in favourable light.[50]

It would be a mistake to attribute China's improved image entirely to its public diplomacy. In other words, it is not just the twisting of minds that matters here. There are real changes, too. China's increasing compliance to and convergence with global norms, rules and values, as discussed before, has contributed to a more positive image of China. It has enhanced the international legitimacy of Chinese power and brought a higher international status for China. The critical question is, however, not how popular China has become in certain parts of the world, but how much China's improved image has increased the trust of the international community in China's growing power and the moral authority and legitimacy of China's domestic and international policies. The evidence in this regard is at best patchy.

If the exercise of China's soft power is not agenda-setting, if it is China that is at the receiving end of the co-optive power of international society, and if China's recent popularity does not lead to either the trust in, or the enhanced legitimacy of, Chinese power, why should we trouble ourselves with the discourse of China's soft power? After all, popularity is often transient and is always difficult to sustain. Power, soft or hard, makes friends as well as enemies.[51] Moreover, China's hard military power, though growing expansively, is likely to remain weak in terms of its capability of power projection. It will hardly be a match to that of the United States even in the long term.

What is then the political logic behind the raging discourse of China's soft power? Clearly the United States is deeply concerned about the rise of China as a transformative force in global politics and world economy in the twenty-first century. "Embrace and hedge," a strategy widely advocated in Washington in regard to the rising China, reflects scepticism, uncertainty and cynicisms on the part of the United States, the sole hegemon, about China's self-claimed peaceful rise. After the initiation of the East Asia Summit without the U.S. participation in 2005, Nye specifically called for the United States to pay more attention to the balance of soft power in Asia. Kurlantzick's description of the rise of China's soft power is particularly illustrative of the U.S. concerns. It is worth quoting at length.

> While the US has been focused on Iraq, it has ignored a subtle—but enormous—change in the world. Since only the early 2000s, and under the US radar, China has changed from a country that barely interacted with the world into a growing foreign power. In fact, China savvily has amassed significant "soft power" around the world through aid, formal diplomacy, public diplomacy, investment, and other tools. Here in Washington, where China's image is not great, it's hard for us to understand how popular China has become in Africa, Asia, and Latin America.[52]

A deeper anxiety in the United States is, however, about the precarious pre-eminence and the uncertain prospects of the American power. The rise of a potential adversary espousing different political values accentuates such anxiety. Small wonder it is that Orville Schell claimed that China's growing soft power "has begun to transform the world balance of power in a way that makes it essential for Americans to recalibrate their presumption of U.S. preeminence."[53] Kurlantzick is more specific when he states that

> No one amassed chits with other nations for no reason. Now, China can begin to use its soft power. It will be able to utilize its popularity in regions where the US and China have potentially competing interests in resources. China is already trying to draw upon its charm to push back against American power in Asia. In the future, China could prod countries like the Philippines or Thailand, which are already using China as a hedge, to downgrade their close relations with the United States.[54]

CONCLUSION

Nye's conception of soft power helps generate a discourse that is directed at resolving a number of genuine puzzles concerning China's rising international status. The rapid growth of China's economic power, its expanding influence in global politics, its unprecedented popularity and its assertive global diplomacy in the last few years are no mean achievements. How a recent pariah state in international society advocating and practicing a political system contrary to the prevailing liberal democratic values could have achieved such a power status in so short a period of time is not a trivial question. The implications of this phenomenon for the emerging global order are significant.

The discourse of China's soft power, however, has been carried out with significant conceptual twists. More often than not, Nye's conceptual clarity and nuances have been either abandoned or simply ignored. This is partly because this discourse could be regarded as a proxy of the debate about the nature and the prospects of American power. The fact that China's soft power rises exactly at the same time when the American soft power is perceived as being in decline, that China is seen as providing an alternative model—the Beijing Consensus vis-à-vis the Washington Consensus—of economic development for developing countries, that China is claimed to be working diligently to undermine American influence in many regions of the world, and the call for urgent American response to balance China's soft power—all could well be part of the discourse about the U.S. soft power. The ultimate paradox is that if Nye's conceptualisation and logic apply, then China could and should never have lasting soft power in the first place.

Perhaps, China's real soft power lies somewhere else. In examining historical fascination about China in the West, Jonathan Spence describes China's lasting charm in terms of its capacity "to attract and retain the attention of others." He further states

> This capacity is evident from the very beginnings of the West's encounter with China; the passing centuries have never managed to obliterate it altogether, even though vagaries of fashion and shifting political stances have at times dulled the sheen. The sharpness of the feelings aroused by China in the West, the reiterated attempts to describe and analyze the country and its people, the apparently unending receptivity of Westerners to news from China, all testify to the levels of fascination the country has generated.[55]

Since the Enlightenment period, China has managed to inspire feelings that alternate between fascination and frustration, admiration and condemnation, as well as excitement and disappointment. The latest rage about China is in part a testimony to the charm that China continues to hold beyond its borders.

NOTES

1. Pei Minxin, "The Dark Side of China's Rise," *Foreign Policy* 153 (2006): 32.

2. For such claims, see for example Joshua Kurlantzick, *Charm Offensive: How China's Soft Power Is Transforming the World.* (New Haven: Yale University Press, 2007); Ether Pan, "China's Soft Power Initiatives," *Backgrounder.* Council on Foreign Relations, www.cfr.org/publication/10715/; Michael Elliott. "China Takes on the World." *Time*, January 11, 2007; and Joseph Nye, "The Rise of China's Soft Power." *Wall Street Journal Asia*, December 29, 2005. http://www.ksg.harvard.edu/ksgnews/Features/opeds/122905_nye.htm.

3. Zbigniew Breczinski and John J. Mearsheimer, "The Clash of the Titans," *Foreign Policy* 146 (2005) 46–9.

4. Alastair Iain Johnston, "Is China a Status Quo Power?" *International Security*, 27, no. 4 (2003): 5–56; Nicholas Taylor, "China as a Status Quo or Revisionist Power? Implications for Australia," *Security Challenges* 3, no.1 (2007): 29–45.

5. Thomas J Christensen, "China's Role in the World: Is China a Responsible Stakeholder?" (Remarks before the U.S.-China Economic and Security Review Commission, Washington D.C., August 3, 2006); Robert B. Zoelick, 2005. "Whither China: from Membership to Responsibility?" (Remarks to National Committee on U.S.-China Relations, New York City, September 21, 2006), www.state.gov/s/d/former/zoellick/rem/53682.htm. (accessed September 23, 2008).

6. This certainly does not mean that the internal discourse is unimportant. In fact, Hu Jintao, in the capacity of the General Secretary of the Chinese Communist Party (CCP), used 'soft power' several times in his report to the 17th CCP National Congress in October 2007. Where appropriate, I have incorporated the internal discourse of China's soft power in my discussions throughout the chapter.

7. Joseph Nye, *Bound to Lead: the Changing Nature of American Power* (New York: Basic Books, 1990), ix.

8. Nye, *Bound to Lead,* 188.

9. This is indeed Nye's major argument in his 1990 article.

10. Joseph Nye, *Soft Power: The Means to Success in World Politics* (New York: Public Affairs, 2004).

11. Joseph Nye, "Soft Power," *Foreign Policy* 80 (1990): 166.

12. Nye, *Soft Power: A Means to Success in World Politics*, 5.

13. Joseph Nye, "Think Again: Soft Power," *Foreign Policy* 152 (February 2006): Web exclusive. www.foreignpolicy.com/story/cms.php?story_id=3393.

14. Nye, *Soft Power: A Means to Success in World Politics*, 11.

15. Nye, *Soft Power: A Means to Success in World Politics*, 11. For further elaborations about these three resources of soft power of the United States, see pages 33–72.

16. See in particular, Joseph Nye, "Ignoring Soft Power Carries a High Cost," *Chicago Tribune*, May 16, 2004.

17. Janice B Mattern, "Why 'Soft Power' Isn't So Soft: Representational Force and the Sociolinguistic Construction of Attraction in World Politics," *Millennium—Journal of International Studies* 33 (2005): 583–612.

18. Kat Schmidt, "Harvard's Stanley Hoffman offers 'A Critique of U.S. Foreign Policy' in speech," *Tufts Daily*, October 15, 2004, http://tuftsdaily.com/2.5511/1.599451 (accessed September 23, 2008).

19. Robert Kagan, *Of Power and Paradise: America and Europe in the New World Order* (New York: Alfred A. Knopf, 2003), 3.

20. Joseph Nye, "Europe's Soft Power." *The Globalist* 2004, www.theglobalist.com.

21. See Elsa Tulmets, "Can the Discourse on 'Soft Power' Help the EU to Bridge its Capability-Expectations Gap?," *European Political Economy*, 7:195–226 (2007); and Eneko Landaburu, et al. "Defining Europe's Soft Power," Café Crossfire Evening Debate, April 25, 2006; www.friendsofeurope.org/.

22. See Ogoura Kazuo, "The Limits of Soft Power," *Japan Echo* 33 no. 5 (2006); Nissim Kadosh Otmazgin, "Contesting Soft Power: Japanese Popular Culture in East and Southeast Asia," *International Relations of the Asia-Pacific* 8 (2007): 73–101.; Nye, *Soft Power: A Means to Success in World Politics,* 85–8.

23. Nye, *Soft Power: A Means to Success in World Politics,* 31.

24. Nye, *Soft Power: A Means to Success in World Politics,* 73–5.

25. Joseph Nye, "Our Impoverished Discourse," *Huffington Post*, November 1, 2006, www.huffingtonpost.com/joseph-nye/. (accessed September 23, 2008).

26. Nye, *Soft Power: A Means to Success in World Politics,* 31.

27. Lillie Chouliaraki, "Introduction: the Soft Power of War—Legitimacy and community in Iraq war discourses," *Journal of Language and Politics* 4, no.1 (2005): 2–3.

28. Joseph Nye, "Assessing China's Soft Power," *Boston Globe,* April 19, 2006.

29. Nye, *Soft Power: A Means to Success in World Politics,* 88.

30. Nye, *Soft Power: A Means to Success in World Politics,* 89.

31. Joseph Nye, "The Rise of China's Soft Power," *Wall Street Journal Asia* December 29, 2005, www.hks.harvard.edu/news-events/news/op-eds/the-rise-of-china-s-soft-power (accessed September 23, 2008). For a comprehensive discussion of the "Beijing Consensus," see Joshua Cooper Ramo, *Beijing Consensus* (London: Foreign Policy Centre, 2004).

32. Nye's *Soft Power: Means to Success in World Politics* published in 2004 stimulated and inspired the discourse of soft power within China. The Chinese elites greeted the idea of China's soft power initially with mixed feelings, for fear that this is a masqueraded claim of the 'China threat.' This is particularly acute when such a discourse and assessment is conducted outside China. The idea is, however, also inherently attractive, as rising China tries to rediscover and redefine its power and to identify means to enhance its attractiveness and its influence. One thrust of this discourse is directed at the search for the sources of China's soft power. See, for example, Xinhua News Agency

"Experts Comment on Soft Power and China's Strategic Choice in Enhancing its Own Soft Power" (in Chinese), www.xinhuanet.com and "The Charm of China's Soft Power," *People's Daily Online*, March 14, 2006 english.peopledaily.com.cn/200603/10/eng20060310_249577.html.

33. Robin Zachary, "The Lure of Asia: Amid the Backwaters of Beijing, a Cultural Heart Is Beating," International Herald Tribune, (December 1, 2004).

34. Jane Perlez, "Chinese Move to Eclipse U.S. Appeal in Southeast Asia," New York Times, (November 18, 2004).

35. Robert Sutter, *China's Rise in Asia: Promises and Perils* (Lanham MD: Rowman & Littlefield Publishers, 2005), 201.

36. The first Confucius Institute was launched in Seoul in November 2004. By November 2008, more than 300 were established all over the world. Even the Chinese increasingly associate the establishment of Confucius Institutes with the projection of China's soft power. See "Confucius Institute: Promoting Language, Culture and Friendliness," *People's Daily Online*, October 2, 2006, english.peopledaily.com.cn/200610/02/eng20061002_308230.html. (accessed September 23, 2008)

37. Bates Gill, and Yanzhong Huang, "Sources and Limits of Chinese 'Soft Power'." *Survival* 48, no.2 (2006): 18.

38. For example, Gill and Huang noted in particular reports about India and Africa looking at China as a model for economic development. Elsewhere, Gill and others claim that "China's historical experience and development model resonate powerfully with Africa." Bates Gill, Huang Chin-Hao and J. Stephen Morrison, "Assessing China's Growing Influence in Africa," *China Security* 3, no.3 (2007): 5.

39. Gill and Huang, *Sources and Limits,* 20.

40. Joshua Kurlantzick, "China's Charm Offensive," *TPMcafe* 2007, www.tpmcafe.talkingpointsmemo.com/2007/06/25/chinas_charm_offensive/. (accessed September 23, 2008). Kurlantzick further argued that "it has appeal to elites in nations in the region—and in other places like Africa—alienated by the Washington Consensus and American intervention around the world."

41. Gill and Huang, *Sources and Limits,* 21.

42. Lee, Kuan Yew, "China's Soft Power Success." *Forbes*, (June 18, 2007).

43. Nye, *The Rise of China's Soft Power*.

44. Kurlantzick, *Charm Offensive: How China's Soft Power is Transforming the World*.

45. Joshua Kurlantzick, *Charm Offensive: How China's Soft Power Is Transforming the World* (New Haven: Yale University Press, 2007), 6.

46. Johnston, *Is China a Status Quo Power?,* 5.

47. See Johnston, *Is China a Status Quo Power?*, 14–22.

48. Ivan Cook, "Australians *Speak 2005: Public Opinion and Foreign Policy*. Sydney: Lowy Institute for International Policy," (2005); BBC News, "China's Influence Seen Positive," March 5, 2005. news.bbc.co.uk/2/hi/asia-pacific/4318551.stm (accessed September 23, 2008).

49. Kulantzick, *How China's Soft Power is Transforming the World,* 120.

50. Kulantzick, *How China's Soft Power is Transforming the World,* 134–35.

51. Josef Joffe, "The Perils of Soft Power," *Hoover Digest*, no. 3 (2006), www.hoover.org/publications/digest/4634921.html. (accessed September 23, 2008).

52. Kurlantzick, *China's Charm Offensive*.

53. Orville Schell made this claim in praise of Kurlantzick's book in 2007. See Kulantzick, *How China's Soft Power is Transforming the World*, back cover.

54. Kurlantzick, *China's Charm Offensive*.

55. Jonathan Spence, *The Chan's Great Continent: China in Western Minds* (London: Allen Lane The Penguin Press, 1999), xi.

Part II

SOFT POWER IN CHINA'S RISING STRATEGY

Chapter Four

The New Hard Realities: "Soft Power" and China in Transition

Yong Deng

As is well known, Joseph Nye first coined the term "soft power" nearly two decades ago to debunk the then popular view that the global status of the United States was in decline. He later developed the concept to detail how the United States could take advantage of its unique strengths—beyond its material power—to revive and prolong its leadership in world politics.[1] It is remarkable that a concept originally applied to a reigning great power would find its popularity in the study of a rising power, the People's Republic of China (PRC).

Although Nye himself lately has applied the concept to the PRC, the notion of China now being a real contender for soft power must have caught him by surprise. When he first popularized the notion, the PRC was mired in potentially the worst crisis in its modern history. With the government struggling for survival, soft power was the farthest thing on the minds of the Chinese policy elites or foreign observers. Even Nye's 2004 book did not take China's soft power seriously. His discussions of the country are buried in the few pages on Asia. For him, Chinese soft power paled in comparison with Japan, which "has more potential soft power resources than any other Asian country," an amount comparable with India. "But the real promise for China and India still lies in the future," he declared.[2] But this does not jibe with the reality of increasing acceptance of China as a leading (if not the central) power in Asia and the country's great leap upward in the international hierarchy. Since a nation's soft power cannot possibly develop in only several years, this raises the question as to how meaningful the concept is for the study of Chinese foreign relations. This chapter addresses that question by investigating how soft power is treated in the rhetoric and practice of China's international strategy in the post-Cold War era.

Soft power generally means the ability to "get your way" in world politics without coercion, although the relationship between soft and hard power remains vague. Heavily influenced by Nye's writings, existing definitions invariably stress the ability of a country to generate genuine affection and strong identification from others. In fact, Nye made it clear that he was concerned with how hegemonic power, which he called "the dominant state" or "leading states," effectively uses the spread of its cultural and ideological influence, dominance in international institutions, and control of prevailing norms and principles to consolidate its material supremacy.[3] I argue that this approach, when applied to the PRC, is misplaced. First and foremost, the United States and China differ in status; i.e., the sources, means, and objectives of their soft power differ. For China, soft power, to a large extent, means the ability to influence others in world politics with the goal of achieving great power status without sparking fully fledged traditional power politics of hostile balancing or war. This is only achievable through a prudent use of its power in deeds and words. Viewed this way, soft power is integral to China's strategy.

I first examine the gap between China's rhetorical silence and practice of soft power in the 1990s and sketch how soft power is being pursued in a more deliberate way in the new century. The second section examines the various dimensions of China's soft power. In the third section, I offer a preliminary evaluation of the success, limits, and implications of China's soft power politics. I argue that the essence of China's post-Cold War foreign policy is to avoid a collision with the established great powers and the international status quo. Soft power thus represents the core of China's foreign policy. To enhance it, the PRC has pursued economic, multilateral, and cooperative diplomacy. It has contested Western dominance in values and standards, but has done so by cultivating its political and cultural influence in the context of a more pluralistic world. From strictly Nye's perspective, David Shambaugh correctly notes that "China seems to have little in the realm of soft power."[4] But judged by its own objectives, China's soft power campaign has succeeded remarkably, suggesting hope for its peaceful rise. The Chinese elites now no longer consider soft power as a lopsided battle in favor of the West; rather it's an arena they too must and can win. Considering soft power in terms of governance at home and influence abroad, they are also aware of myriad weaknesses and hard realities in China's domestic and international transitions.

CHINA'S SOFT POWER: FROM DEEDS TO WORDS

In the 1990s, the notion of soft power did not figure into Chinese foreign policy, although the country pursued elements of what would later be called soft power. In the decade following the Tiananmen incident, the country's foreign policy was first focused on how to break away from its international isolation, and then on managing a string of crises. It was a period marked by heightened domestic insecurity and international turbulence. Pervasive among the educated elites were emotionally charged reactions to the seemingly endless provocations and bullying of the West.

When soft power was mentioned by Chinese analysts, it was attributed to the West or the United States. The implicit reasoning was that Western countries, as the dominant parties in world politics, controlled international discourse, institutions, and rules. They manipulated these soft power instruments to justify and legitimize their political practices. Case in point was the NATO war on Yugoslavia in 1999. From the Chinese perspective, what started out as civil strife between two ethnic groups within a sovereign country was portrayed by Western media and politicians, and later accepted in international society, as genocide. NATO members recast the nature of the conflict and launched a well-coordinated international campaign to promote "humanitarian interventionism," a new principle that paved the way for its military attacks against the Republic of Yugoslavia in the name of stopping ethnic cleansing.[5] Soft power was thus considered a Western privilege, an essential part of the moral and political high ground commanded by the West, which disadvantaged countries like China. Chinese strategists believed that China should guard against this subtle form of power, just as it should against Western hard power.

Besides insecurity in the Western-dominated world, another explanation for the lack of explicit interest in soft power was a series of foreign crises that characterized China's foreign relations in the 1990s. Except for a brief period, the first decade following the end of the Cold War ushered in an intensely unstable era in the Sino-American relationship. In the early 1990s, a host of issues, notably pertaining to China's human rights record, "most favored nation" status, and arms proliferation, threatened the very foundation of the bilateral relationship.[6] Nationalist emotions ran high among the educated Chinese populace, culminating in the publication of the wildly popular anti-American bestseller, *China Can Say No*, in 1995. The Taiwan crisis at the same time added fuel to the fire. After a brief respite, yet another major incident erupted in 1999 over NATO's accidental bombing of the Chinese embassy in Belgrade. These rancorous disputes and crises underscored the dangers that China faced, whereas nationalist reactions brought to the forefront a sense of victimization dating back to the nation's experience as a semi-colony following the Opium War of the 1840s.

In the rare cases when Chinese soft power was mentioned in the 1990s, it was about the country's *domestic* politics. Chinese authors invariably used the term to call for domestic institutional reforms, which they saw as neglected but critical components of China's modernization.[7] In fact, the Chinese notion of comprehensive national power (*Zonghe Guoli*), which was first popularized in the late 1990s, stressed technological and economic capacity, but also entailed non-material power in terms of national cohesion and domestic governance.

Insecurity at home and abroad did not create a permissible environment for explicit talk of soft power as part of a deliberate Chinese foreign policy pursuit. Nonetheless, in practice, the country did pursue a foreign policy that eschewed hardcore power politics. The emphasis was on domestic development, economic diplomacy, and participation in the global mainstream. The imperative of economic modernization dictated much of the choice. Internationally, the U.S.-led global order was structured such that a confrontational hard-power strategy appeared prohibitively costly, while at the same time a softer approach appeared plausible in achieving both the Chinese leadership's domestic agenda and international aspirations.

By the mid-1990s, the West's "China threat" theories had been replaced by "China collapse" theories. The former, which are essentially foreign fears of China as a destabilizing, aggressive, and harmful actor in world politics, started to gain currency. By then the United States had become poised to consolidate its forward presence in the west Pacific, dissipating earlier doubts about its security commitment in the region. A drastic realignment of regional order detrimental to China's interests appeared to be under way. To preempt such a development, Chinese leaders realized they needed to promote a gentler and softer approach to their country's foreign relations. A campaign of rhetoric thus followed. Chinese analysts rejected negative portrayals of China that fanned fear of, and hostilities toward, their nation as biased, malicious, or simply reflective of a Cold War mentality, while at the same time they maintained that their country's rise presented an opportunity for peace, prosperity, and stability in the world. But as E. H. Carr noted more than half a century ago, "Every country wanted to achieve the aims of its policy without war, and therefore stood for peace."[8] Thus, such rhetorical protestations did not suffice, but required corresponding behavioral adjustments to lend credence to the counter-China threat campaign in order to improve China's image. In practice, the Chinese government began to openly embrace the idea of responsible power, to pursue partnership diplomacy with countries near and far, and to establish itself as a constructive, cooperative member in Asia and vis-à-vis the international status quo.

At the same time, events between 1997 and 1998 added impetus to China's pursuit of cooperative, economic, and multilateral diplomacy. During the two years, the Sino-American relationship experienced unprecedented stability since the end of the Cold War. Leaders in Beijing and Washington publicly committed to building a strategic partnership. They joined hands in spearheading an international response to the nuclear proliferation crisis in South Asia. The financial crisis in East Asia was soon to pass, but had enduring effect on China's foreign policy transformation. The PRC stood firm in not devaluing its currency, in contrast to Japan's manipulation of yen exchange rate for apparently myopic self-interest. Beijing also provided funds to their hardest hit Southeast Asian neighbors. While the funds were relatively small, the gesture showed genuine sensitivity to neighboring states' economic difficulties. Moreover, by comparison, neither other powers nor international institutions, including the International Monetary Fund, demonstrated leadership in crafting an effective response, further accruing image gains for the PRC. In any case, Chinese behavior during the crisis scored it high diplomatic points.[9]

The financial crisis fostered East Asian regionalism while lifting China's relationship with southeast Asia to a new level. The principal mission of the Association for Southeast Asian Nations (ASEAN) is to reverse security dilemmas, lessen competition for relative power, and delegitimize the use of violence in regional relations. The ASEAN approach, coupled with its inclusive and reassuring style and adherence to the sovereignty principle, has proved to Beijing's liking. With the creation in 1994 of the ASEAN Regional Forum (ARF), the multilateral security platform that draws in all major powers in the Asia-Pacific, ASEAN had effectively abandoned its long-standing policy of keeping great powers at arm's length in favor of a policy of keeping them engaged and constrained on ASEAN's terms. Amidst and after the financial crisis, the PRC and the ASEAN discovered that the compatibility between their international approaches would be both beneficial and eminently possible. Mutual suspicion subsequently began to give way to mutual accommodation, whereby China's pursuit of a softer, gentler diplomacy fit nicely with the ASEAN style of diplomacy, generating a positive, interactive momentum unprecedented in the Sino-ASEAN relationship.[10]

Against this backdrop, a renewed interest in East Asian regionalism resurfaced, kicking off the ASEAN "ten plus three" (China, Japan, and Korea) dialogue. Around the same time, ideas such as responsible power, nonconventional threats, new security, win-win policy, and the Shanghai spirit, started to make inroads into China's international thinking. These ideas underpinned a multilateral turn in China's Asia diplomacy that both dovetails with and reinforces its bilateral ties with individual states and its regional position as a whole.[11] Diplomatic successes in opening up opportunities for China abroad vindicated these ideas, further locking in the strategic choice with a corresponding definition of national identity in world politics.

As the 1990s drew to a close, the NATO war against Yugoslavia and the embassy bombing incident would further mute any self-congratulatory talk of soft power. During this time, out of necessity and by choice, the PRC pursued economic diplomacy and a set of foreign policy choices reflective of pro-status quo international orientations. But the country was not yet secure or strong enough to brandish soft power in its foreign policy rhetoric.[12]

The new century did not start auspiciously for China-U.S. relations. Having labeled the PRC a strategic competitor during the presidential campaign, newly inaugurated President George W. Bush appeared ready to reverse much of the President Clinton's engagement policy. The EP-3 crisis in 2001 dealt yet another setback to the already volatile bilateral relationship. But the crisis quickly passed, and the Bush administration reengaged the PRC on an even more extensive bilateral, regional, and global agenda. The Sino-American relationship has since seen unprecedented strength, although the Chinese side has refrained from an overly optimistic characterization of the new cooperative dynamics between the two countries. As it has moved to the center stage of world politics, China's soft power discourse and practice have gained even greater steam. Chinese analysts have become less reticent in talking about China's soft power and the frequency of such references picked up particularly after the Iraqi War in 2003.

Specifically, Chinese commentators since 2004 all agree that the U.S. soft power has been damaged, while some have expressed confidence that this in turn creates an opportunity for China to improve its own image. At the same time, policy-makers started to articulate a global vision designed to showcase China's soft power assets. However, Chinese leaders and officials have remained cautious about the use of the term to characterize foreign policy. Tellingly, President Hu Jintao's report to the 17th Chinese Communist Party (CCP) in October 2007 only mentioned "soft power" in reference to the need for China to build up a national value system best suited for the party's domestic agenda on building a "harmonious society."[13] Even after the image-boosting Olympic Games in August 2008 and amidst the subsequent global financial crisis, caution, wariness, and realism continued to characterize what has become a more deliberate and confident Chinese quest for soft power.

Since the end of the Cold War, Chinese-style soft power has been a key component of the PRC's foreign policy. The need for positive recognition as an international actor became particularly acute after the Tiananmen incident. In line with Deng Xiaoping's "lie low" policy, the Chinese leadership opted to focus on domestic development while pursuing a generally conservative, non-confrontational approach abroad. Since the new century begun, the PRC has more consciously pursued soft power. The various refrains in its diplomatic language throughout the past twenty some years invariably reflect a softer, gentler foreign policy approach to facilitate the overall Chinese goal of joining the global mainstream,[14] to pave its own path abroad, and to define responsibilities on its own terms. Even on Taiwan, Chinese analysts have argued that soft power gives them more options and diplomatic tools to keep pro-independence forces on the island in check.[15] Interestingly, under the new KMT administration since May 2008, Taiwan too has come to see soft power beyond military deterrence against the mainland as an indispensible part of its national security.[16]All in all, Chinese foreign policy is now more than ever marked by a deliberate effort to incorporate soft power into the nation's international strategy.

SOFT POWER, CHINESE STYLE

China's foreign policy has attempted to reassure others of its nonthreatening intent, enhance acceptance by the international community, and proactively realign the international environment to its liking. It is with these goals in mind that the instruments of soft power are conceived and pursued. Some of these are more "natural" insofar as they extend from the domestic path of reforms and opening up since the late 1970s. Other soft power practices, however, result from more deliberate choices.

Despite internal debates over its foreign policy since the end of the Cold War, the PRC has largely stuck to the line of "peace and development." This has paid off in its diplomacy, not least in terms of ensuring decades of stable growth on the domestic front. As the economy grows, its trade, investment, and aid have cemented ties with the rest of the world while strengthening its leverage in foreign relations. As noted earlier, the East Asian financial crisis, in particular, underscored how a win-win approach in economics and finance was possible, and when effectively pursued could spill over into positive mutual recognition in world politics at large.

The success of China's modernization has led to talk by foreign observers of a "Beijing consensus," supposedly a distinctive Chinese-style development philosophy that defies the "Washington consensus," a set of liberal values based on Western experience and interests.[17] Coined by Joshua Ramo, the idea has quickly caught on, owing mostly to China's continued economic success. Chinese officials initially showed little enthusiasm to such talk, but have quickly warmed up toward variants of reference to China's developmental approach. They are well aware that their country's domestic transition is still in such a state of flux that it's simply premature to declare an exemplary role of a so-called Chinese development model. Also, it could be counterproductive for its image abroad, as China has disavowed any attempt to export its ideology or developmental model. Much of China's soft power stems from managing its own business of domestic transition. To the extent that the "Beijing consensus" is presented as antithetical or an alternative to the "Washington consensus," it's debatable whether such a model of third-world development exists at all. But like the once-exalted East Asian developmental model, China's spectacular economic growth, particularly as experienced by certain sectors and geographic areas of the society, naturally tempts outside observers to attribute this success to some uniquely Chinese experience. Indeed, the path to the reforms of the past thirty years is paved with much trial-and-error experimentation by the Chinese leadership itself. The reformist leaders embraced globalization while at the same time insisting on a strong central role of the CCP in engineering sustained growth and resisting hasty "Western-style" political liberalization.

As China's global presence grows, interest in Chinese language and culture has also grown. In response, the government has done its part to promote both, with the most notable success being the swift proliferation of the Confucian Institute across the world. According to the official Chinese report, from 2004, when the first Confucius Institute opened in Seoul, South Korea, to the end of 2008, "Two hundred forty-nine Confucian Institutes and fifty-six Confucian Classrooms (Kongzi Xuetang) had been created in seventy-eight countries across five continents of the world," whilst at the same time "applications from over 100 universities and institutions of over forty countries were still awaiting for review and approval."[18] Under the supervision of the PRC's Ministry of Education-based Hanban (The Office of Chinese Language Council International), which is tasked with promoting Chinese language studies abroad, each institute is essentially a partnership program between a Chinese educational institution and its counterpart in the host country. Hanban would offer a seed grant of $100,000 and will continue to provides teaching staff, textbooks, and other educational materials to facilitate Chinese language teaching.[19] The quick spread of the institutes have caught the Chinese sponsors by surprise, as Hanban scrambles to search for enhanced quality control to these highly variegated, disparately run forms of collaboration. In addition to resource support, the institutes also serve as vehicles for cultural and educational exchange. As the name indicates, China has tapped its thousands of years of history to spread its cultural influence and appeal. Foreign institutions favor such an arrangement for the additional opportunities and resources for enhancing learning about, and ties with, China.

Increasingly, however, China's contemporary cultural products and arts are also gaining some popularity beyond its borders. For example, Chinese movies won the top prize at the Venice Film Festival three times in a row between 2005 and 2007. The spectacular opening ceremony of the 2008

Beijing Olympics similarly highlighted the traditional culture and ancient advancements in the Chinese civilization. Also given some play were themes of contemporary China's embrace of globalization and openness. Undoubtedly, there is growing global interest in all things Chinese, including its cuisine, but one can hardly speak of a distinct Chinese brand of popular culture that rivals that of the United States.

Compared with the West and Japan, the country is also woefully inadequate in terms of its innovative domestic institutions, science and technology, and institutions of higher learning, all of which are often associated with soft power. Due to a preoccupation with the myriad problems of domestic transition, the Chinese government has not shown much zeal in promoting its brand of politics. Chinese elites have been interested more in how the "Beijing consensus" concept vindicates China's self-paced reforms than its applicability to other developing countries. The spread of Chinese language and culture mainly results from the country's extending global presence and the associated economic opportunities. Compared with the political and cultural arenas, the Chinese government has been more focused and deliberate in cultivating soft power on the foreign policy dimension.

Through the post-Cold War era, Chinese leaders and analysts have promoted various ideas about foreign policy and world politics, including most recently "peaceful rise" and "harmonious world." These are not particularly new ideas. They boil down to a respect for sovereignty, emphasis on development, and mutual respect for differences in political system and culture. In practice, China's foreign policy has been geared toward adapting to the imperatives of deepening economic globalization, cultivating acceptance abroad, and bringing about change to the regional and international status quo such that its domestic and international paths are legitimized and mutually supportive.

Perhaps the most remarkable change was the country's embrace of multilateral diplomacy. China's accession to the World Trade Organization represented a landmark event in its path to joining the global world economy. International institutions such as the United Nations acquire particular significance insofar as China is a permanent member of the Security Council.[20] At the regional level, the PRC has pursued multilateral diplomacy, a drastic departure from its past refusal to be so entangled. In northeast Asia, its substantive role since 2003 in facilitating the Six-Party Talks toward the goal of denuclearization has been widely hailed as a remarkable example of this new course. In central Asia, China and Russia have turned what started out as a border security mechanism (namely, the Shanghai Five) into the Shanghai Cooperation Organization, which has now evolved into a comprehensive institution serving China's political, economic, and security interests while fending off turmoil and Western encroachment in this strategically pivotal region.

In Southeast Asia, the PRC has strengthened its ties with ASEAN and ASEAN-centered regional initiatives, having acceded to the ASEAN Treaty of Amity and Cooperation, signed a free trade agreement with all ten Southeast Asian economies, and pledged jointly with other regional contestants not to unilaterally enforce its claims over the South China Sea disputes. The PRC's approach to ASEAN-centered cooperative initiatives, such as the ASEAN Plus Three and the ARF, has been marked by both activism and deference to the regional organization. Similarly, Beijing has played along with the Asia-Pacific Economic Cooperation (APEC) forum and the latest East Asian Summit (2005–) rather than throw its weight around. This multilateral turn has even reached Africa in the form of the Forum on China-Africa Cooperation (FOCAC) Ministerial Conference. While the FOCAC was created with much fanfare in 2000, it soon sunk into oblivion. However, several years into the new century, the Forum has found a new life. Particularly after the second FOCAC meeting in Addis Ababa, Ethiopia in December 2003, China has helped invigorate the Forum as it rediscovered the importance of Africa for its economic and diplomatic interests.

China's soft power can be better understood and evaluated in the Chinese context. Its activism in these formal and informal institutions and processes,[21] coupled with its omni-directional partnerships and economic diplomacy, has proven to be an effective instrument to promote its economic interests, reassure others of its foreign intentions, and realign regional and international relations. Some countries, particularly in the developing world, have identified with the PRC's priority on sovereignty and its success in domestic and international transition. As China's rise creates more opportunities, economic and otherwise, foreign interest in its culture and language has also grown. China's emphasis on economic ties, non-violence, and multilateralism, has been somewhat vindicated. Skepticism toward China's international intent has decreased, and more countries seem willing to give the PRC the benefit of the doubt.

The country has largely refrained from projecting soft power on the political front, presumably because it is an area of China's comparative disadvantage. However, a few years into the new century, Chinese officials and scholars are increasingly vocal in arguing that their nation should not back down on the political front. For example, former spokesman of the Chinese Foreign Ministry Shen Guofang recently argued that soft power must entail some say in political discourse, agenda-setting, and the "moral high ground" in world politics.[22] The influential scholar Yan Xuetong dismissed the idea that China's ancient culture could itself turn into soft power; rather, he contended, cultural power ultimately depended on political power, which he defined as the government's ability to harness and promote its cultural resources abroad. The corollary is that Chinese should not cede its political ground, but rather should directly contest Western political domination.[23] His argument will find greater resonance amongst Chinese intellectual and political elites, as they increasingly believe that their nation's rise must entail an intellectual and political struggle with prevailing Western ideas and values.

Indeed, the Chinese are more forthcoming now than in the 1990s in propounding a global vision that supposedly goes beyond their parochial concerns about national security. Perhaps most notable is the call for building a "harmonious world," an idea rooted in Chinese traditional culture while intimately connected to the current Chinese leadership's agenda of building a harmonious society at home.[24] This notion may find some resonance with the domestic audience or even in other Asian countries. But from the perspective of mainstream thinking in the West, such a world reflects a utopianism divorced from the reality of world politics. As the leading American international relations scholar Robert O. Keohane writes, "Harmony refers to a situation in which actors' policies (pursued in their own self-interest without regard for others) automatically facilitate the attainment of others' goals. . . . Where harmony reigns, cooperation is unnecessary."[25] Ultimately, it remains unclear what concrete solutions the Chinese can offer to solve the myriad real world problems and conflicts.

The Chinese conception of soft power entails simultaneously addressing concerns to strengthen domestic stability, governance, and vibrancy, on the one hand; and cultivating acceptance and influence abroad, on the other. The domestic-international nexus compels the Chinese leaders to be highly attentive to their country's vulnerabilities in both fronts, with particularly acute sensitivity to how the unresolved problems in domestic transition impede soft power practice abroad. The protests on the streets of London, Paris, and San Francisco against the Olympics torch relay surrounding the March 14, 2008 incident in Tibet literally drove home how ill-quipped China's domestic politics was to deal with the new reality of eroded state power and decentralized control under globalization and information revolution. [26]

SOFTENING THE PATH FOR GREAT-POWER STATUS

The reformist CCP leaders' domestic reforms are closely tied to an embrace of economic globalization, although they emphatically resist Westernization. While complaining about the unfairness and discriminatory nature of the international arrangement, they also recognize that the globalized world creates opportunities that align with their nation's international aspirations and are amenable for gradualist change in their favor. The current domestic track of reforms and global integration has given rise to a particular national identity that predisposes the political elites to imagine their nation's "greatness" in terms of a positive interactive process between China's rise and the evolving world order. The country's deepening economic globalization cements the symbiotic ties between the prevailing interests and institutions at home and abroad.[27]

Beyond the economic benefits, globalization and the liberal world order also rein in the containment impulse in great-power politics to provide an orderly, institutionalized mechanism hospitable to China's aspirations.[28] Indeed the United States has signaled its positive message in welcoming China to become a "responsible stakeholder," and so have other established powers in their "engagement" with China.[29] Thus, to the extent that China's soft power emphasizes a mutually supportive domestic and international agenda, a balance between power and acceptance, and a pursuit of change through cultural influence, economic diplomacy, and institutional participation, it fundamentally defines the country's foreign policy strategy in general. Understood in the Chinese context, much of the so-called "soft power" is essential ingredients of the Chinese model that have enhanced governance at home and presence abroad.[30] As such, soft power should not be treated as a tool for some exigency, but rather as embedded in China's domestic and international transition.

China's soft power may be distinctive, but its reliance is not *sui generis* in great-power politics. In fact, both Germany and Japan after World War II utilized economic diplomacy, international institutions, and their model of technological advancement, to forge new international roles. Comparing contemporary China with postwar Germany and Japan this way by no means suggests that the Chinese are simply repeating their paths. In fact, the international trajectories of the two U.S. allies were themselves quite divergent, with the German success in securing a leadership role in Europe contrasting with the ambivalence between Japan and its Asian neighbors.[31] If the foreign policy patterns of the two pivotal states in the American hegemony are so divergent,[32] then we should expect the PRC, as an out-group member vis-à-vis the established great powers in the post-Cold War world, to pursue a diplomacy that is markedly different, with a greater challenge to the regional and international status quo.[33]

In any case, the PRC has pursued a foreign policy designed to soften competitive power politics while realigning its international relations. In the early years of the twenty-first century, China's soft power has seen phenomenal growth, particularly in southeast Asia and many developing countries in Africa and Latin America.[34] The country has gained a great deal of legitimacy, the one thing Beijing lost badly after Tiananmen. Today its power is less feared and more accepted. As Shi Yinhong recently wrote, in the "asymmetrical race" between the U.S. reliance on "military deployments, military advances, and the building of military alliances," and Chinese use of "peaceful economic forces, on foreign trade, and on its diplomacy," his country has won. Like him, many other Chinese analysts have argued that the U.S. unilateralism has undercut its role in Asia and the world. However, Shi subsequently noted the striking absence of China's contribution to liberal political values and the equally stunning costs of his country's single-minded pursuit of economic growth on the environment and "social justice" at home.[35] While keenly aware of the daunting challenges in their country's domestic transition, Chinese strategic analysts at present generally feel that the United States is somewhat constrained. There is a growing sense that things are going their way, albeit not necessarily at the expense of other established powers.

There is no doubt that China has gained a great deal in international status, particularly since the onset of the new century. But more difficulties lie ahead in U.S.-China relations. According to Iain Johnston and Daniela Stockmann, even after 2003, survey data indicated that residents in Beijing had a deep suspicion that the United States was trying to hold back their nation's rightful quest for great power status.[36] As China grows stronger, power transition will intensify to fuel frictions between the two countries. Sophisticated Chinese analysts, aware of the challenge in managing the Sino-American relationship, are not in a self-congratulatory mood. They are not rushing to declare that the United States is in irreversible decline, nor are they rejoicing about the onset of a new world order, presumably because of an awareness of the necessities and difficulties in managing the unwieldy Sino-American relationship.

As with hard power, soft power projection encounters resistance and contestation. Most notably, Beijing's practices in Africa have elicited criticism of neocolonialism, allegedly repeating the pattern of rapacious Western plundering of local economies. The so-called "Beijing consensus" remains nebulous in telling other countries what inspiring values and ideas China really stands for. China's soft power is ultimately limited by weaknesses on its domestic front. In this connection, it is useful to recall what Deng Xiaoping said in the 1980s: China is both a big power *and* a small power. [37] China is big, given its population, scale, U.N. permanent seat, and now growing comprehensive power. But it is also small, in the sense that the country still suffers from the common "third world syndrome": the government has to combat myriad sources of insecurity and challenges as it struggles to sustain balanced growth, build institutions, and maintain stability on the home front.

Internationally, China's regional and global environment remains deeply uncertain, particularly with regards to the United States, Japan, and Taiwan.[38] The leadership remains wary of the momentum of "color revolution" along its borders, as well as the various forms of hard balancing against Chinese power by its neighbors. The potency of nationalism based on official remembrance of victimization and humiliation at the hands of the West and Japan during a bygone era reflects a real sense of vulnerability. Thus, the Chinese leadership must carefully navigate the turbulent and uncertain waters of domestic and international transition.

History and scholarship on international relations in the United States have shown again and again that the power transition prompted by redistribution of power has led to war, often between the reigning great power and the rising one. In fact the international relations field has produced two findings that are generally regarded as empirically "scientific": one is democratic peace and the other is the inevitability of hegemonic war. China's emphasis on soft power reflects an implicit acceptance of a single, unified power and authority arrangement in contemporary world politics within which China can attain its status interests. That does not mean that China's rise will be harmonious and friction-free. The reality is that this non-Western country's soft power is differently endowed compared to the United States. For its strategic, political, and cultural interests, the PRC will try to modify the predominant ideas, institutions, and values in world politics in order to gain an advantage in competing with the United States and the West.[39]

The gap in polity could potentially be played up to drive a wedge and accentuate a strategic divide between China and the liberal democratic powers.[40] If soft power competition becomes an unmitigated, zero-sum ideological struggle, it would only harden competitive power politics. Vowing to avoid another Cold War, Chinese leaders and analysts alike appear quite aware of the danger and have thus stressed its soft power growth as a positive sum game with the rest of the world. They have focused on the domestic construction of soft power, which for them means refurbishing an institutional system in a CCP-led society that is vibrant enough to stand its ground in the age of Westernization and globalization. Chinese leaders do not like to talk about Chinese diplomacy in terms of soft power, preferring instead to use various euphemisms to characterize China's subtle initiatives.[41] Such caution is analogous to their approach to the concept of the "peaceful rise." The Chinese leadership quickly dropped the idea of the "peaceful rise" in 2004, presumably because of calculations that an unconditional declaration of peace undermines China's deterrence posture, whereas premature declaration of a rising status feeds into China threat theories. Perhaps similar concerns are behind Chinese reticence in playing up soft power in its foreign policy discourse.

While cautious, the country has high expectations for soft power development as its growth is considered as woefully inadequate, especially when compared with China's fast growing hard power. Chinese elites take solace that soft power has now become a tool at their disposal, but they are by means satisfied with what they have. While to a large degree it is a matter of choice for the United States whether to turn to soft power, for China, soft power is not readily available. They will have to work hard to discover, identify, harness, and foster such new sources of influence from the past, present, and future.

CONCLUSION

All in all, China's foreign policy has been amenable to positive-sum competition among great powers and as such has so far softened its path to great-power status. "Soft power" has provided a platform for the United States and China to negotiate the meaning of "responsible stakeholder," which the United States wishes the latter to be. For the next fifteen to twenty years, the PRC will remain a developing country with a continued need for international support to address its daunting domestic agenda. And more likely than not, the great-power politics will not relapse to cut-throat hard power competition. Globalization has reordered how states interact with each other. The bright side of it—multilateralism, economic interdependence, and unifying forces that cross boundaries and erode barriers—has tied countries together in ways never seen before. The dark side—financial crisis, environmental degradation, epidemics, terrorism, and weapons of mass destruction—represents transnational, unconventional challenges calling for collective efforts by all the states involved, particularly the major powers. Under these conditions, soft power has become an ever-greater part of great-power politics with each pushing its strengths and advantages in areas of competition besides hard power. Given the foregoing discussions, barring an unexpected economic meltdown or a major foreign policy crisis, it is in all likelihood that soft power will become an even greater part of China's foreign policy.

China's approach to soft power is characterized by a focus on domestic renewal, an emphasis on the benign history, and an embrace of globalization, which has curbed its ambition to push an alternative world vision. The country's heavy reliance on soft power indicates awareness of its own weaknesses at home, a sense of citizenship in international society, and a conscious attempt to reverse the hardcore power transition. It also reveals a new confidence, a discontent with the Western-dominated world order, a heightened sense of vulnerabilities, and a determined pursuit of comprehensive material power commensurate with a traditional great power. China's diplomacy does suggest the possibility of a pattern of great-power politics as reconfigured by a non-confrontational competition over soft power. If that paradigm shift is to hold, a new global consensus transcending the polarized thinking of the "Washington consensus" versus "the Beijing consensus" will have to be negotiated. How to navigate such a transition to a more pluralist world in an age of globalization is at the core of the questions regarding both the future of China's foreign relations and the future of world politics at large.

NOTES

1. Joseph Nye, *Bound to Lead: The Changing Nature of American Power* (New York: Basic Books, 1990); Joseph Nye, *Soft Power: The Means to Success in World Politics* (New York: Public Affairs, 2004).

2. Nye, *Soft Power,* 83–9 on Asia. (Quotes on 85 and 88).

3. Nye, "*Bound to Lead,*" 32–5.

4. David S. Shambaugh,"Introduction: The Rise of China and Asia's New Dynamics," in David Shambaught, ed., *Power Shift: China and Asia's New Dynamics* (Berkeley: University of California Press, 2005), 2.

5. Yuan Zhibing, "What is 'New' About New Interventionism," *Renmin Ribao*, July 29, 1999, 6. Open Source Center (hereafter cited as OSC, formerly Foreign Broadcast Information Service): FTS 19990729000569; Liu Ming and Guo Suping, "Beware of the Influence of 'Soft Attacks' on the Nation's Image," *Zhongguo Dangzheng Ganbu Luntan*, January 6, 2007, 18–19. in OSC: CPP20070417332001.

6. The classic treatment on this period is Harry Harding, *A Fragile Relationship: The United States and China since 1972* (Washington, DC: Brookings Institution, 1992).

7. Jen Hui-wen, "China Establishes the Building of Soft Power as a Strategic Mission," March 30, 2007, 15, OSC: CPP20070330710009; Chu Shulong, "China's National Interest, National Power, and National Strategy," *Zhanlue Yu Guanli*, October 26, 1999, 13–8, OSC: FTS19991026000196.

8. E. H. Carr, *The Twenty Years' Crisis, 1919–193: An Introduction to the Study of International Relations* (2nd edition) (London, MacMillan, 1946; reprinted in 1961), 140.

9. Thomas G. Moore and Dixia Yang, "Empowered and Restrained: Chinese Foreign Policy in the Age of Economic Interdependence," in David Lampton, ed., *The Making of Chinese Foreign and Security Policy in the Era of Reform, 1978–2000* (Stanford, CA: Stanford University Press, 2001), chapter 7.

10. Amitav Acharya, *Constructing a Security Community in Southeast Asia: ASEAN and the Problem of Regional Order* (New York: Routlege 2001); Amitav Acharya, "How Ideas Spread: Whose Norms Matter? Norm Localization and Institutional Change in Asian Regionalism," *International Organization*, 58 (Spring 2004): 239–275.; Alastair Iain Johnston, "The Myth of the ASEAN Way? Explaining the

Evolution of the ASEAN Regional Forum," in *Imperfect Unions: Security Institutions over Time and Space*, eds. Robert O. Keohane, Helga Haftendorn, and Celeste Wallander (New York: Oxford University Press, 1999), 287–324.; Donald K. Emmerson, "Security, Community, and Democracy in Southeast Asia: Analyzing ASEAN," *Japanese Journal of Political Science*. 6, no. 2 (August 2005): 165–85.; Alice D. Ba, "Who's Socializing Whom? Complex Engagement in Sino-ASEAN Relations," *Pacific Review* 19, no. 2 (June 2006): 157–79.

11. Pang Zhongying, "Zhongguo De Yazhou Zhanlue: Linghuo De Duobian Zhuyi" [China's Asia Strategy: Flexible Multilateralism], in *Zhongguo Waijiao Juan* [China's Foreign Affairs], ed. Niu Jun (Beijing: New World Press, 2007), 132–42.; Xiao Huanrong, "Zhongguo De Daguo Zeren Yu Diquzhuyi Zhanlue" [China's Great Power Responsibility and Strategy of Regionalism], in *Zhongguo Waijiao Juan* [China's Foreign Affairs], ed. Niu Jun (Beijing: New World Press, 2007), 143–56.

12. Wang Hongying finds very few references to "soft power" in Chinese journals during the 1990s. See her "Chinese Conception of Soft Power and Its Policy Implications," *Journal of Contemporary China* (forthcoming), ms, 2.

13. *Renmin Ribao* (overseas edition, hereafter cited as RMRB), Oct. 25, 2007, 3.

14. Jeffrey W. Legro, "What China Will Want: The Future Intentions of a Rising Power," *Perspectives on Politics* 5, no. 3 (2007): 515–34.

15. Liu Hong, "Zhao Qizheng: Taiwan Issue Should be Resolved with Soft Power First," *Zhongguo Xinwen She*, January 12, 2005, OSC: CPP20050124000189.

16. On Taiwan, see Su Chi, "Soft Power + Defensive National Defense=National Security," Lienho Pao online, Jan. 24, 2009, OSC: CPP 20090114312008.

17. Joshua Cooper Ramo, "The Beijing Consensus," *Foreign Policy Institute Report* 2004, fpc.org.uk/fsblob/244.pdf (accessed October 2, 2007).

18. RMRB, Dec. 16, 2008, 3.

19. RMRB, Jan.12, 2009, 6.

20. Yong Deng, "Better Than Power: International Status in Chinese Foreign Policy," in *China Rising: Power and Motivation in Chinese Foreign Policy,* eds. Yong Deng and Fei-Ling Wang (Lanham, MD: Rowman & Littlefield, 2004), 51–72.

21. Alastair Iain Johnston, *Social States: China in International Institutions 1980–2000* (Princeton, NJ: Princeton University Press, 2008). See also Bates Gill, *Rising Star: China's New Security Diplomacy* (Washington, D.C.: Brookings Institution Press, 2007).

22. Shen Guofang,"Theory and Practice of China's New Diplomacy," Shijie Zhishi, July 1, 2007, 42–4, OSC: CPP20070713508001.

23. Yan Xuetong, "Political Application of Cultural Resources," Huanqiu Shibao, August 2, 2007, 11, OSC: CPP20070822329001.

24. Liu Jiansheng, "'Hexie Shijie' Sixiangwenhua Suyuan" [The Intellectual and Cultural Origins of "Harmonious World"], China Institute of International Studies. www.ciis.org.cn/ (accessed March 6, 2007); Yin Chengde, "Jiangou Hexie Shijie" [Building a Harmonious World), China Institute of International Studies]. www.ciis .org.cn/ (accessed March 6, 2007).

25. Robert O. Keohane, *After Hegemony: Cooperation and Discord in the World Political Economy* (Princeton, NJ: Princeton University, 1984), 51. (original emphasis).

26. Yang Jiemian, "Chinese Diplomacy and Theoretical Innovations off 30 Years of Reform and Opening Up," Guoji Wenti Yanjiu, Nov. 13, 2008, pp. 6–11, OSC: CPP20090110267; Interview with Wang Yizhou and Wang Zaibang, "China: Crisis Diplomacy 2008," Shijie Zhishi, Dec. 1, 2008, pp. 14–23, OSC: CPP20090101267 1002. Qin Yaqing, "The World Strucutre, Security Threats and International Actors," Xiandai Guoji Guanxi, Sept. 20, 2008, pp. 1–3, OSC: CPP20081118671001.

27. David Zweig, *Internationalizing China: Domestic Interests and Global Linkages* (Ithaca, NY: Cornell University Press, 2002).

28. G. John Ikenberry, "The Rise of China and the Future of the West," *Foreign Affairs* 87, no. 1 January/February 2008): 23–37.; Yong Deng and Thomas G. Moore, "China Views Globalization: Towards a New Great Power Politics?" *Washington Quarterly* 27, no. 3 (summer 2007): 117–36.

29. Robert Zoellick, "Whither China: From Membership to Responsibility?" National Committee on US-China Relations, New York, Sept. 21, 2005, www.ncuscr.org/articlesandspeeches/Zoellick.htm (accessed Oct. 7, 2007).

30. See David M. Lampton, *The Three Faces of Chinese Power: Might, Money, and Minds* (Berkeley: University of California Press, 2008).

31. On Japan, see Peter Katzenstein and Takashi Shiraishi, eds., *Japan and Asia: Network Power* (Ithaca, NY: Cornell University Press, 1997). On Germany, see Peter Katzenstein, *Tamed Power: Germany in Europe* (Ithaca, NY: Cornell University Press, 1997); Thomas Banchoff, *The German Problem Transformed: Institutions, Politics, and Foreign Policy, 1945–1995* (Ann Arbor, MI: University of Michigan Press, 1999).

32. Peter J. Katzenstein, *A World of Regions: Asia and Europe in the American Imperium* (Ithaca, NY: Cornell University Press, 2005).

33. Robert Jervis, "Theories of War in the Era of Leading-Power Peace," *American Political Science Review* 96, no. 1 (March 2002), 1–14.

34. Joshua Kurlantzick, *Charm Offensive: How China's Soft Power Is Transforming the World* (New Heaven: Yale University Press, 2007).

35. Shi Yinhong, "China's Rise and Prospects of China's Relations with the United States, Japan," *Hong Kong Zhongguo Pinglun*, no. 114 (July 2007): 16–20, OSC: CPP20070604710001, 1; Shi Yinhong, "China's Soft Power and Peaceful Rise," *Hong Kong Zhongguo Pinglun*, no. 118 (October, 2007): 10–12, OSC: CPP20071017710002. See also Yang Jiemian, "New Features of Sino-U.S. Relations in the Transformation Period of the International System," *Shijie Jingji Yu Zhengzhi*, December 1, 2007OSC: CPP20080104587004.

36. Alastair Iain Johnston and Daniela Stockmann, "Chinese Attitudes toward the United States and Americans," in *Anti-Amerianism in World Politics,* eds. Peter Katzenstein and Robert Keohane (Ithaca, NY: Cornell University Press, 2007): 157–95.

37. Deng Xiaoping, "Heping Fazhan Shi Dangdai Shijie De Liangda Wenti" (Peace and Development Are the Two Major Issues in Contemporary World), Deng Xiaoping, *Deng Xiaoping Wenxuan*, Vol. III [Selected Works of Deng Xiaoping] (Beijing: Renmin chubanshe, 1993), 105.

38. Susan Shirk, *China: Fragile Superpower* (New York: Oxford University Press, 2007); Yong Deng, "Reputation and the Security Dilemma: China Reacts to the

China Threat Theories," in *New Directions in the Study of China's Foreign Policy,* eds. Alastair Iain Johnston and Robert S. Ross (Stanford: Stanford University Press, 2006), chapter 7.

39. Deborah Welch Larson and Alexei Shevchenko, "Shortcut to Greatness: The New Thinking and the Revolution in Soviet Foreign Policy," *International Organization* 57 (Winter 2003), 77–109.

40. Mark Haas, *The Ideological Origins of Great Power Politics, 1789–1989* (Ithaca: Cornell University Press, 2005); Azar Gat, "The Return of Authoritarian Great Powers," *Foreign Affairs* 86, no. 4 (2007): 59–69.

41. See, example, Wang Jiarui, "Actively Explore New Pattern of Party Diplomacy with Chinese Characteristics," *Renmin Ribao*, September 28, 2007, 7, OSC: CPP20070928710005.

Acknowledgement

I am grateful for the helpful comments on an earlier version of the chapter by Harry Harding and Hongying Wang. Thanks are also due to Mingjiang Li for inviting me to write this chapter and for his subsequent advice. I also benefitted from discussions with participants of the conference, "The Rise of China and Its Soft Power," held at the S. Rajaratnam School International Studies, Nanyang Technological University, Singapore, October 18–19, 2007.

Chapter Five

The Practice of the Mean: China's Soft Power Cultivation

Jianfeng Chen

The existing literature on soft power in China and other countries demonstrates a wide and often contradictory range of views. A variety of proposals have been put forward by Chinese scholars about how the country should build its soft power; via a "Chinese model,"[1] a constitutional state,[2] policies and strategic choices that match most nations' interests,[3] learning from the lessons of the United States during its soft power build-up,[4] and emphasizing its cultural heritage.[5]

The impact of China's soft power on the rest of the world is also disputed. Fearing the negative impact of China's soft power, some scholars have called for countermeasures against its development. Nye, for instance, notes: "Although China is far from America's equal in soft power, it would be foolish to ignore the gains it is making. It is time for the United States to pay more attention to the balance of soft power in Asia."[6] Kurlantzick advocates that the United States should be wary of China's "charm offensive."[7] Other commentators on China's soft power have been less alarmist. As one scholar argues, "the purpose of the soft power offensive is to spread Chinese values throughout the world and to project a more benign view of the country, one that is unquestionably committed to a peaceful rise."[8] Hunter is optimistic about China's soft power projection, writing:

> Given a historical and cultural background in "soft-power" and "moral leadership"; [and] given the intense but hopefully non-military competition with the U.S. and other states; perhaps it is logical to expect that China will increasingly project itself on the world stage by peaceful means, for example by culture, education, media presence and other means.[9]

This chapter will explore how China can effectively cultivate soft power from a cultural and philosophical point of view. A nation's soft power increases as it provides more public goods for the international community. In the international arena, the most significant public goods are stability and other beneficial conditions for common prosperity. China's soft power is growing in tandem with its contributions to world stability and prosperity. China is able to contribute to world stability and prosperity because there is a profound philosophical tradition in Chinese thinking and statecraft called the "Golden Mean."[10] I contend that the wisdom of this traditional Chinese concept can provide Chinese leaders with the intellectual capacity to approach major international issues in a balanced way, which will be more acceptable to the international community, and thus confer significant soft power on China.

The discussion in this chapter is also pertinent to the heated debate about the impact of China's rise, which is causing unease in some quarters. Many scholars have predicted that China will change the status quo and challenge American world domination. Regionally, China is seen as a threatening competitor by Japan and India and a rising power with an uncertain future by Southeast Asian nations. This chapter advances the argument that if China bases its international strategies on the Doctrine of the Mean—as Beijing is currently doing—it will be able to maintain rather than revise the international status quo. The Doctrine of the Mean would dictate China to follow the status quo because it is easier, psychologically speaking, to accept something familiar instead of something brand new and uncertain. I suggest that Chinese practice of the Mean will defuse the anxieties felt by much of the outside world in response to its rise on the world stage.

THE DOCTRINE OF THE MEAN: THE CONCEPT AND INTERSTATE RELATIONS

Different political systems are grounded in different cultures. People of the West and the East hold different beliefs about the international order based on their different cultural concepts, such as the Greek city-states or the ancient eastern Asian international system. One of the core values of Chinese culture is the Mean, the nature of which implies balanced relationships in the universe. The Mean is achieved when things develop and stay at their proper degree. Peace among nations is maintained by realizing the value of equilibrium, which generates "a happy order" throughout heaven and earth, and then "all things will be nourished and flourish."

Culture and International Order

Civilizations display many variations of cultural and social arrangements, although they are also somewhat homogeneous in the sense that there exists a fundamental and shared human nature. A nation is a cultural system and "international relations are therefore by definition also intercultural relations."[11] Culture is a concentric web with its core values encircled by its corresponding outer layers such as social structure and economical and political forms. Once its core is formed, culture, like an organism's genome, shapes a nation's behaviors and its development pattern.

If a nation produces successive economic miracles, it is taken for granted that its culture is robust, and vice versa. On the other hand, the rise and fall of a nation is closely associated with its culture in specific historical periods. When a culture is able to resolve major contradictions for a nation, it accommodates the circumstances and needs of the nation's development. When a culture is opposed to the needs for social and economic development, the nation is bound to fall. Of course, a nation's strategies, and even its political system and international relations, do not necessarily remain confined to the boundaries of its culture. But there indeed exist close relations between a state's strategies and the core values of its culture.

The cultural influence on international order is quite obvious. This can be seen in scholars' characterization of the evolution of international systems. Wight identified three interstate systems: the Hellenic-Hellenistic or Greco-Roman, the Chinese during the time of Spring-Autumn and Warring States, and the Western systems.[12] Bull recognized five international societies: the classical Greek city-state system, the Hellenistic international system in the period between the disintegration of Alexander's empire and the Roman conquest, the states system of China during the period of Warring States, the states system of ancient India, and the modern international system that formed in Europe and is now predominant on the global stage.[13] Toynbee, furthermore, characterized international relations as "Janus-headed" in the sense that the relations among states with the same civilization are different than those between states with different cultural identifications.[14]

Each of these systems was formed in a particular cultural sphere, which implies that the core values of a culture do shape a nation's behaviors and development pattern. Moreover, man is a "culture-laden" or "culture-bound" creature who makes institutions, systems, policies, and strategies. The United States has been struggling to promote democracy worldwide because the core values of the West are furnished with concepts such as freedom, equality, individualism, and competition. To universalize those values ultimately becomes an American national interest. China upholds the concept and practice of building a "harmonious world"[15] and Iran complies with Islamic fundamentalism. All these policies and strategies result from core values of the nations' respective cultures.

The Mean: A Core Value in Chinese Culture

The Mean is one of the core values in Chinese culture. The nature of the Mean encompasses the notion of appropriately balanced relationships between man and man, man and society, man and nature, and well-adjusted relations among nations. Carrying out the Mean implies that one is being neutral and is finding a balance between *Yin* (feminine or negative principle) and *Yang* (masculine or positive principle), black and white, right and left, good and bad, and them and us. The Mean focuses on self-cultivation so as to adjust interpersonal and even interstate relations, which leads to universal peace. The Confucian doctrine of the Mean is similar to the golden mean in ancient Greek philosophy. Such an analogy provides human beings with inspiration to construct a universal balance. "Confucian thought, thus, has also universal qualities and tendencies, but it could be classified as belonging more to a soft (aesthetic) universalism in contrast to a hard (rational) universalism in the West."[16]

According to the doctrine of the Mean, the right or ideal course of action is always at the middle way between the two extremes of excess and deficiency. Confucius' *Doctrine of the Mean* begins with clarifying the content and relations of Nature (*xing*), The Path of duty (*dao*), and Instruction or Cultivation (*jiao*): "What Heaven has conferred is called The Nature; an accordance with this nature is called The Path of duty; the regulation of this path is called Instruction."[17] Nature is the root and The Path of duty incarnates Nature. The Path of duty is the end and Instruction is the means. Through self-cultivation as well as the cultivation of others, man can reach The Path. The Path of duty, the aim that man needs to reach, is of vital importance. Therefore, "the path may not be left for an instant. If it could be left, it would not be the path."[18] In this account, "the superior man does not wait till he sees things, to be cautious, nor till he hears things, to be apprehensive."[19] Confucius wrote that

> Shun [an ancient Chinese emperor] indeed was greatly wise! Shun loved to question others, and to study their words, though they might be shallow. He concealed what was bad in them and displayed what was good. He took hold of their two extremes, determined the Mean, and employed it in his government of the people. It was by this that he was Shun.[20]

The Mean also implies harmony within difference:

> All things are nourished together without their injuring one another. The courses of the seasons, and of the sun and moon, are pursued without any collision among them. The smaller energies are like river currents; the greater energies are seen in mighty transformations. It is this that makes heaven and earth so great.[21]

This state of equilibrium is like a well-prepared soup, which is delicious because all the ingredients are mixed together in their proper proportions. Unlike religions that worship only one god, Chinese culture is much more inclusive. Christianity, Islam, and Judaism have been living and developing side-by-side harmoniously with Confucianism and Daoism for thousands of years in China.

Concerning the way to achieve the Mean, Confucius stated:

> While there are no stirrings of pleasure, anger, sorrow, or joy, the mind may be said to be in the state of Equilibrium. When those feelings have been stirred, and they act in their due degree, there ensues what may be called the state of Harmony. This Equilibrium is the great root from which grow all the human actions in the world, and this Harmony is the universal path which they all should pursue.[22]

The Mean is achieved when all chaos has been eliminated and order is preserved; i.e., when a state of Equilibrium has been reached. "Let the states of equilibrium and harmony exist in perfection, and a happy order will prevail throughout heaven and earth, and all things will be nourished and flourish."[23]

Applied to international relations, the Mean implies that peace and order are achieved by taking a neutral position and choosing compromise so as to establish a balance among diverse interests. The Mean not only stands for a "middle way," but also integrity. Both Confucianism and Moism (Mo Zi) insist on treating other nations with kindness and morality and believe that tenderness is the antidote to roughness. Balance can thus be maintained among nations by trading interests. Sun Zi advocated winning over the enemy without fighting. Lao Zi said: "He who would assist a lord of men in harmony with the Tao will not assert his mastery in the kingdom by force of arms. Such a course is sure to meet with its proper return."[24] Concerning interstate relations, he said:

> What makes a great state is its being [like] a low-lying, down-flowing [stream]; it becomes the center to which tend [all the small states] under heaven. [To illustrate from] the case of all females: the female always overcomes the male by her stillness. Stillness may be considered [a sort of] abasement. Thus it is that a great state, by condescending to small states, gains them for itself; and that small

> states, by abasing themselves to a great state, win it over to them. In the one case the abasement leads to gaining adherents, in the other case to procuring favor. The great state only wishes to unite men together and nourish them; a small state only wishes to be received by, and to serve, the other. Each gets what it desires, but the great state must learn to abase itself.[25]

In this way, trust is built between big nations and small ones. Therefore, the Mean is achieved and balanced relations are maintained.

THE PRACTICE OF THE MEAN: THE CHINESE TRADITION OF MANAGING INTERSTATE RELATIONS

The Mean is an ideational factor that surely has had an impact on the strategic thinking of Chinese decision-makers. Looking at the major patterns of China's foreign relations throughout history, one can safely say that this doctrine has had a great impact on China's international behavior. Rising powers in the West, such as Spain, France, Russia, the UK, Germany, the US, and Japan, followed a bloody path. They increased their strength and expanded their influence by military force and colonizing weak nations. On the contrary, ancient China highly valued harmony among peoples.

Unlike the European system, which was replete with confrontation and wars, the ancient East Asian international order, namely the tribute system, was more stable. The system was "one that involves a dominant power that does not fold secondary states under its wing in empire, and yet also does not cause other states to balance against it."[26] As a matter of fact, the tribute system was more a cultural and economical configuration than a political one in East Asia. Most of the time, China's neighboring countries, such as Japan, Vietnam, and Korea, enjoyed full political independence within the system. Their emissaries presented tributes to the Chinese emperor and to ask for recognition, symbolically at least, of their rule. This system, comparable to a family of nations with China as the center, was an extension of the Confucian social order based on rites and morals. The order was maintained and managed according to virtue (*Li*) and culture assimilation. "In the Chinese world order, hierarchical power relationship, therefore, was by definition more 'moral' than in the West."[27]

For centuries, thanks to the tribute system, China's relations with other states were based on a "taking less and giving more" (*Houwang Bolai*) approach. Because of this trading behavior, its neighboring countries enjoyed much trade surplus. "The emissaries received lavish gifts of cloth, silks, gold, and other luxuries that often far exceeded the value of what they had brought."[28] Some historians believe that the trade deficit was so big that the

Ming emperor stopped the great explorer Zheng He's expeditions to restore the trade balance. China, the unique power in the system, followed its culture's demands and made concessions in order to maintain balanced relations with other "members of the family." As Lao Zi advocated: "A great state, by condescending to small states, gains them for itself; and small states, by abasing themselves to a great state, win it over to them."[29]

Another example illustrates what the Mean implies. When Christopher Columbus first stepped on "the new continent", he formally declared that the land belonged to the Kingdom of Spain. By contrast, Zheng He decades earlier had conducted seven voyages with more than 20,000 crew members:

> He had sailed on the South China Sea and the Indian Ocean, further south to Java in today's Indonesia, then northwest to Iran and the Holy City of Mecca and further west to today's Somalia in East Africa. During his visits to more than 30 countries, he brought with him the desire of Chinese emperors to build up friendly contacts by presenting valuable gifts and inviting the rulers to send emissaries to China.[30]

His voyages were guided by the Mean-bound cultural principle of not conquering other people to expand China's territory, but instead of building friendly relations.

Of course, not all of China's behavior has followed the principles of the Mean, especially since the founding of the People's Republic of China. Mao Zedong, a revolutionary opposed to Chinese traditions, employed extreme strategies to solve the nation's problems both at home and abroad. The historical context in which he was born and raised made him embrace extremes instead of the Mean. China's then semi-colonial society led to his belief that the outside world was not trustworthy and China had to adopt a policy of self-reliance. Moreover, the unfavorable international environment–containment from the West and threats from the USSR-led Mao Zedong to expand China's diplomatic sphere in the Third World, while at the same time try to protect China from any foreign interference in its internal affairs. Domestically, he launched the Cultural Revolution to release his anti-tradition sentiment. For him, a Mean-based culture was too mild for China to "stand tall" in the East. The case of Mao's era demonstrates that his revolutionary zeal and the Cold War context played a more important role in shaping China's international strategy than cultural traditions. Since Mao's time, in the absence of such a political ideology and international environment, the doctrine of the Mean is expected to play a larger role in China's foreign policy.

Indeed, since the end of the 1970s, China's foreign policy and strategy have been established on the basis of restoring the Mean and of transcending the international order embedded in military alliances and ideological confrontation. Regarding international disputes, Deng Xiaoping stated that "some international territory disputes can be solved for the moment by joint exploration while laying aside sovereignty"[31] and "agreement can be reached while both you and we make concessions."[32] As for interstate relations, he advocated: "Do not try to gain benefit for one party only. It should be mutual to both nations and their peoples,"[33] and "we hope you are flourishing as well as we are prospering."[34]

Deng's dictums conform to the essence of the doctrine of the Mean. According to the principles of the Mean, concession, mutual benefit, and common prosperity should all be in a state of equilibrium where human nature is satisfied and harmony ensues. If you get what you want and give what the others want, both parties reach the Mean. As Confucius insisted, "Do not do to others what you would not want others to do to you." To give consideration to others is to take care of oneself, which is the Mean. For the practice of the Mean, Chinese President Hu Jintao warned in a speech to party members, at the opening ceremony of a seven-day training course in the Party School of the CPC Central Committee on Feb. 19, 2005, that "without a common ideological aspiration or high moral standard, a harmonious society will be a mansion built on sand." To the Chinese, a righteous government should use power to solve problems in conformity to the principles of the Mean and to maintain balanced relations among nations.

According to the Doctrine of the Mean, the "righteous point" is a situation in which all parties' interests are acceptable by and beneficial to all. From the 1990s onward, China has worked together with neighboring nations to settle territorial disputes in a rational and peaceful manner. For example, during the past ten years, China and Russia have found their "middle way" by jointly exploiting several islands in the bordering waters so that by the end of 2007, they had agreed on a mutually accepted demarcation of their common boundary. Thanks to agreements signed between China and India in 1993, 1996, and 2005, both countries' interests are now being protected in the border areas. The quarrels over the South China Sea islands calmed down in 1995 when China agreed to discuss the problem multilaterally within the ASEAN framework. In 2002, China, Vietnam, Malaysia, the Philippines, and Brunei found themselves at the "righteous point" when they signed "*The ASEAN-China Declaration on the Conduct of Parties in the South China Sea*" based on the principle of engaging in joint exploitation while shelving the sovereignty issue. The declaration was followed in 2005 by a joint agreement by China, Vietnam, and the Philippines' national oil companies that aimed at carrying out surveys of hydrocarbon resources in a disputed area of the South China Sea. Finally, China shelved a sovereignty issue over the Diaoyu Islands in order to develop a "strategic and mutually reciprocal" relationship with Japan. "With the principle of equal consultation as well as mutual understanding and accommodation, China has signed boundary treaties or agreements with twelve of its fourteen neighbors, demarcating ninety percent of its 22,000 km land border. . . . [As a result,] former battlefields are witnessing booming cross-border trade."[35]

Since the establishment of Deng Xiaoping's reform and opening strategy, China has not only embraced a market economy and foreign currency, but also a constellation of foreign music, movies, fashion, cuisine, books, languages, education, institutions, and norms. From a political point of view, a world with different cultures and ideologies is better than a homogeneous one. If a democratic or a socialist system is imposed on nations of different cultures and at different stages of development, the world risks conflict rather than equilibrium because it is departing from the principles of the Mean. The American strategy of global democratization ultimately reduces its soft power. According to a survey by the French-American Foundation in June 2007, the percentage of Britons having a positive view toward America declined from eighty-three percent in 2000 to fifty-one percent in 2007, for the French it declined from sixty-two percent to thirty-nine percent, and for Germans it declined from seventy-eight percent to thirty percent.[36] This shows that the most efficient way to resolve conflicts is to maintain equilibrium, just as the sea maintains its size by balancing inflow and outflow.

Due to an insufficient understanding of the pacific nature of its culture, China's rise has been viewed as a threat from the perspective of power politics. Seen through the prism of experience—i.e., most rising powers emerge from conflict and bloodshed—China's fast economic growth is doomed to cause unease and suspicions. "The West now needs to face the possibility that it has welcomed a Trojan horse into the international community."[37] To break the historical template in which rising powers are born out of bloodshed, Deng Xiaoping created the basic national policy known as the "Guiding Principle of Twenty-four Characters" He said: "Watch the world with a calm mind; stand firmly; confidently deal with the difficulties; keep a low profile; never act as a leader; and do things well" so as to build a benign China. He further stated:

> We must not act as the head. Those practicing hegemony have a bad reputation, so acting as the head of the Third World will also be ill-reputed. This is not a word of courtesy, rather, a realistic political consideration. Even though we are powerful in the future, China will never serve as the head, never practice hegemony, never seek spheres of influence, never pursue alignment, and never interfere in the internal affairs of other countries.[38]

The "Twenty-four Characters Guiding Principle" aims at safeguarding the Mean. If China achieves a dominant position of power, the Mean is vitiated and the international system is out of equilibrium. As China's power rises, it ought to rise softly by taking a position at the "righteous point" between the two extremes of "excess and deficiency" so as to balance interests among neighboring countries as well as major powers. Only in this way can the impact of a rising power be diluted.

THE PRACTICE OF THE MEAN IN CHINA'S RISING STRATEGY

In today's world, China intentionally promotes a Mean-based culture so as to maintain friendly relations with the other nations while avoiding hegemony and political disputes. Doing so also opens up markets to foster common prosperity, it promotes cultural exchanges to unite the hearts and minds of people of all races, it sacrifices some of its interests in order to maintain a stable international environment, and it focuses on how to successfully solve its numerous domestic problems. Furthermore, China's soft power increases whenever it embraces heterogeneous values rather than maintaining cultural homogeneity.

Building a New World Order: China's Prudent Move

The soft power of China's practice of the Mean is perhaps best illustrated in the process of building a "new world order." The world is currently evolving from an old system to a new one and "is still in reconciliation as well as conflict between [the] two halves: economically the north and south, politically the might and right, and culturally the West and non-West."[39] Under such circumstances, developing and developed countries are both calling for the new order, but with different definitions of what this entails.

The United States wants to build a new world system in accordance with American values and ideals. The Clinton administration aimed at building a new world order according to the principles of neoliberalism and globalization so as to maintain American world leadership. The Bush administration used the phrase "global democratization" to promote liberty worldwide. Former British Prime Minister Tony Blair advocated that Europe and the United States should work as "one polar power" to tackle the world's problems rather then bickering as they did over Iraq. Qatar's First Deputy Prime Minister and Foreign Minister stressed the urgency of establishing a new world order leading to an equitable distribution of wealth nationally and internationally.

Meanwhile, China has tried to build a new world order based on the "five principles of peaceful coexistence." The old world was dominated by power politics and ideological confrontation. The new world should be a diversified one consisting of various social systems, ideologies, values, cultures, and religions. According to the principles of the Mean, Deng Xiaoping in 1988 enunciated a new world economic and political order of independence, equality, and mutual benefit. Former Chinese president Jiang Zemin in March 1999 further interpreted China's will to democratize international order. In his speech on May 28, 2003, Hu Jintao put forward four propositions: democratization of international relations, a world of diversity, a new concept of security, and even development and respect for U.N. institutions. To some extent, the Chinese concept of a new world order maintains the basic principles and norms of the international order established in the aftermath of World War II.[40]

Building or transforming a new international order requires cooperation among the major powers. Unfortunately, there is a great discrepancy among the nations' concepts of international order, which makes cooperation difficult and undermines world stability. Furthermore, one nation by itself cannot reconstruct the world order. The U.S. has been trapped in Iraq and Afghanistan while attempting to build a unilateral order, which has decreased its soft power to a certain extent. The new world order China is calling for is arguably in accordance with international moral standards and is an ideal structure for an international system. But establishing a new order involves challenging the existing one. A rising power's attempt to reconstruct the world order implies that its ambition is to transcend the dominant power's order, which, in turn, is likely to cause regional and global tensions. In this sense, it is a deviation from the principles of the Mean.

Since the reform era, China has moved away from extremes and toward the Mean. It has evolved from a revolutionary outsider into a participant or "stakeholder" within the system. China participates actively in U.N. reforms, Six Party talks, anti-terrorism campaigns, nuclear weapon nonproliferation negotiations, environmental protection initiatives, regional and global cooperation, as well as in international organizations such as the APEC, SCO and ASEAN+3. Meanwhile, China has also been adjusting its economic policies in order to cope with situations both at home and abroad. On issues such as market share, intellectual property rights, and currency, China is willing to follow international rules and norms. The eleventh "Five-Year Plan" explicitly states that China needs to transform its export-oriented economy to one of domestic consumption for the sake of the balance of international payments. As a matter of fact, China is fully aware that the "body" of the international system becomes sick when it departs from the Mean.

During the fourth session of National People's Congress in March 2006, Chinese premier Wen Jiabao declared that China is a participant in, and supporter of, the international system. He stated: "We have participated in more than 100 international organizations and signed almost 300 treaties. We are willing to make great efforts together with fellow countries to build a peaceful world." The will he expressed is the manifesto that clarifies China's role in international society. Even so, China's declaration and strategic moves are viewed as cunning by the international community. In essence, China does not have the capability or the wish to revise the international system. Why would it seek a change of the system from which it has benefited ever since embracing the outside world?

As Lao Zi stated:

> Embracing the Way, you become embraced; [. . .] clearing your mind, you become clear; [. . .] opening your heart, you become accepted; accepting the world, you embrace the Way. Bearing and nurturing, creating but not owning, giving without demanding. This is harmony.[41]

In this regard, China's primary strategic option is to cope with both strong and weak nations so as to safeguard world stability while downplaying its leading role in constructing a new world order.

China's "Middle Way": Neither Encouraging Nor Seeking Hegemony

China, as its foreign policy has demonstrated in the past few decades, does not follow any of the following four strategies: hegemonic domination, expansion by challenging the status quo, bandwagon with the dominant power, or closed-door development. The road China is currently taking and will continue to take is the "middle way" in which the "righteous point" is achieved by skillfully combining all four strategies so as to maintain the equilibrium of the international system. In other words, the strategy China practices is to "accept the world" by means of cooperation instead of encouraging or seeking hegemony, because the Mean cannot be reached without avoiding extremes.

There are two opposing views concerning China's strategic moves and the future role it will play on the world stage: one is represented by Mearsheimer, the other by Zoellick and Johnston. In the prologue written for the Chinese version of *The Tragedy of Great Power Politics*, Mearsheimer demonstrated that if China continues its dramatic economic growth in the next decade, it could build a gigantic military force that could dominate Asia as America does in the western hemisphere. He maintains that China will seek regional hegemonic status because survival is almost guaranteed when a nation achieves predominant status. It is logical to believe that if China becomes increasingly powerful, its elites will emulate the U.S. and depict China's foreign policy with idealistic rhetoric. China, like the U.S., will thus seek to maximize its power. China has no other options if survival is its ultimate aim. This is the tragedy of great power politics[42] Mearsheimer believes that China will eventually challenge U.S. domination of the international system. To him, the world is full of powers with revisionist intentions unless there is an extraordinary and absolute dominating power who ardently strives to prevent any other great power from achieving similar status.

Former U.S. Deputy Secretary of State Robert Zoellick regarded China as a "stakeholder" that could transcend the traditional way a great power emerges. "As a responsible stakeholder, China would be more than just a member—it would work with us to sustain the international system that has enabled its success."[43] Johnston established five criteria to assess whether a state intends to revise or keep the status quo. Based on China's behaviors in the past, he believes that China is an actor willing to sustain the international system. China respects international institutions now more than any other time in the past, which explains why it does not have revisionist or imperial ambitions.[44] Brzezinski argues that China is more of a participant than a challenger. "China's leadership is not inclined to challenge the United States militarily, and its focus remains on economic development and winning acceptance as a great power."[45]

There are two reasons underlying China's choice to get involved in the international system. First, China's strategic choices are bound to have cultural implications. To practice the Mean or to build a world of balanced relations requires China to work in parallel with other nations. If China withdraws from international society as it did in the 1950s to the 1970s, it would depart from the Mean and turn itself into a polar power, which would cause confrontation between the dominant power and itself, the rising power. Moreover, China recognizes that the international system helps sustain its development.

Second, the U.S., the sole superpower, is not willing to allow China, a socialist power with nuclear weapons, to be independent from the system. As Mearsheimer writes:

> It is clear from the historical record how American policymakers will react if China attempts to dominate Asia. The United States does not tolerate peer competitors. As it demonstrated in the twentieth century, it is determined to remain the world's only regional hegemon. Therefore, the United States will seek to contain China and ultimately weaken it to the point where it is no longer capable of dominating Asia. In essence, the United States is likely to behave toward China much the way it behaved toward the Soviet Union during the Cold War.[46]

The American motive is to contain China within the system and prevent China from becoming a power that challenges American interests.

There are two explanations why China's booming economy attracts more suspicion than approval. First, China is viewed through the prism of the political culture and historical experience of the West, which values equality, independence, competition, and conflict. Western culture cherishes progress by sacrificing harmony whereas Chinese culture prioritizes harmony by downplaying progress. The experience of past great powers often leads to the conclusion that power transition results in inevitable conflict. China's enormous economic growth reminds the Western countries of their own rapid rise and leads to the conclusion of a "China threat." To pessimistic realists, competition between the dominant power and the rising one is inescapable. A realist like Mearsheimer does not believe that there is any status quo power in the international system. A rising China is the most dangerous potential threat to the United States in the early twenty-first century. A wealthy China will not be a status quo power but rather a state determined to ambitiously achieve regional hegemonic status[47] Gilpin elaborated that "a state will attempt to change the international system only if it has relative advantage over the other state, that is, if the balance of power in the system is to its advantage."[48] China's worldwide expansion of products, hunger for resources, military build-up, and currency and trade disputes with the U.S. and European countries support the notion that "relations between a superpower and an emerging rival are bound to be touchy."[49]

Second, China is not a democratic country and has quite a different political ideology from most of the developed world. China's fast growth causes more unease in developed countries than in developing ones. It is undeniable that ideological differences have been at play in international relations. When the United States rose in the nineteenth century, and Japan and West Germany rose after WWII, they were not contained by developed nations. On the contrary, the economic, political, and military build-up of the Soviet Union brought about containment from capitalist countries and led to tensions and, ultimately, to the Cold War. In today's world, China, India, and even Brazil all enjoy remarkable economic development. Why is only China regarded with suspicion? The answer might be that the United States, Germany, Japan, India, and Brazil share a similar political ideology that China does not. China is not "one of us" for the West. At the same time, it is a nation with a long history, a rich culture, a large territory, and a huge population. Thus it has the potential to change the international system even if it does not have such an intention.

In fact, whether a rising power gets contained or not has to do with the strategic choices made by the rising power as well as by other powers. During a time of transition, the international society first contains those who are apparently playing the role of the challenger or who present unclear strategies. By the same token, the source of the "China threat" concept may not be found in the increase of China's wealth but rather in the unknown strategies for its transition economy. In order to mitigate this unease, China has articulated new strategies and has conveyed to the world such intentions as peace and development (by Deng Xiaoping), being a responsible power (by Jiang Zemin), and a harmonious world (by Hu Jintao).

The post Cold-War international order is still uncertain. For the benefit of China and global stability, the best approach for China is to adopt Mean-oriented policies. As discussed previously, the Mean signifies a neutral situation in which differences are harmonized. The physical world was born in chaos, developed epistemological dichotomies, and then the Mean was found. In the context of international relations, the Mean refers to a world where different factions coexist in harmony, and where there is no absolute peace or absolute chaos. Chinese tradition emphasizes practicing the Mean positively rather than passively. Pang Pu writes that practicing the Mean reveals neither egocentricity in interpersonal relations nor anthropocentricity in the universe. Otherwise, it polarizes itself into a state of duality and departs from the true meaning of the Mean. The Mean offers a solution to many of the entrenched dichotomies of modern times: East versus West, China versus the world, traditions versus modernity, matter versus spirit, and science versus humanity. This does not mean that Confucianism can unify the world or China can serve as the center on the world stage; if that were so, the principles of the Mean would be violated.[50]

After the founding of the People's Republic of China, China played the role of a challenger in the international system with the intention to oppose hegemony. This strategy, a deviation from the Mean, did not benefit China but rather isolated it. At the end of the 1950s, China began to oppose the Soviet Union's hegemonic behavior. By the 1960s, China established the grand strategy of "fighting with two fists," which referred to fighting the two hegemons of the United States and the Soviet Union. As a result of this policy, China was plagued by both internal and external difficulties. It has paid a high price for going to the extremes.

Historical experience demonstrates that the costs and benefits of being a challenger are inversely related. In his theory of long cycles of world politics, Modelski posited that since 1500, Spain, France, Germany, and the Soviet Union acted one after another as the challenging power, yet none had won a global war. On the contrary, the new leading power was usually one that had been the ally or partner of the old dominant power.[51] It is thus not a prudent approach for China to show any intention of challenging the prevailing international hegemony. It is obvious that the United States would contain China or Japan if either of them tried to dominate East Asia. This does not imply that China is afraid of might, but rather that it avoids conflict for the sake of international stability and its own prosperity.

CONCLUSION

Though culture is not an omnipotent factor, it does shape a nation's internal and external behaviors. A culture is attractive only when it is capable of solving problems and contradictions in the process of development and transition. Democracy is what Europe and the United States provide for the world, whereas the Mean is China's contribution to the international community. The world order today is still characterized by economic, political, and cultural extremes. The Mean is what the world needs most. The lesson of the Mean is to accept differences and harmonize the extremes of excess and deficiency. In this sense, China's soft power is inherent in the Mean.

In accordance with the Mean, China should stay in the "middle way." As such, it must orientate itself as a defensive participant within the system, one who aims not at changing the status quo or opposing hegemony, but at defensively managing both internal and external challenges and avoiding high-cost competition so as to sustain its own development and modernization. China should not position itself at one extreme or another but rather align itself with the mainstream of the international community in order to maintain the system's stability.

China should enhance international cooperation by promoting compromise, as it did during the Asian financial crisis of 1997. This is one way to achieve the Mean. China also must solve international disputes by adopting a soft approach: as Confucianism teaches, the soft overcomes the hard just as dripping water eventually penetrates rock.

China needs to recognize the importance of respecting cultural, political, religious, and ideological diversity and should encourage tolerance, respect, and dialogue among nations. Balanced international relations are achieved by reconciling differences; as Confucius advocated, "men of honor live in harmony with differences, men without honor live in conflict without differences." All these initiatives are possible because China has a deep-rooted cultural emphasis on the Mean, which it has successfully practiced in both its ancient history and in recent decades.

NOTES

1. Yu Keping and Zhuang Junju, "Guanyu 'Beijing Gongshi' Yu Zhongguo Fazhan Moshi De Duihua" [Dialogue about 'Beijing Consensus' and China's model of development], October 26, 2005, www.people.com.cn. (accessed October 6, 2008).

2. Zhang Jianjing, "'Beijing Gongshi' Yu Zhongguo Ruanshili De Tisheng" ['Beijing Consensus' and increasing of China's soft power], *Contemporary World and Socialism* 4 (2004): 7.

3. Zhu Feng "Zhongguo Ying Duo Cezhong 'Ruanshili' Jueqi" [China Should Particularly Emphasize the Rise of Soft Power], *Global Times,* April 30, 2007, 11.

4. Pang Zhongying, "Guanyu Zhongguo Ruanliliang Wenti" [On China's soft power issue] *Forum on International Issues* 42 (Summer 2006): 9.

5. Lu Gang, "Wenhua Shili Ruo Rang Zhongguo Shifen" [China loses score because of her weak cultural power], *Global Times*, June 19, 2007, 11.; Zhu Hong, "Wenhua Xiyingli Yu Guojia Xingxiang" [Culture attraction and national image], *World Culture* 4 (2007): 7.; Li Haijuan, "'Ruanquanli' Jingzheng Beijing Xia De Wenhua Zhanlue" [The cultural strategy on the background of competition among 'soft powers'], *Studies on Mao-Zedong and Deng-Xiaoping Theories* 12 (2004): 73.

6. Joseph Nye, "The Rise of China's Soft Power," *Wall Street Journal/Asia,* December 29, 2005, x.

7. Joshua Kurlantzick, "China's Charm: Implications of Chinese Soft Power," *Policy Brief,* Carnegie Endowment for International Peace, June 2006.

8. James F. Paradise, "Can China's Soft Power Offensive Succeed?" *Asia News Daily,* March 5, 2007, www.asiamedia.ucla.edu/article.asp?parentid=65078. (accessed October 6, 2008).

9. Alan Hunter, "China: Soft Power and Cultural Influence," www.ipra2006.com/papers/CRPBC/ChinaSoftPowerAndCulturalInfluence, x.

10. Pang Pu. "Zhongyong Yu San Fen" [The mean and three divisions], 2000, www.confucius2000.com. (accessed October 6, 2008).

11. Adda Bozeman, *Politics and Culture in International History* (Edison, NJ: Transaction Publishers, 1994), 5.

12. Martin Wight, *Systems of States*, ed. Hedley Bull (Leicester: Leicester University Press, 1977).

13. Hedley Bull, *The Anarchical Society: A Study of Order in World Politics* (New York: Macmillan, 1977).

14. A. J. Toynbee, *A Study of History,* vol. 1 (Oxford: Oxford University Press, 1934–1961).

15. An "equilibrium world" is much closer to the Chinese concept of "*Hexie Shijie*" than a "harmonious world."

16. Karl-Heinz Pohl, "Communitarianism and Confucianism: In Search of Common Moral Ground," in *Chinese Thought in a Global Context: A Dialogue Between Chinese and Western Philosophical Approaches,"* ed. Karl-Heinz Pohl (Leiden, Boston, Köln: Brill, 1999), 262–86.

17. Confucius, The Doctrine of the Mean, trans. James Legge, 1893, www.sacred-texts.com/cfu/conf3.htm. (accessed October 6, 2008).

18. Confucius, "The Doctrine of The Mean".

19. Confucius, "The Doctrine of The Mean".

20. Confucius, "The Doctrine of The Mean".

21. Confucius, "The Doctrine of The Mean".

22. Confucius, "The Doctrine of The Mean".

23. Confucius, "The Doctrine of The Mean".

24. Lao Zi, *Tao Te Ching,* 30, trans. James Legge, 1891, www.sacred-texts. com/tao/taote.htm.

25. Lao Zi, *Tao Te Ching,* 61.

26. David Kang, "Why China's Rise Will Be Peaceful: Hierarchy and Stability in the East Asian Region," *Perspectives on Politics* 3, no.3 (September 2005): 539–75.

27. Mark Mancall, "The Persistence of Tradition in Chinese Foreign Policy," *The Annals of American Academy of Political and Social Science* 349 (September 1963): 14–26.

28. Mark Borthwick, *Pacific Century: The Emergence of Modern Pacific Asia* (Boulder, CO: Westview Press: 1992), 30.

29. Laozi, *Tao Te Ching,* 61.

30. Zhao Xianfeng. "Great Voyage, Peace Envoy," a special news report, July 08, 2005, http://english.chinamil.com.cn/site2/special-reports/2005-07/08/content_245223.htm. (accessed October 6, 2008).

31. Deng, "Deng Xiaoping Wenxuan," 49.

32. Deng, "Deng Xiaoping Wenxuan," 19.

33. Deng, "Deng Xiaoping Wenxuan,"53.

34. Deng, "Deng Xiaoping Wenxuan," 20.

35. People's Daily Online, October 2, 2007

36. Zhang Niansheng, "Ouzhou Qingshaonian Fuza Kan Meiguo" [European youngsters complicate views toward the United States], *Global Times,* August 14, 2007, 4.

37. Hugo Restall, *see* Axel Berkofsky, "The Hard Facts on 'Soft Power'," Asia Times Online, May 25, 2007, www.atimes.com/atimes/China/IE25Ad02.html. (accessed on October 6, 2008).

38. Deng, "*Deng Xiaoping* Wenxuan," 363.

39. Chen Jianfeng and Guo Xuetang, "Maodun Yu Zhenghe:Guoji Shehui Xiang Hechu Qu?" [Conflict and reconciliation: Where the world should head to?], *Social Science* 1 (2003): 37.

40. Zhang, "Beijing Consensus," 316.

41. Laozi, *Tao Te Ching,* 10, trans.Peter A. Merel, 1995, www.chinapage. com/gnl.html.

42. ohn Mearsheimer, *The Tragedy of Great Power Politics* (Chinese version), (Shanghai: Shanghai Century Publishing Group, 2003), 28.

43. Robert B. Zoelick, "Whither China: From Membership to Responsibility?" Remarks to National Committee on U.S.-China Relations, September 21, 2005.

44. Alastair Iain Johnston, "Is China a Status Quo Power?". *International Security.* Vol.27, No. 4 (Spring 2003). 5–56.

45. Zbigniew Brzezinski, "Clash of the Titans," *Foreign Policy*, January/February 2005, web.rollins.edu/~tlairson/easia/chinaforpol.pdf (accessed October 6, 2008).

46. John Mearsheimer, "Clash of the Titans," *Foreign Policy*, January/February 2005, http://web.rollins.edu/~tlairson/easia/chinaforpol.pdf (accessed October 6, 2008).

47. Mearsheimer, "*Tragedy,*" 529.

48. Robert Gilpin, *War and Chang in World Politics* (New York: Cambridge University Press, 1981): 54.

49. Editorial, "Emerging China," *Washington Post*, July 10, 2005, B6.

50. Pang Pu, "Zhongyong Yu San Fen" (The Mean and Three Divisions). www.confucius2000-4-4.

51. George Modelski, "The Long Cycle of Global Politics and the Nation-State," *Comparative Studies in Society and History* 20 (1978): 214–238.

Chapter Six

Education: The Intellectual Base of China's Soft Power

Xiaohe Cheng

According to Joseph Nye, higher education is a significant driver of a country's soft power, "the ability to win the hearts and minds of others."[1] Powerful nations are rarely weak in the educational sector. A strong and prosperous society always attracts foreign nationals for advanced education, and a quality higher education system elevates a nation's international status and reputation. After a decades-long, single-minded pursuit of hard power, Chinese leaders have finally come to realize that it is now time to develop China's soft power. Part of their effort is to transform Chinese universities into world-class institutions. The latest attempts to promote the Confucius Institutes across the world is also a critical indicator that the Chinese government is trying to transform its higher education institutes into world powerhouses, which can then generate and project Chinese influence abroad.

The first part of this chapter is a brief review of Chinese educational history that helps explain Chinese leaders' ambitious "charm offensive" in general and the country's higher education development in particular. Next, I address the efforts by the Chinese government during the reform era to rejuvenate the educational sector. I then discuss the increasing attraction of China's higher education for foreign students. In the last part of the chapter, I analyze some of the challenges for China in its attempt to use education as a means to advance its soft power. I conclude that China has great potential to develop its educational sector as part of its soft power initiative but daunting challenges exist.

EDUCATION IN ANTIQUITY

Education has occupied a central position in Chinese life since ancient times. Confucius, the great educator and thinker, emphasized that human beings are teachable, improvable, and perfectible. Thus, education—together with rituals and family—is one of the three major institutions that people can use to cultivate their virtue. With a few exceptions, the successive dynasties in China have stressed the importance of education. Highly developed educational systems gave birth to cultural prosperity, which in turn helped to shape China's relations with other parts of the world. Yu observed that the introduction of the tributary system in Chinese foreign relations, which was largely derived from the educational system, clearly formed a vision of a world order based on the superiority of Chinese culture.[2]

As the traditional educational system became mature, the civil service examination was introduced for the first time by the Sui Dynasty (581–618). Although the short-lived Sui did not have time to fully implement the new procedures, the introduction of the examination system began a new era in Chinese history. The examination became a convenient instrument for the ruling class to recruit new talent; for the ruled, it offered a valuable way to move upward in a hierarchical society. The Tang Dynasty made good use of the examination system. As the most open and dynamic dynasty in China's history, the Tang gave rise to a vibrant outward-looking culture. As Mu (2001) notes, "current academic thought is that the political and social institutions of the Han and Tang dynasties have not been surpassed."[3]

The Song Dynasty adopted a national strategy of "attaching importance to civil affairs . . . [and] neglecting military ones" (*zhongwen qingwu*), and thus rode another wave of educational advancement and cultural prosperity rarely seen in China's history. The dramatic technological improvements in printing and papermaking helped to facilitate the proliferation of carved wood books. In turn, the availability of printed texts greatly encouraged the spread of knowledge far beyond the privileged class. Private schools (*sishu*) and academies (*shuyuan*) proliferated across China. The enlarged pool of educated people and the emergence of distinguished scholars such as Zhuxi, made the Song Dynasty a standout in Chinese educational history.

As the Mongols began to rule China in the thirteenth century, education became much less important. The traditional civil service examination was suspended, and often abolished, for lengthy periods of time, thus blocking the ability of the Han Chinese to pursue careers within the government through the exam system. Although the continuity of the Chinese educational tradition was interrupted, cultural expansion continued its momentum largely due to the Mongols' endless military campaigns that brought about extensive interactions between China and other parts of the world. For the first time, educational development and cultural expansion diverged: education faltered but culture remained relatively strong.

This divergence was never redressed during the Ming Dynasty even though education was re-established and the civil service examination restored. The Ming's educational system became more complicated as the "eight-legged essay" (*ba guwen*) was adopted as the primary format for civil service exams. Although the eight-legged essay helped to eliminate favoritism by standardizing the exams, its rigid format seriously reduced students' creativity.

As a consequence of the exploration of the New World, Western Christians made their way into China starting in the mid-sixteenth century. Missionaries like Matteo Ricci made great efforts to translate Western books into Chinese. Unfortunately, the sporadic contacts between the Chinese and the West did not significantly change China. As an agrarian country with a highly centralized leadership, China showed little enthusiasm for Western ideas and technologies. As neo-Confucianism began to permeate into Chinese society, education became a mere instrument for people to secure a position in the government. Cultural vigor withered and China increasingly became conservative and inward-looking.[4] In attempt to consolidate their internal control and prevent external attacks, the Ming rulers imposed a ban on maritime trade, forbidding Chinese from going overseas as well as foreigners from coming in to do business. Although the ban was never strictly enforced, it remained in place as a long-term national policy. Except for Zheng He's naval expeditions, which lasted twenty-eight years and were mainly aimed at demonstrating China's superiority in culture and technology, the Ming had no interest in trade or cultural exchanges.

WESTERN IMPACT: STUDIES ABROAD

Traditional Chinese education, which was based on Confucianism, reached its final but highest stage during the Qing Dynasty. At that time, education lost its function of projecting China's influence over neighboring countries. It essentially became an instrument for the Court to maintain the empire's internal order. Government control over academia tightened to an unprecedented degree. Cultural vitality and intellectual dynamics were ruthlessly strangled. Although the Qing rulers continued to regulate their external relations with neighboring countries by exercising the age-old tributary system, they became increasingly inward-looking and gradually slipped into self-imposed isolation: the inherited ban on maritime trade was much more rigorously implemented with only one port, Guangzhou, opened to foreign traders. Private contact between the Chinese and foreigners was strictly forbidden.

The traditional Chinese educational system experienced its first sudden jolt when China's closed-door was ripped off by British gunboats. The Westerners' technological superiority, as revealed by their military might, shocked the Chinese ruling class and forced them to build up the country's hard power. As Ting-Tee Kuo noted, "since European military power appeared to depend on technology, the adoption of this technology was regarded as the primary task."[5] The Qing ruling class adopted a policy of "learn advanced technology from Barbarians in order to oppose Barbarians" (*shiyi changji yi zhiyi*).[6] As a direct result of this policy, new types of schools emerged one after another. The Beijing *Tongwen Guan*, a new school designed to train translators for Chinese diplomats, was established under the Grand Council's auspices in 1860. In addition to formal education, training schools affiliated with big factories and shipyards were established. Hundreds of students under the age of fourteen were recruited from local families in the hope that they could learn how to manufacture guns and ships.

Studying foreign technology at home was not enough for the Qing. In the late nineteenth century, they took the unprecedented step of sending students abroad. In 1872, the first group of 30 Chinese youths was sent to the United States to study. By 1875, the number of students in the United States had increased to 120. Initially, these students had planned to study there for fifteen years, and were strongly advised to study military and industrial engineering. Unfortunately, as anti-Chinese sentiment intensified in the United States and opposition from Chinese conservatives strengthened, the Chinese government decided to call back all the students in 1881.[7] Almost at the same time, the Qing rulers also sent smaller group of Fuzhou school graduates to Europe, including Great Britain and France. Some of them were trained to be future ship captains, who could operate modern warships being ordered in Europe. In contrast with the abrupt termination of the program in the United States, the program in Europe lasted well into the twentieth century.

Although the first government-sponsored overseas study program was small in scale, it produced a number of distinguished scientists, diplomats, and captains. More importantly, for the first time, the Chinese government was willing to learn directly from a foreign land, which opened the door for more Chinese people to study overseas. But the traditional Chinese educational system was not ready to give way to the new learning. The ruling class had not fundamentally overcome its contempt for the "Barbarians." They insisted upon "Chinese learning as the basis, Western learning for practical use" (*zhongxue weiti, xixue weiyong*).[8] In other words, the Chinese wanted Western technology but not its ideas.

As the old education system struggled, schools sponsored by Christian missions began to take root in China. From 1843 to 1860, the Christian church established about fifty schools, which enrolled 1,000 students. But from 1861 to 1874, the numbers of schools and their enrollment jumped to 800 and 20,000, respectively. For the first time, Western-style middle schools, as well as schools for girls, emerged. As the nineteenth century drew to a close, the first group of universities funded by the Christian church appeared in China. From 1901 to 1911, the number of Christian schools surged to over 10,000 with about 300,000 Chinese students attending them. In terms of enrollment numbers and teaching quality, these Christian schools clearly outperformed their Chinese government-funded counterparts.[9]

As the Christian schools developed, more and more Chinese students, disillusioned with the "Self-Strengthening Movement" that had been bankrupted by the first Sino-Japanese war, studied abroad. Ironically, Japan, which traditionally played the role of student of China, became the first destination for Chinese students overseas. The first generation of Chinese revolutionaries, such as Sun Yat-sen, Huang Xing, Zhou Enlai, and Chiang Kai-shek, were educated in Japan. As a response to the humiliating defeat in the war with Japan, Emperor Guangxu attempted to carry out sweeping reform by issuing some forty decrees, including the abolition of the civil service examination system. As Fairbanks (1998) noted, "the old order was losing its intellectual foundation and therefore its philosophical cohesion."[10]

As China was poised to embrace the Western educational system, the great powers intensified their efforts to attract Chinese students. In 1906, in the wake of a nationwide boycott of American goods due to the resumption of the Chinese Exclusion Act in 1905, Edmund J. James, then President of Illinois University, sent a memo to President Theodore Roosevelt, suggesting that the American government should take measures to attract more Chinese students to the United States on the grounds that American-educated Chinese leaders might be more receptive to American influence.[11] In 1907, in an effort to address Chinese grievances and to compete with Japan who had already made some inroads in Chinese educational sector, the American government decided to refund half of the Boxer Indemnity on the condition that the money would be allocated to scholarships for Chinese students sent to American colleges. From 1909 to 1910, 118 Chinese students were awarded the indemnity scholarships and were sent to the United States.[12] By 1911, there were 650 Chinese students in the United States, 443 of whom were self-funded.[13]

However, this last-minute reform failed to save the Qing rule. The final collapse of the dynasty in 1911 pushed "learning from the West" to a new level: the mere emulation of Western technology and institutions gave way to the study of Western "isms." A variety of "isms,"—including anarchism, liberalism, and socialism—made deep inroads into Chinese intellectual life, which in turn gave birth to various political parties, including the Nationalist Party (KMT) and the Communist Party (CCP). In 1912, the new republican regime formulated a new educational system, which turned out to be short-lived because of President Yuan Shikai's attempt to restore monarchy. After years of debate, influenced by the ideas of American philosopher John Dewey and educator Paul Monroe,[14] an American-style educational system was finally established in 1922. This system still forms the basic framework of Chinese education today.[15] As predicted by Westerners, many returning students became political activists and played a leading role in overthrowing the Qing dynasty. Sun Yat-sen, a Japanese-educated student, even became the interim President of the Republic of China.

A new twist on "learning from the West" occurred when the CCP established the People's Republic of China (PRC) in 1949. To administer the war-ravaged country, the new regime needed a large skilled work force. As the PRC adopted the "lean-to-one-side" policy, the Soviet Union replaced the United States as the main destination for Chinese students. The older American-style educational model underwent a thorough reconstruction in accordance with the Soviet model, which stressed the specialized training of scientific personnel in natural sciences. The Western-style colleges of liberal arts were transformed into polytechnic colleges that produced more engineers, Soviet curricula and textbooks made their way into Chinese campuses, and Russian became the most popular foreign language to study (approximately eighty percent of high school students learned Russian at that time).[16] In 1953, China sent 583 students to the Soviet Union but by 1956, that number jumped to 2,000.[17]

However, the Sino-Soviet split in the late 1950s made this educational boom short-lived. As China gradually slipped into self-imposed isolation in the 1960s, the whole educational system became increasingly politicized. Party affiliation took precedence over expertise, enrollments were mainly based on class background rather than academic merit, and educational exchanges with other countries nearly stopped. The whole educational system was in a shambles as large numbers of high school and college students and their teachers were sent to the countryside for "reeducation." Interestingly, even though Chinese higher learning was in bad shape, China became a study destination for students from some third-world countries. As Pepper (1986) observed, "it became fashionable to explore what could be learned from the Chinese experience and applied elsewhere."[18] Unfortunately, the number of foreign students was very small: by the end of 1966, only 190 African students from fourteen countries came to China.[19]

Deng Xiaoping's initiation of reform and the open-door policy in late 1970s fundamentally changed the Chinese educational landscape. In 1978, the Chinese government resumed the massive overseas study program, and more than 480 government-funded Chinese students were sent abroad that year.[20] With the passage of time, the government's control of self-funded overseas study was also relaxed. After 1980, Chinese students were allowed to accept scholarships provided by foreign institutions and individuals. "Studying abroad" became a huge phenomenon in Chinese society, as hundreds and thousands Chinese students pursued academic degrees overseas. From 1978 to 1989, about 60,000 government-funded students were sent out, including 20,000 graduates and 1,000 undergraduates. During the same time, the number of self-funded overseas students was over 20,000.[21] Hu Yaobang, former General Secretary of the CCP, announced in 1983 that "we've sent nearly 20,000 students to study abroad; such a large scale has never been seen in China's history."[22]

The purpose of sending out so many students was simple: "to learn advanced science, advanced technology, and advanced managerial skills in order to facilitate China's 'Four Modernizations.'"[23] But Western ideas also fueled the students' movements that occurred in 1986 and 1989. "Learning from the West" was so strong that the Tiananmen incident did not derail the state-run overseas study program even though the program was somewhat scaled back.

In sum, for the last 150 years, the Chinese have demonstrated a strong commitment to education as an essential component of their strategy to make China wealthy and strong. During this "catch-up" period, the aura of the Chinese traditional education quickly dimmed and foreign systems became the main source of inspiration.

EDUCATIONAL PHILOSOPHY: FROM *DIYI SHENGCHANLI* TO *KEJIAO XINGGUO*[24]

As Deng Xiaoping re-emerged as China's top leader in the Post-Mao era, he made a sober assessment of China's educational situation: (1) "Now it appears that China is fully 20 years behind the developed countries in science, technology and education,"[25] (2) "The key to achieving modernization is the development of science and technology" and "unless we pay special attention to education, it will be impossible to develop science and technology,"[26] and (3) Initially education and science lined up in third place in Chinese strategic priorities;[27] later, in Deng Xiaoping's "three-step" strategy of development formally announced in 1987,[28] the first priority became "to develop education and science and technology."[29]

With these pronouncements, the battered school system was put back on track, the suspended national entrance examination for college was restored, academic merit was again emphasized, and previously denounced intellectuals were welcomed back. Deng Xiaoping's call to "respect knowledge, respect trained personnel" gradually took root, and hundreds of thousands of underprivileged students went to college.

The new series of measures produced impressive results. As the Chinese government tried hard to promote nine years of compulsory education, higher education also leapfrogged to become a global enterprise. The enrollment of full-time students in higher education institutions jumped from 1,140,000 in 1980 to 1,750,000 in 1985[30] and 2,701,000 in 1988.[31] From 1979 to 1989, higher education institutions produced 3,821,600 graduates, exceeding the total produced in the first thirty years of the PRC's history. In 1982, for the first time, China began to train its own doctoral students. As of 1989, 147,948 students with master's degrees and 4,827 students with doctoral degrees had joined the workforce.[32] From 1978 to 1989, more than 80,000 students traveled abroad to study in over 70 countries, with 600,000 of them state-funded.[33]

As public higher education institutions proliferated, the Chinese government took further steps in 1985 to reform the outmoded educational system with an aim to produce more talent students as quickly as possible. In 1985, in order to enhance the role of science and technology and root out the remaining prejudice against intellectuals, Deng Xiaoping began to emphasize that "science and technology are productive forces."[34] Deng's tone sharpened further as the 1980s ended. At a meeting with President Gustav Husak of Czechoslovakia in 1988, Deng announced that "science and technology are the *primary* productive force" [emphasis mine].[35] In order to develop science and technology, Deng pledged that "we should try every way to expand education, even if it means slowing down in other fields."[36]

The Tiananmen incident did not disrupt China's efforts to promote education inside China. After Jiang Zemin took over the leadership of the PRC, he faced two kinds of challenges: the first was the new technological revolution introduced by information breakthroughs and the second was the "peaceful evolution" initiated by the Western countries. In 1994, during the National Educational Conference, Jiang Zemin emphasized that "education is a fundamental issue concerning the general situation of socialist modernization and the historical fate of socialism."[37] Accordingly, it would be China's basic strategy to shift from economic development to a new track mainly based on technological progress, improving the quality of the labor force, placing a priority on education, and raising the national level of ethics, science, and culture.[38] These proposals were included in the "Outline of Educational Reform and Development in China," which systematically detailed the general objectives of educational development that were announced in 1990.[39] For the first time, the outline revealed the "211 Project," which was designed to push 100 Chinese universities into the highest rankings in the world.

In 1995, Jiang Zemin further left his personal mark on China's educational strategy by coining the concept of "rejuvenating the country through science and education" (*kejiao xingguo*). *"Kejiao xingguo"* became the new strategy for China's development following the promulgation of the landmark "Decision on Accelerating the Progress of Science and Technology." This Decision made it clear that "science and technology is no longer the province of the old Soviet-style institutes; universities and the private industry should do research as well." Furthermore, it called on research and institutions of higher education to create joint ventures with Chinese or foreign companies in order to accelerate the transfer of science and technology to China's industry.[40] A few years later, then Premier Zhu Rongji echoed, "The implementation of the *Kejiao Xingguo* is a matter of vital importance for economic development and national modernization."[41]

Over time, China's leaders have come to realize how essential education is for the country's development. Education has jumped from being the third priority to the first, from one of the necessary prerequisites to the Four Modernizations to a "fundamental strategy" (*gengben daji*). This paved the way for the Chinese government to shift gears from merely catching up with the West to overseeing the spectacular rise in education seen today.

BECOMING A GREAT EDUCATIONAL POWER

Due to its rapid economic development, China has more resources than ever before, which in turn has whet its appetite for transforming Chinese universities into heavyweight, respected global institutions. As early as in 1994, the Chinese government launched the "211 Project," the largest direct investment ever made by the government in PRC's history.[42] This project envisaged that after several years' effort, 100 universities and 100 key disciplines would have greatly improved their quality of education, scientific research, management, and institutional efficiency. Consequently, they would become the bases for training highly skilled workers, who would then solve the major problems of the country's economic and social development.[43] From 1996 to 2000, China invested more than 18 billion Yuan (US $2.2 billion) on the project.[44] However, 100 universities competed for the limited funds and the results were not encouraging. In 1998, after Jiang Zemin's call to promote a number of elite Chinese universities to world-class rank, the Ministry of Education launched the "985 Project," in which the government allocated significant funds to a small number of these elite universities. Thirty-four top universities, which were also awarded funds by the "211 Project," would receive three-year grants ranging from 200 million to 1.8 billion Yuan. As Mohrman (2005) wrote, "The 985 Project reflects a conscious strategy to concentrate resources on a handful of institutions with the greatest potential for success in the international academic marketplace."[45] The launch of the "985 Project" set in motion an unprecedented large-scale expansion of China's higher education: the total number of new students admitted into higher education institutions in 1999 jumped to 1.3 million, a twenty percent year-over-year increase. In 2006, this number skyrocketed to 5.42 million.[46] Postgraduate education also experienced the same stunning growth: in 1998, higher education and research institutions enrolled about 58,000 postgraduates, but in 2006 the number reached about 400,000. The total number of students in higher education institutions hit a record 23 million in 2005.[47] During the same period of time, college mergers also took place. Tsinghua University led the merger movement in 1999. A number of mega-sized universities, like Zhejiang and Jilin Universities, emerged overnight.

As higher education expanded, the Chinese government carried out the "bring-in strategy" (*qing jilai zhanlue*) aimed at encouraging more foreign students to study in China. The "bring-in" strategy is essential for Chinese universities to embark on the path of internationalization. In fact, attracting foreign students is not new for China. From the founding of the PRC to 1979, China has received 9,757 foreign students.[48] After pausing during the Cultural Revolution, China resumed its student exchange program in 1973. From 1973 to 1978, a total of 2,498 international students studied in China.[49] The 1979 Working Conference on Foreign Students emphasized that "accepting foreign students not only helps friendly countries to train their talented students, but also facilitates understanding and friendship between the Chinese people and the people of the other countries." The Conference decided to create favorable conditions for a gradual increase in foreign students in China.[50] Subsequently, from 1979 to 1984, the number of foreign students jumped to about 17,800.[51]

As foreign students flocked to China, the Chinese government gave more resources to student exchange programs. At the 1984 National Work Conference on Foreign Students, then Vice-Premier Li Peng reiterated, "Foreign student work is an integral part of diplomacy, and must serve the general foreign policy. . . . With the economic development and the growth of international stature, China will accept more foreign students."[52] The Conference stressed that accepting and training foreign students was a strategic initiative and that government agencies at all levels had to pay enough attention to it.[53] In 1988, following the line drawn by the Conference, Chinese higher institutions enrolled 3,800 new foreign students from 110 countries.[54] In order to encourage more foreign students to study in China, in 1991, 1995, and 1999, the Chinese government substantially increased stipends for foreign students who were awarded scholarships. In 1990s, the number of foreign students increased at a much quicker pace. In 1992, the number jumped to 13,000,[55] then to 32,758 in 1995, and to 52,150 in 2000, according to data in the 1996 and 2001 editions of the China Education Yearbook. More importantly, nearly ninety percent of the foreign students were self-funded by 2000.[56] Nonetheless, China attracted far fewer students from other parts of the world than Western countries. For example, in 1995, there were 452,000 foreign students in the U.S. but only 32,758 in China.[57]

Aware of this huge gap, the Chinese government intensified its efforts to court more foreign students to come to China. In 1999, the Chinese Service Center for Scholarly Exchange held its first-ever "Study in China Seminar" (*Liuxue Shuoming Hui*) in Japan. In 2000, a similar promotion seminar was held in South Korea. In order to encourage more foreign students to come to China, the Chinese central government also significantly increased scholarship quotas allocated to them, from 5,211 in 1999 to 11,000 in 2007.[58] Chinese local governments and companies also joined in and began to provide financial support to foreign students.

While the "211" and "985" Projects were well under way, Chinese universities also became enthusiastic about bringing more foreign students onto their campuses because maintaining a certain percentage of international students was one of the critical requirements to raise their internationalization level. As a critical step to lure foreign students, more and more universities offered scholarships and English-instructed courses, ranging from acupuncture to international trade. In 1999, Beijing University for the first time offered scholarships to thirty-five foreign students.[59] Fudan and Renmin Universities began to offer two-year English-instructed Master Programs in 2006. These programs attracted diplomats, members of NGOs, and employees of multinational corporations. As a result of these concerted efforts, the number of foreign students in China skyrocketed from 52,150 in 2000 to 162,695 in 2006.[60] China overtook Japan and became the number one study destination in Asia.

The dramatic expansion of foreign students in China is a useful barometer, since it not only demonstrates the reversal of the trend of talent outflow from China but also reveals the strength of Chinese soft power. The rapid increase of foreign students studying in China, and especially the significant ratio of self-funded students, clearly shows the increasing attractiveness of Chinese higher education. More importantly, the attractiveness of traditional disciplines, such as Chinese medicine and Chinese language, began to spill over into other fields, such as science and engineering. In addition to bringing in more foreign students to China, the Chinese government has also adopted an aggressive strategy of "going global" (*Zou chu qu*) in an attempt to promote Chinese language and culture overseas in a systematic way.

"Chinese learning" became a new phenomenon in the 1970s when China regained its seat in the United Nations Security Council. Nonetheless, "Japanese learning" overshadowed "Chinese learning" during the 1980s as Japan experienced its economic miracle. From 1978 to 1987, about 27,000 students came to China to learn Chinese for short-term courses.[61] In order to improve the quality of Chinese learning, the Chinese government introduced the "Chinese Proficiency Test" (HSK) in 1990, which is a standardized national examination to assess the Chinese proficiency of non-native speakers. It also issued the "Evaluation Method for Teachers' Qualification in Teaching Chinese as a Foreign Language (TCFL)," which aims to recruit qualified teachers. As of 1991, about 120 higher institutions engaged in the TCFL and hosted about 16,000 foreign language students.[62]

In the 1990s, as the Japanese economy struggled and the Chinese economy boomed, Chinese learning regained its popularity across the world. From 1988 to 1999, more than 251,900 foreign students came to China to learn Chinese.[63] The Chinese government seized the chance to promote Chinese learning. In December 1999, the Second National Work Conference on TCFL was convened in Beijing. On that occasion, Vice-Premier Qian Qichen pointed out that teaching Chinese as a foreign language was "a national cause" and had "important and far-reaching meaning in expanding China's influence."[64] Echoing Qian's analysis, Chen Zhili, Minister of Education, called for intensifying efforts to promote Chinese learning overseas.[65] In 2002, the Chinese government announced plans to set up institutions overseas to systematically promote Chinese culture and language. In 2004, the government finally put forward an ambitious plan of setting up 500 Confucius Institutes throughout the world by 2010.[66] The Chinese government acted swiftly: the number of overseas Confucius Institutes multiplied to 155 by May 2007[67] and to 209 by November 2007.[68] The pace of this expansion was spectacular: about one Confucius Institute was built every four days. Xu Lin, director of the Chinese Language Council International (CLCI), jubilantly described the current chance to be "once in a blue moon" and "if China misses the chance, it would be very hard for it to do the same job again, even with tremendous effort".[69]

The Confucius Institutes were publicly endowed with the primary task of teaching Chinese as a foreign language. Since language itself is the principal instrument used by human beings to communicate with one another, as well as being an effective medium for transmitting ideas, beliefs, values, and tradition, promoting Chinese language learning overseas is the first step to promote Chinese culture abroad. As Yan Juanqi, former Vice Mayor of Shanghai, said, "to promote Chinese learning overseas is beneficial to the revival and the spreading of traditional Chinese culture, to the projection of a benign image of China on the international stage, as well as to the expansion of China's influence in the world."[70] The ultimate goal for the Confucius Institutes is to "carry forward the great Chinese culture and promote Chinese culture to the world".[71]

In summary, over the years China has become a nation where higher education is promoted and nurtured. As of today, there are 18 million students in China's higher education institutions. Moreover, it has produced 1.8 million postgraduates in the past twenty-nine years.[72] In less than thirty years, China has overtaken the United States as the country with the largest student population and is now the fourth-largest destination of international students.[73] Keenly aware of the negative consequences that this spectacular expansion might have on the quality of higher education, the Chinese government has begun to consolidate its achievements by trying to focus more on quality control than on mere numbers.

CHALLENGES AHEAD

There is no doubt that Chinese higher education helps to generate and project China's soft power abroad: more and more foreign students flock into China, the Confucius Institutes continue to proliferate across the world, and academic interactions between China and the outside world multiply. But when we analyze in detail China's higher education strategy, we find that the overall results of China's "charm offensive" are mixed and could face significant challenges in the future.

The exponential increase in foreign student enrollment in China tells only one side of the story. The origin of these students tells the other side: in 2006, seventy-four percent of the students came from Asia, with Korea accounting for almost fifty percent of that total.[74] This extremely uneven distribution reveals that China's educational influence is largely confined to its periphery. Although the international students coming to China originate from the same countries as those going to the United States,[75] the gap between China and the United States is quite wide on a number of key indicators: (1) While in China, only thirty-four percent of international students pursue degrees, while eighty-six percent do so in the United States. In other words, a significant proportion of international students stay much longer in the United States than in China, and American higher educational institutes receive much higher tuitions and fees from international students than their Chinese counterparts; (2) Among the degree-seeking students, only sixteen percent are graduate students in China, but they are forty-five percent in the United States. This large percentage disparity indicates that many more American-educated students have advanced degrees than their counterparts in China, and so they would likely have more promising careers back in their homeland; and (3) In China, according to the 2007 China Education Yearbook, more than sixty percent of international students focus on Chinese learning, and only four percent major in science and engineering, while in the United States, eighteen percent of international students major in business and management and fifteen percent in engineering.[76] In 2006, non-U.S. citizens earned forty-five percent of all doctorates in science, technology, engineering, and mathematics in the United States.[77]

As China received more and more foreign students, the exodus of Chinese students to Western countries also increased. Although the Chinese government has taken a number of measures to encourage overseas Chinese to return to China, and although the number of returning students is on the rise, the majority of these students choose to stay where they have been studying. In 2004, more than 114,700 Chinese students, among whom 91 percent were self-funded, went to study abroad, but only 25,100 returned home.[78] This "brain drain" has not significantly changed since then.

Any euphoria derived from the apparent progress made by China in higher learning should be tempered by these facts. The lackluster attractiveness of China's higher education in comparison with some developed countries has to do with its weak historical foundation on the one hand and the side effects of its exponential growth on the other. Liu Daoyu, former President of Wuhan University, criticized this expansion by labeling it a "New Great Leap Forward" that has caused a crisis of quality (*zhiliang weiji*), a crisis of study style (*xuefeng weiji*), and a financial crisis (*caizheng weiji*). According to Liu, these three crises influence each other and severely undermine the quality of higher learning.[79] In November 2005, a task force led by Yang Jie, Vice Director of the Institute of Higher Education at Shanghai Jiaotong University, released a report warning that "the quality of graduate education in China's key universities is fairly low" and the future of higher education in the country "is vague."[80] Certainly, the lasting attractiveness of a Chinese education depends on its quality, but quality improvement takes time; compromised educational quality would discourage foreign students from coming to China to study.

Although Chinese officials have denied that the development of Confucius Institutes was, as critics put it, a "blind great leap forward," establishing one Institute every four days has caused problems that cannot be ignored. The problems are three-fold: First, there is the difficulty of learning the Chinese language. Although more people speak Chinese as a native language than any other language in the world, it is largely confined to mainland China, Taiwan, Hong Kong, Macau, and Singapore. As a non-alphabetic language, Chinese has a reputation as one of most difficult languages to learn.[81] The difficulty of learning Chinese may scare away some people who are interested or force some to give up prematurely.

Second, Chinese officials have acknowledged that the absence of high quality textbooks and the shortage of certified teachers are the two major bottlenecks in the development of Confucius Institutes. In fact, the challenges that the Institutes face extend far beyond the textbooks and teachers. The prospect of long-term financial relations between the Chinese government and the local host universities is troublesome. The Chinese government pledged that each branch of the Institute would receive funding during its first three years, and then it would have to find ways to become self-sufficient. This arrangement triggers a thorny question: why would the host universities agree to make a long-term financial commitment to Institutes tasked with boosting China's soft power? In fact, the host universities tend to seek more sources of funding from Hanban by leveraging their cooperation with China. With regard to the future locations of the Confucius Institutes, the critical questions are: What benefits accrue to the host universities? For how long and to what extent is the Chinese government willing to give money?

Finally, fierce international competition could make China's "bring in" and "go global" campaigns an uphill struggle. Chinese higher education and the Confucius Institutes do not have the privilege of being a one-man show on the world stage. They have to compete for influence with their foreign counterparts sponsored by the Western powers. China cannot ignore the facts that Germany has run its Goethe Institutes for more than five decades, the United Kingdom and France both are strong players in the field thanks to a chain of British Councils and Alliances Françaises, and the United States and Japan are also trying to maintain their leading position. Therefore, "ensuring the quality of teaching, establishing and improving the quality of the certification system, and publishing high quality Chinese teaching materials"[82] is not enough to make China's voice heard above this boisterous chorus in the long run.

China's enhanced educational attractiveness is, to a large extent, an outgrowth of its incredible economic success. But rapid economic growth has caused a variety of social and environmental problems, which in turn threaten development sustainability. Although the recent reforms and the open-door policy have brought tangible benefits to ordinary people, many Chinese are now struggling with the so-called "New Three Mountains": the high cost of housing, schooling, and medical care. Drinking clean water and breathing clean air have become luxuries that many Chinese dream about. As Chinese economist Hu Angang acknowledged, the challenges that a rising China are facing mainly come from within rather than from outside. A "green" environmentally friendly development model is a welcomed alternative to the current "black" model, which is characterized by high-energy consumption and severe pollution.[83]

CONCLUSION

China has the longest tradition of education in the world. As a convenient governing tool, education once helped to create a united and strong Chinese empire and spread China's culture and influence across its borders. As the traditional education system became more sophisticated and stable, it was blamed for being the root of China's backwardness and weakness. This century-long humiliation transformed China from a role model for its neighbors to a humble imitator. The Western countries became its source of inspiration, from technology to institutions to political philosophy. In addition to emulating foreign educational systems, the Chinese began to travel to foreign countries in order to seek knowledge and technology. After 150 years, the process of emulation is not yet finished and the momentum of overseas studies continues to grow.

Nonetheless, after generations of painstaking efforts, the Chinese educational enterprise has finally been experiencing rapid development and has begun to produce soft power by attracting more foreign students and promoting Chinese culture and language abroad. The logic that underlines China's efforts to lure more foreign students has actually been spelled out by former American Secretary of State Colin Powell, who said: "I can think of no more valuable asset to our country than the friendship of future world leaders who have been educated here."[84]

But China has a long way to go to become a great educational power. It is still in the process of catching up with Western countries, as shown by the exponential growth of higher education and the apparent scarcity of strong academic disciplines. China's ambition to transform itself from a global factory to a center of high-quality education faces a number of internal and external challenges. The prospects of this transformation, which, to a large extent, hinges on the sustainability of its economic success, remain to be seen.

NOTES

1. Joseph Nye, "You Can't Get Here From There," *New York Times*, November 29, 2004.

2. Yu Ying-Shih, "Han Foreign Relations," *The Cambridge History of China* 1: *The Chin and Han Empires, 221 B.C.–220 A.D.*, eds. Denis Twitchett and Michael Loewe (Cambridge: Cambridge University Press, 1986), 383.

3. Qian Mu, *Guoshi Xinlun* [New comments on Chinese history] (Shanghai: SDX Joint Publishing Company, 2001), 356–357.

4. Zhang Weihua, *Zhongguo gudai duiwai guanxishi* [History of Chinese external relations in antiquity], (Beijing: Higher Education Press, 1993), 270.

5. Kuo Ting-Tee, "Self-Strengthening: the Pursuit of Western Technology," T*he Cambridge History of China* 10: *Later Ching 1800–1911* ed. Dennis Twitchertt & John K. Fairbank (Cambridge: Cambridge University Press, 1986), 492.

6. Wei Yuan, "*Haiguo Tuzhi·xu*" [Illustrated treatise on the maritime kingdoms. Xu], in Zhao Lixia ed., *Muo Gu: Seleced Works of Wei Yuan* (Shenyang: Liaoning People's Publishing House, 1994), 270.

7. Liu Xuyi and Lin Jie, "The First Group of Government-sponsored Overseas Students and Sino-US Cultural Exchange," *Symposiums on the Sino-US Cultural Exchange,* (1999): 171.

8. Zhang Zhidong, *Quan Xue Pian* [Exhortations to Study], *Complete Collection of Zhang Zhidong's Works* (Shijiazhuang: Hebei People's Publishing House, 1998), 9703–9770.

9. Wang Rongsheng, *Complete History of Qing Dynast* 9 (Shenyang: Liaoning People's Press, 1991), 417–9.

10. John K. Fairbank & Merle Goldman, *China: A New History*, enlarged edition (Cambridge: Harvard University Press, 1998), 243.

11. "Memorandum for President Roosevet sent by the President of University of Illionis to," *Dictionary of China's Diplomacy* (Beijing: World Affairs Press, 2000). 395.

12. Su Yunfeng, *From Qinghua School to Qinghua University* (Beijing: SDX Joint Publishing Cmpany, 2001), 16.

13. *Education Journal*, no.6 (1911), cited in *the Historical track of Overseas Chinese Students 1872–1949*, ed. Wang Kesheng, (Wuhan: Hubei Education Press, 1992), 17.

14. John Dewey once held a lecture series in China during 1919–1921; Paul Monroe first visited China in 1913 and lectured in China in 1921.

15. Shen Xiaoyun, "The Formulation and Implementation of the 1922 Educational System and the American model Adopted in China's education," *Symposiums on the Sino-US Cultural Exchange* (1999): 116.

16. Sun Qiming, *History of Sino-Soviet Relations* (Shanghai: People's Publishing House, 2002), 207.

17. Wang Taiping, *Diplomatic History of the People's Republic of China 1949–1956* (Beijing: World Affairs Press, 1998), 42.

18. Susanne Pepper, "Education," *Cambridge History of China 14: The People's Republic* (Cambridge: Cambridge University Press, 1986): 389.

19. "Jiaoyu Hezuo: Fazhan Jingji Yuren Weixian"[Educational Cooperation: To Develop Economy, Education Takes the Lead], *People's Daily*, Sept.12, 2000.

20. "Woguo Qunian Paiqian Yipi Renyuan Chuguo Liuxue, Xiang Ershi Baguo Paichu le Sibai Bashi Duoren" [Our Country Send a group of Students Overseas Last Year, More Than 480 Peoples sent to 28 Countries], *People's Daily*, Jan. 4, 1979.

21. Li Tieying, "Guanyu Woguo Jiaoyu Gongzuo Ruogan Wenti de Huibao" [Report On the Educational Works in Our Country], *People's Daily,* Jan. 3, 1990.

22. "Hu Yaobang Zhao Ziyang Peng Zhen Deng Yinchao Mianli Zaimei Liuxue Renyuan, Ba Yiqie Xianjin de Zhishi Xuedaoshou Zuo Shehui Zhuyi Xiandaihua Jianshe Shenglijun"[Hu Yaobang, Zhao Ziyang Peng Zhen and Deng Yinchao Encourage Students Who Are Studying In the United States: to Master the Advanced Schientific and Technological Knowledge and to Be Fresh Constructors for the Socialist Modernization] *People's Daily,* Dec. 31, 1983.

23. *Ibid.*

24. *Diyi Shengchanli* means "science and technology are primary productive force"; *Kejiao Xingguo* means "Rejuvenating the country through science and education."

25. Deng Xiaoping, *Selected Works of Deng Xiaoping* II (Beijing: Foreign Languages Press, 1995), 40.

26. Deng, "*Selected Works,*" 40.

27. The first is agriculture; second, energy resources and communications. See *Selected Works of Deng Xiaoping* III (Beijing: Foreign Languages Press, 1994), 11.

28. China is developing its economy in three steps. Two steps will be taken in this century, to reach the point where out Chinese people have adequate food and clothing and lead a fairly comfortable life. The third step will take China 30 to 50 years into the twenty-first century.

29. State Education Commission, *China Education Yearbook* (1995) (Beijing: People's Education Publishing Press), 1.

30. Zhao Ziyang, "Guanyu Diqige Wunian Jihua de Baogao" [Report on the Seventh Five-Year Plan], *People's Daily*, April 14, 1986.

31. Lie Tieying, "Report On the Educational Works in Our Country," *People's Daily*.

32. State Education Commission Department of Planning and Construction, *Educational Statistics* (1989)(Beijing: People's Education Press), 16.

33. "Paiqian Liuxue Renyuan Fangzhen Bubian, Li Ruihuan Li Tieying Yan Jici He Sibai Duo Liuxue Guiguo Renyuan Lianhuan" [The Policy of Sending Student Abroad Remains Unchanged, Li Ruihuan Li Tieying Yan Jici celebrate New Year With More Than 400 Returned Students], *People's Daily*, Jan. 21, 1990.

34. Deng, "*Selected Works* II," 107.

35. Deng, "*Selected Works* III," 274–6.

36. *Ibid.*

37. "Jian Fuqi Lingdao de Zhongren—Quanguo Jiaoyu Gongzuo Huiyi Xunli" [Shoulder Leaders' Heavy Responsibility—a Brief on the National Educational Conference], *People's Daily*, June 18, 1994.

38. "Dangzhongyang Guowuyuan Zhaokai Quanguo Jiaoyu Gongzuo Huiyi"[Central Committee of the CPC and State Council Convene National Educational Conference], *People's Daily,* June 15, 1994.

39. The tasks included universalizing the 9-Year Compulsory education and illiteracy eradication among young and middle-aged groups, proactively developing vocational and adult education, developing higher education properly, optimizing the educational structure, improving education quality and efficiency, etc.

40. "Kejiao Xingguo" [rejuvenating the country through science and education], *People's Daily*, May 22, 1995.

41. "Jianchi Shishi Kejiao Xingguo Zhanlue" [Adhere to Implementing the Kejiao Xingguo Strategy," *People's Daily,* March 6, 1999.

42. "'211 Gongcheng' Shishi Shunli Chengguo Fengshuo" ['211 Project" Smoothly Implemented and Bears Rich Fruits], *People's Daily*, Dec. 12, 2000.

43. *Ibid.*

44. "'211' Schools Lead Pack In research, Students," *China Daily*, Sept 5, 2002.

45. Kathryn Mohrman, "World-Class Universities and Chinese Higher Education Reform" *International Higher Education,* Spring 2005, www.bc.edu/bc_org/avp/soe/cihe/newsletter/News39/text013.htm (accessed October 16, 2008).

46. "China's Colleges to Enroll 5 pct More Students," *China Daily*, Jan. 24, 2007.

47. *Ibid.*

48. "Laihua Liuxuesheng Qunian Zuiduo" [The Number of Foreign Students Reaches Record High Last Year], *People's Daily,* Feb.8, 1993.

49. *China Education Yearbook* (1949–1981), 668.

50. *Ibid.*

51. "Li Peng Huijian Quanguo Waiguo Liuxuesheng Gongzuo Huiyi Daibiao Shishuo Woguo Jiang Jinyibu Kuoda Jieshou Waiguo Liuxuesheng de Renshu" [Li Peng Says Our Country Will Receive More Foreign Students When He Meets Delegates to the National Educational Conference], *People's Daily,* Dec. 21, 1984.

52. *Ibid.*

53. *Ibid.*

54. "Duiwai Jiaoliu Sishinian: Chuguo Liuxue Qiwanren, Xuecheng Guilai Siwanduo, Jieshou Waiguo Laihua Liuxuesheng Liuwanduo" [Forty Years of Foreign Educational Exchange: 70,000 Students Go Abroad, 40,000 Return, and Receive More Than 60,000 Foreign Students], *People's Daily,* Sept.16, 1989.

55. "The Number of Foreign Students Reaches Record High Last Year", *People's Daily,* Feb. 8, 1993.

56. *China Education Yearbook* (2001), 282–3.

57. *China Education Yearbook* (1996), 358.

58. Xinhuanet, Dec. 21, 2006, news.xinhuanet.com/edu/2006-12/21/content_5517742.htm (accessed on Oct. 20, 2008).

59. "Beida Xiang Waiguo Zifei Liuxuesheng Panfa Jiangxuejin" [Beijing University Offers Scholarship to self-funded Foreign Students], *People's Daily,* July 5, 1999.

60. *China Education Yearbook* (2007), 345.

61. "Shijie Xuduo Guojia Chuxian Hanyure, Quanguo Duiwai Hanyu Jiaoxue Gongzuo Huiyi Zaijing Jiesu" [Chinese Learning Fever Emerges in Many Countries, the National International Chinese Language Teaching Conference Draws to Conclusion], *People's Daily*, Sept. 26, 1988.

62. *China Education Yearbook* (1992), 270.

63. "Qian Qichen zai Dierci Quanguo Duiwai Hanyu Jiaoxue Gongzuo Huiyishang Qiangdiao Nuli Kaichuang Duiwai Hanyu Jiaoxue Gongzuo Xinjumian" [Qian

Qichen Reiterates at the Second National International Chinese Language Teaching (ICLT) Conference to Create a New Situation for ICLT], *People's Daily*, Dec. 11, 1999.

64. *Ibid.*

65. *Ibid.*

66. "2010 Nianqian Zhongguo Jiang Jian 500 Suo Kongzi Xueyuan" [China Will Set Up 500 Confucius Institutes by 2010], news.xinhuanet.com/newscenter/2007-11/08/content_7036268.htm (accessed October 16, 2008).

67. "Chen Zhili zai Chuxi Dierci Kongzi Xueyuan Dahui bing Zuo Zhuzhi Yanjiang" [Chen Zhili's Keynote Speech at Second Conference of Confucius Institutes], www.gov.cn/ldhd/2007-12/11/content_831067.htm (accessed October 16, 2008).

68. "Juren Xuqiu Cuisheng 'Kongzi Xueyuan Sudu'" [The Giant's Need Gives Birth to a Speed of Confucius Institute], *Global Times,* Dec. 3, 2007.

69. *Ibid.*

70. "Zhengxie Weiyuan Jianyi Jiakuai Hanyu 'Zou Chu Qu'" [Members of CPPCC Encourage Chinese to "Go Abroad"], *Beijing Daily*, March 13, 2006.

71. "Li Changchun Yaoqiu Dali Fazhan Wangluo Kongzi Xueyuan, Hongyang Zhonghua Wenhua" [Li Changchun Requests to Vigorously Develop Online Confucius Institute to Promote Chinese culture], *Xinhuanet,* April 25, 2007, news.xinhuanet.com/overseas/2007-04/25/content_6025148.htm. (accessed October 16, 2008).

72. "China Grants 1.8m Postgraduates in Three Decades," *China daily,* Jan. 15, 2008.

73. The top three include USA, Australia and Canada.

74. *China Education Yearbook* (2007), 346.

75. Asia accounted for 59 percent of total U.S. international enrollments, see The Boston College Center for International Higher Education, *International Higher Education* 50 (Winter 2007), 13.

76. *International Higher Education* 50, 13–4.

77. National Science Foundation, 2007, www.nsf.gov (accessed October 17, 2008).

78. *China Education Yearbook* (2005), 463.

79. "Liu Daoyu: 'Gaoxiao Dayuejin Haiku Xuesheng, Gaodeng Jiaoyu Cun SanweiJi'" [Liu Daoyu: "Universities' great leap forward threatens students, Higher Education Is Faced With Three Crisis"], sohu.com June 4, 2007, learning.sohu.com/20070604/n250379477.shtml (accessed October 17, 2008).

80. Lu Ling, "Graduate Education's Trying Times," *Beijing Review* 49, no.02 (2006): 28–9.

81. John King Fairbank, *The United States and China*, 4th edition, (Cambridge, Harvard University Press, 1980), 42–3, 77–8.

82. "The Number of Confucius Institutes reaches 155 globally," *People's Daily* Online, May 29, 2007, english.peopledaily.com.cn/200705/29/eng20070529_378769.html (accessed October 27, 2008).

83. "Hu Angang: Zhongguo Bujin Yao Heping Jueqi Yeyao Luse Jueqi" [Hu Angang: China Should Rise in Peace and in Green", news.sina.com.cn/c/2007-02-12/063611221191s.shtml (accessed October 20, 2008).

84. Colin Powell, "Statement on International Education Week 2001," cited in Joseph Nye, "Soft Power and Higher Education," *The Internet and the University: Forum* (2004): 42.

Chapter Seven

China's Soft Power Dilemma: the Beijing Consensus Revisited

Zhongying Pang

> "Success or failure, Xiao He is the man behind it." (Cheng ye Xiaohe, bai ye xiaohe)
>
> —A Chinese proverb

In any study of China's soft power, it is crucial to discuss economic development. Development has been a major driving force in China since the late 1970s and the resultant meteoric economic transformation has awed the world. The story of Chinese economic achievement itself is an important source of its soft power. Meanwhile, some countries in the developing world have been inspired by China's economic development and want to learn about the Chinese experience and its development model. In particular, its strategy for poverty relief has been acknowledged as a good example to other poor countries. In the words of one observer, "China's emergence as part of the modern world gives hope to many people in other developing and newly-industrializing countries. . . . China's success provides a model, and the country is therefore an attractive partner for many Africans."[1]

However, it is risky and premature to overestimate the significance of China's development model for its soft power. Development is, in China's case, a double-edged sword: its benefits have been accompanied by many social, environmental, political, and diplomatic challenges. In this sense, it also weakens or even undermines China's efforts to strengthen its soft power because of the numerous negative aspects of the Chinese experience. If China's development can become a more effective model for the developing world, the country will eventually be able to command powerful and important soft power. Conversely, failing to address China's long-term challenges will put the growth of its soft power in jeopardy. The relationship between China's development path and its soft power very much resembles the proverb noted above.

This chapter is organized as follows. First, I describe how China's development has engendered so much soft power for China. Second, I examine some of the negative aspects of China's development to show that the Chinese model is rife with shortcomings. In the third section, I examine the lack of competition for the Chinese model in the world and argue that China's development both generates soft power and harms it. Finally, I present the view that not only is there a political gap between China and the West, but there is also a growing values gap between China and some parts of the developing world, especially in Asia and Africa.

THE LINK BETWEEN CHINA'S SOFT POWER AND ITS DEVELOPMENT

In late 1970s, China launched its long-awaited modernization plan, which was to be focused on the industrial, agricultural, defense, and science and technology sectors. The country's leaders and the state machinery at that time were eagerly doing everything they could to get rid of the material poverty after the end of the Cultural Revolution. They sought to solve the problem of a shortage of food and clothing, to achieve a universal "freedom from want" in China. Needless to say, there was no mindset of cultivating soft power at that time. In the earlier stages of the modernization, particularly in 1980s, the goal of China's development was simply to let the people make money. Deng Xiaoping encouraged some Chinese who wanted to have wealth to boldly "get rich first."

Throughout the 1990s, despite the harm caused by the 1989 Tiananmen incident, China continued to focus on its "economic construction." The party and its state tried to solve China's social problems and overcome political challenges by focusing on economic development rather than seeking further reform of the system. As a result, the party told the country that all the country's problems could be easily solved as long as there was more development. Deng Xiaoping, by devising the developmental doctrine—i.e., "development is the most important means to solve China's problems" (*fazhan si ying daoli*)[2]—was seen as China's founding father of development.

Even with new leadership in the beginning of the twenty-first century, one of China's top political slogans was the same as the old: "development is the first task in ruling and governing" (*fazhan shi zhizheng xingguo de di yi yaowu*). In fact, China's development strategies (poverty relief and other problem-solving initiatives) gradually paid off. China's economy finally experienced a "take-off" moment and its economic growth trajectory has been sustained for more than two decades. Internationally, as China successfully entered into the global economy, China was assessed by the global community as a "miracle" and a "rising great power" geo-politically.

Previous Chinese development initiatives were really about the development of "hard power" in terms of the economy, technology and military rather than about the development of soft power. We still have little evidence to support a strong correlation between this kind of development and the rise of soft power. However, this does not mean that historically, China's soft power had made no progress.

This rapid and continuous growth has indeed brought much fame for China from political leaders and pundits throughout the world. With the outside world continuously applauding China's economic achievements, China has received a significant amount of intangible soft power. Many developing countries and international economic institutions (mainly the World Bank and the International Monetary Fund) praised China's economic performance. As the former president of the World Bank, for instance, noted: "In the last quarter century, over 300 million people have escaped poverty in China. With ingenuity and pragmatism, they have pursued a path that offers valuable lessons for the 600 million people in sub-Saharan Africa who still struggle to find the path out of poverty."[3]

The good reputation that China has harvested from its economic rise is in particularly sharp contrast to the reduced influence of the "Washington Consensus" based on Western liberal political economy. The Washington Consensus has a history of more than two decades in Africa.[4] In the past years, however, the development assistance policies of both the United States (US) and the European Union (EU) were not well received in the developing world, and several grand development proposals that the West initiated in various developing countries have been demonstrated to be ineffective. The Consensus' liberal market orthodoxy has been resisted in the majority of African countries. Growing numbers of developing countries do not simply want to learn about the Chinese experience; they also believe that the Chinese model of economic development may be an alternative to Western prescriptions.

In this context, Ramo coined the buzzword "Beijing Consensus." The Beijing Consensus was a new development model that described the effect of the China experience on developing countries in Africa, Asia, and Latin America. Ramo predicted that the Beijing Consensus would replace American-dominated development model hegemony.[5] An Oxford-trained Chinese scholar, he nicely summarized the Chinese model. He writes that one of the key features of the "Beijing consensus" is a strong state that is capable of shaping a national consensus on modernization, ensuring overall political and macroeconomic stability, and pursuing wide-ranging domestic reforms. What makes the Chinese experience unique is that Beijing has safeguarded its own policy space as to when, where and how to adopt foreign ideas." He criticizes "the ideology driven" American model that failed to bring democracy and development to Africa and elsewhere. Rather, the Chinese model "has enriched the world's political discourse and wisdom and hence expanded the policy options."[6]

Indeed, many developing countries have shown interest in the Chinese experience. Zimbabwe's "Look East Initiative" exemplifies the influence of China's economic growth path. The Look East Initiative was proposed for the sake of trade, investment, and political agreements with China rather than Harare's traditional Western partners, Britain and America. Zimbabwe's senior leader Robert Mugabe recently said in a speech that

> during the past year, the Government continued to implement the 'Look East' policy. This effort received a boost from my State Visit to the People's Republic of China in July this year, and has been expanded by our ever-deepening relations with most countries in Asia and the Middle East. This region has stood by us in our time of need and has created and offered new trade and investment opportunities.[7]

Zimbabwe is a small African country, but Mugabe's China policy is not just an isolated and insignificant case. In the eyes of many Africans, China's economic achievements serve as a good example.[8] Coupled with the attraction of the Chinese model, "China is seen as more willing than the West to help develop the predicates of industrialism in the global South and to do so at a lower cost to the continent, without imposing what many find to be onerous requirements for African states' policies."[9]

Africa's interest in the Chinese model comes at least partially from the failures of imported policies. The neo-liberal paradigm has not been a cure for Africa's developmental ills. Since the 1970s, Africa has never lacked donor-dictated socio-economic reforms, but the continent as a whole has nonetheless become the most indebted, marginalized, and aid-dependent region in an increasingly globalized world. "The African people were not given a chance to determine their own development paths. They were coerced to implement those preferred by the donors and creditors."[10] In 2006, leaders of forty-eight African countries gathered in Beijing and expressed that "the African countries are greatly inspired by China's rapid economic development."[11]

DEMYSTIFYING CHINA'S DEVELOPMENT

While there is no denying that China's impressive economic growth has attracted the world's attention, provided food for thought for various leaders in the developing nations, and conspicuously elevated China's international status, it is clear that the Chinese model, if there is a coherent model at all, is fraught with problems. To a large extent, the Chinese themselves are still in the process of searching for a model of modernization. These factors are likely to serve as constraints for the influence of the Chinese experience.

Thirty years after the modernization movement began, the Chinese are only now seriously and openly reflecting on their development in its various forms. Since 2003, Chinese leaders have been promoting their new political slogan: "scientific development" (*kexue fazhan guan*), by which they mean placing more emphasis on balanced and sustainable development. These new considerations clearly highlight the following shortcomings in the Chinese development experience.

First, China has repeated many old methods, strategies, and policies that other industrial countries have already tried. Instead of learning from others' unfortunate mistakes, China has followed their path. For example, in the 1980s, Chinese leaders and reformist elites solemnly vowed to not follow the similar road of economic growth at the expense of environmental degradation. However, China has quickly become the most polluted country in the world; it has paid an over enormous environmental price for its development. China's environmental challenge is quickly becoming a diplomatic disadvantage as global climate change takes center stage in international negotiations. Europe, Japan, and the US—the world's most developed country—is asking China—the world's largest developing country—to take action to control its emissions.[12]

Second, it is commonly acknowledged that China's development has mainly followed a gradual, trial-and-error, market-oriented path rather than a well-designed comprehensive reform strategy that includes democratic political reform. China's economic changes have happened quickly but the pace of political change toward a Chinese-style democracy has been slow. This has seriously hampered the expansion of China's soft power, which is currently limited around the world mainly for this reason. After the collapse of the Soviet Union, the international environment turned against China's political ideology. To secure and stabilize China's global economic interests, Beijing has had to claim that it wants to go beyond the political and ideological differences with the West. This "ideology-free" or "value-neutral" political strategy served China's economic and security interests well during the 1990s. The China-West economic relationship was strengthened, and some unnecessary political disputes were avoided. Since then, China no longer "exports" its values.

Third, China's economic growth has been fueled by direct foreign investment. However, the policy of attracting and using foreign investment has led to China becoming the world's producer of cheap value-added products. As an inevitable result, the development of home-grown Chinese brands was very slow; they "occupy an infinitesimal piece of the export pie. . . . In fact, the share of Chinese exports under the control of foreign-invested entities grew in the decade between 2005 and 2006 to almost sixty percent."[13] According to Overholt, China is "a far more open economy than Japan and it is globalizing its institutions to a degree not seen in a big country since Meiji Japan."[14] The foreign investment driving the Chinese economy has negatively impacted the increase of China's hard power—and perhaps its soft power as well. China is flooded with other nations' soft power, including foreign cultural products but its own cultural industry is still in a less-developed stage. As a result, a soft power deficit has emerged and is growing bigger: on the whole, China exports few soft power products but imports many more.

Fourth, as China follows a dependent economic development path like other developing countries, its economic and social vulnerability in the global arena has been fully exposed. A highly outward dependent economy lacks necessary protection and is easily attacked by others' politically motivated trade and investment protectionism. Currently, in the United States, Europe, and Japan, dominant opinions have continuously focused on the quality and safety issue of the "made in China" products. Of course, many export firms in these developed countries have acknowledged their economies still largely need "made in China" products. "China's [reputation] as a quality 'factory for the world' has been damaged."[15] In response, the Chinese government needs to propose international dialogues to deal with the challenges from "made in China" products. Some bilateral agreements such as China-United States and China-Japan, and multilateral mechanisms such as the Asia Pacific Economic Cooperation (APEC) Food Safety Cooperation Forum, have begun to address how to improve the quality and safety of Chinese goods. The proliferation of the issue of the safety and quality of "made in China" goods not only damages China's export prospects but also damages its reputation and credibility around the globe.

Fifth, China's economic gains are at the expense of political losses. It is now falling into several political traps because of economic engagements in Asia and elsewhere. To meet its dramatically increasing demand for energy and raw materials, China has had to conduct "resource/energy diplomacy." However, this development-driven diplomacy may be not conducive to increasing China's soft power. Many in the West and elsewhere have been outspoken in their criticism of China's expanded energy relations with resource-rich, so-called "rogue states" in Africa and Asia, such as Sudan and Myanmar.

A price China has paid for its economic relations with countries like Sudan is that the Western-dominated international community closely links China with human rights violations and humanitarian crises. Both Western governments and NGOs have taken advantage of these Chinese engagements in Asia and Africa to press China take up a "responsible" role in mediating domestic conflicts in Sudan and Myanmar. Moreover, some Africans (for example, South Africans), despite the fact that their countries generally have benefited greatly from China's economic engagements, including development assistance, have unexpectedly accused China of pursuing a neo-colonialism strategy. "China is not immune to accusations of exploitation."[16]

Clearly, China's current development path has resulted in various constraints on its soft power. Some of these constraints are related to drawbacks of its development model, whereas others originate from its expanding need for energy and raw materials to fuel its domestic economic growth.

CHINA'S RELUCTANCE TO EXPORT ITS DEVELOPMENT MODEL

Normally, if a country has indeed been successful, it will not hesitate to promote itself to other parts of the world. Successful models can be parlayed into an increased ability to influence other countries. For instance, Taiwan has actively exported the so-called "Taiwan experience"—its half-century history of economic and political self-proclaimed successes—to other countries, including African, South Pacific, and Central American states. During the Chinese Nationalist Party's (KMT) ruling period, Taiwan attempted to sell its experience in the Chinese mainland too. However, China has not followed Taiwan's example. Instead, it has intentionally tried to avoid actively promoting its model. If China really has valuable development and governance experience, why doesn't it share it with others?

The reality is this: while the outside world is interested in talking about and learning from the Chinese experience, China modestly claims that it respects other countries' choices and that it is not interested in being an exporter of development models. The simple reason for this posture is that the Chinese model is incomplete, besieged by the Western liberal political economy model, and politically assaulted by Western elites. Analysts and critics in the West are worried that African countries are following in the footsteps of China, perhaps rightfully so. If the "allure" of the Chinese model is true[17], it conflicts with the established development models that the West has exported to Africa. The adoption of the Chinese model in Africa has been widely seen in the West as having negative political consequences.[18]

In the following section, I provide an analysis of the popularity of the Western model, Africa's model "demands," and China's model "supplies." I hope to make clear the clash of the Chinese and Western development models, and to advise that Western concern of the influence of the Chinese model in Africa is an overreaction. China has neither exported its model to Africa nor has Africa imported the model from China. African countries will of course learn from some aspects of China's development, but to say that they will copy the Chinese model is simply unwarranted.

The Assertiveness of the Western Model

The West exports a wide range of values to the rest of the world, including China. Indeed, China has been the biggest recipient of the Western models. The United States has been a leading exporter of such a "product." The European Union, as a newly emerged global actor, has limited hard power but has nonetheless also become an exporter of values and models.[19]

In the late 1980s and early 1990s, one of the United States' biggest exports was the "Washington Consensus," a standard reform package promoted to crisis-stricken countries. It quickly evolved into a neo-liberal formula for promoting economic growth in the developing or less developed world. "In this sense, it is argued that the Washington Consensus policies propose to introduce various free market-oriented economic policy prescriptions which are theoretically designed to make the targeted nation's economy function more like that of First World countries such as the United States.[20]

The West's strategy, however, has been about more than the promotion of liberal economic policies in the rest of the world. "The policies of Western governments towards Africa have come to reflect a more normative and reform-oriented edge in recent years, and despite pervasive ambiguities, have broadly sought to promote democracy, human rights and conflict prevention."[21] The export of development models from the West has been described as the West "flexing its soft power muscles" or conducting "soft diplomacy."[22]

The West has not only proactively promoted its model, but has been very vigilant for the influence of other models, especially from China. Africa has been learning lessons from China and this move has made some in the West feel uneasy, threatened, and even panicky. The West has also flooded China with repeated criticisms, such as (emphasis mine): "Chinese loans help reluctant reformers escape the International Monetary Fund's clutches" and "Beijing is intent on securing raw materials and commodities to fuel its *own* booming economy, and on finding new markets for *Chinese* exports. That sounds very much like the past strategy of Western colonial powers." Dominant opinion in the West has consistently warned African countries that "the Chinese model is no panacea for Africa" and that "China's policy in Africa is not an alternative to neo-liberalism."[23]

China as a Weak Competitor in the International "Model Market"

China is a weak competitor in the international "model market" because of the ambiguity in defining its model, the still strong influence of Western liberal ideology, and the increasingly international scrutiny of China's political influence in some parts of the world.

Reception to Ramo's description of the Beijing Consensus has been mixed in China. Nevertheless, the emergence of the concept has provided a good opportunity to re-think China's development. Chinese scholars have acknowledged that there probably is a "Chinese development model," but that the Beijing Consensus fails to accurately summarize it.[24] Other scholars in China believe a more accurate term is neither "Beijing Consensus" nor "Chinese model" but rather "Chinese experience" or "lessons from China." This subtle distinction is meant to convey that China still has not successfully produced a new development model; it has just provided many lessons of both success and failure.[25]

Growing numbers of scholars in the West now conclude that the Chinese model means a market economy/capitalism combined with political authoritarianism and repression. China is now an "autocratic superpower whose seemingly unstoppable economic ascent shatters the comfortable belief that capitalist development leads to democracy. Should the liberal west brace itself for a new global 'Beijing consensus' of authoritarian modernity?"[26] The global media, led by the West, increasingly describes China as an "illiberal" polity just as Russia is an "illiberal democracy."[27] It has been alleged that both Chinese and Russian political elites are

> pursuing an alternative to the prevailing Western model. The new Russo-Chinese model is authoritarian rather than democratic. . . . Rather than relying on democracy or communist ideology to create loyalty to the political system, the Russian and Chinese elites increasingly stress a combination of economic growth and nationalism. The two ideas are related because rising prosperity not only offers individual citizens new comforts—it also holds out the promise that the nation will be more respected around the world.[28]

Africa has been learning lessons from China and this move has made some in the West feel uneasy threatened and panicky. The West has also flooded repeated criticisms to China (for instance, "Chinese loans help reluctant reformers escape the International Monetary Fund's clutches," "Beijing is intent on securing raw materials and commodities to fuel its *own* [present author's italics] booming economy, and on finding new markets for *Chinese* [present author's italics] exports. That sounds very much like the past strategy of western colonial powers"). Dominant opinions in the West have consistently warned African countries that, "the Chinese model is no panacea for Africa", and that "China's policy in Africa is not an alternative to neo-liberalism."[29]

Chinese Reluctance to Export its Model

There is no evidence demonstrating that China has promoted, or has ambitions to promote, its model in Africa. Since the late 1970s, China has not offered an alternative political model to the developing world. Although it is prevalent in the political imagination in the West, China is actually cautious and reluctant to sell its social-economic experiences to other developing countries. Deng Xiaoping told the visiting president of Ghana, Jerry Rawlings, in September 1985: "Please don't copy our model. If there is any experience on our part, it is to formulate policies in light of one's own national conditions."[30] In 2006, China and Africa declared to the world that "each country has the right to choose, in its course of development, its own social system, development model and way of life, in light of its national conditions."[31]

Intentionally promoting its own experience would sharply contradict one of China's staunch foreign policy principles. For a long time, China has maintained that countries that vary from one another in terms of social system, stages of development, historical and cultural background, and values have the right to choose their own approaches to promoting and protecting human rights. Moreover, Beijing has also claimed that the politicization of human rights and the imposition of human rights conditionality on economic assistance should be vigorously opposed as they themselves constitute a violation of human rights.[32] This Chinese-African joint statement is of course a declaration against the West's political intervention in the developing world, including China, but it also implies that China has no intention of exporting its political models. Therefore, Africa's demand for "alternative models" is not being fully met by China.

There is a gap between Africa's high expectations for alternatives that could be supplied by China and China's reluctance to supply such a model. Although China rhetorically supports Africa's independent choice of development paths, it does not want to compete with the world's dominant model exporters in the West. It does not want to violate its own policies of 1) "no political conditionality" (i.e., "no strings attached") in giving aid to less developed countries, and 2) non-interference in others' internal affairs. That is why accusations that China promotes its model in Africa are irresponsible and groundless. One of the "neo-con" policy analysts in Washington asserts that "Beijing actively promotes its development model, based on a limited market economy controlled by a totalitarian government."[33] However, there is little evidence to support this assertion.

As a matter of fact, China has been at the receiving end of soft power influence. One indication of China's soft power deficit is that it has been one of the major markets for American values based on neo-liberal market economics since the 1970s. The "Chinese" model actually contains major ingredients of the Washington Consensus, most notably in the domestic and international economic arena. China is ironically a good student of Washington.

After the end of the Cold War, China eagerly and completely joined the America-led world economic order. In other words, today's China is already a part of a U.S.-centered international system. Some American analysts acknowledge that "all of China's economic successes are associated with liberalization and globalization," which the United States architected and dominated.[34]

> China is no longer a vacuum that sucks the world's great powers into gigantic conflicts. China no longer sponsors insurgencies in Southeast Asia, Africa and Latin America. China no longer seeks to undermine the global financial institutions. We obtain benefits from a China that supports stable capitalist democracy in Thailand and the Philippines; that joins the IMF, World Bank, and WTO; and that counsels its neighbors about the benefits of political stability, free trade, and free investment.[35]

China Supports Africa's Neo-Liberal Development Model

Africa's new inter-continental development plan, called the New Partnership for Africa's Development (NEPAD), is based on essentially the neo-liberal principles of liberalization and privatization. NEPAD is basically a continuation of projects inspired by international financial institutions (for instance, the Structural Adjustment Programs), "albeit ostensibly now advocated by Africans themselves."[36] Various Western actors proposed partnerships with Africa for development purposes.[37] NEPAD's application of neo-liberal prescriptions is a new starting point in Africa's quest for an effective development model. It "provides another mechanism for implementing the "Washington Consensus/post-Washington Consensus framework."[38] Both the European Union and the United States have repeatedly endorsed, encouraged, and praised NEPAD for its role in Africa's development.

Naturally, China has been a strong supporter of NEPAD. The Forum of China-Africa Cooperation (FOCAC) and its China-Africa summit in Beijing is the kind of "development partnership" that NEPAD has been pursuing. This NEPAD-based China-Africa connection shows that the Chinese model is a variant of neo-liberal principles. Any supposed "conflict" between China and the West over development models in Africa is imaginary. The Chinese model is really a Western product "made in China" (but not "made by China").

THE EXPANDING VALUE GAP BETWEEN CHINA AND THE DEVELOPING WORLD

Many countries in Africa have benefited greatly from China's non-ideological economic engagement. However, the influence of China's African policy has been weakened by the West's persistent and overstated opposition. The West is worried that Beijing's economic presence in Africa may undermine Western efforts to create democratic administrations in African countries. The West has accused China of not being concerned about accountability, good governance, and human rights in Africa—issues that the West has been trying to export.

My purpose here is not to stimulate a political debate between China and the West over issues such as governance and rights, but rather to address fundamental questions about China's soft influence on developing countries. As discussed above, the West has exported values and development models to Africa and most African countries have experienced democratization since the end of the Cold War. As a consequence, is there a values gap between China and other developing countries in general and Africa in particular?

China and other developing countries share many common ideas and values. However, a values gap exists and is increasing. China needs to be aware of how its values differ from those of other developing countries.

Africa's Political Changes Strain Africa-China Relations

In 2000, the African Union (AU) replaced the Organization of African Unity (OAU) and adopted a new pan-African continental constitution that embraced new principles and norms in order to accommodate new realities in both Africa's domestic politics and international relations. The AU constitution explicitly codifies the terms of direct intervention into a member state if the Peace and Security Council (PSC) finds that there are gross violations of human rights or other humanitarian crises. The New Economic Partnership for Africa's Development (NEPAD) is empowered to go through an independent review process to investigate whether an African country adheres to good governance criteria. This is clear evidence that Africa is moving closer to accepting Western norms. Furthermore, the functions of the African Commission on Human and Peoples Rights' have been strengthened.

All of this moves the emerging continental architecture of Africa a considerable distance from the unconditional support for unlimited state sovereignty promoted until recently by the Organization of African Unity. . . . For Beijing this has troubling implications: a bloc of states that could once be counted on to defend the prerogatives of sovereignty in multilateral settings (with the exception of the case of apartheid South Africa) is no longer wedded to this position.[39]

Scholars such as Alden overstate Sino-African friction over values because they don't adequately consider the history of relations between the two regions.[40] But if we consider China's current worsening domestic corruption, including business bribery, bad governance, low moral standards, and the shortage of rights protection, Western worries cannot be easily ignored by the Chinese. If African countries continue to struggle for good governance based on the principles NEPAD advocates, and if China's domestic governance still has serious problems, the values gap will continue to widen.

Southeast Asia's Widening Values Gap with China

The financial crisis from 1997 to 1999 was a turning point for domestic politics and international relations in East Asia. Indonesia finally terminated the country's dark days of the "New Order" created by Suharto's highly authoritarian and military-controlled government and began to make a halting transition to democracy. Other Southeast Asian countries also deepened their domestic reforms and improved their governance by pushing democratization. Since then, like the African Union, most of the Association of Southeast Asian Nations (ASEAN) countries have reconsidered their old norms—norms that have been used to manage their intra-regional relations for more than four decades. In December 2005, ASEAN published the Kuala Lumpur Declaration on the Establishment of the ASEAN Charter for the first time. In January 2007, ASEAN released the Cebu Declaration on the Blueprint of the ASEAN Charter. In November 2007, "the Heads of State or Government of the Member States of ASEAN, assembled in Singapore on the historic occasion of the fourth anniversary of the founding of ASEAN, agreed to this Charter."[41] According to the ASEAN Charter, while member countries respect "the fundamental importance of amity and cooperation, and the principles of sovereignty, equality, territorial integrity, non-interference, consensus and unity in diversity," they adhere "to the principles of democracy, the rule of law and good governance, respect for and protection of human rights and fundamental freedoms."[42] This is a fundamental change from previous agreements.

The West has been satisfied to closely watch the drafting and approval process of the ASEAN Charter and has seized the opportunity to notice a growing values gap between China and its Southeast Asian partners. U.S. President Bush loudly praised the ASEAN Charter, saying at the 2007 APEC Summit in Australia that it "includes democratic and human rights principles."[43] At the EU-ASEAN summit to celebrate the thirtieth anniversary of their partnership, the regional groups commended "the adoption of the ASEAN Charter which marks a new level in ASEAN regional integration and sets a firm basis for its further community building" and express "support for the realization of the ASEAN Community by 2015."[44]

There is some evidence that ASEAN is truly embracing the new values. In the current Myanmar crisis, ASEAN's 2007 chair country Singapore issued a statement in New York against Yangon. The ASEAN foreign ministers

> were appalled to receive reports of automatic weapons being used and demanded that the Burmese government immediately desist from the use of violence against demonstrators. They expressed their revulsion to Myanmar's Foreign Minister, Nyan Win, over reports that the demonstrations in Myanmar are being suppressed by violent force and that there has been a number of fatalities. They strongly urged Myanmar to exercise utmost restraint and seek a political solution. They called upon Myanmar to resume its efforts at national reconciliation with all parties concerned, and work towards a peaceful transition to democracy. The Ministers called for the release of all political detainees including Daw Aung San Suu Kyi.[45]

It is important to mention that one of the reasons for ASEAN's revision of the principle of non-interference was the influence from the West and Japan. The United States has been promoting democracy in the region, the European Union has been pursuing its regional policy in Southeast Asia by addressing the issue of international intervention, and Japan has been doing its "values-oriented diplomacy" in the region in recent years. The United States and Japan, together with several ASEAN members and India, the world largest democracy, is now forging a "Concert of Asia-Pacific Democracies."[46] Under Foreign Minister Taro Aso, Japan is seeking to implement an "arc of freedom and prosperity" in Asia.

It is also necessary to emphasize that that China and the developing world still have many solid shared values, including age-old principles such as sovereignty, equality, non-interference in others' domestic affairs, and a common commitment to peaceful resolutions to conflict.[47] China has various reasons to reassure the developing world that its current value-free policy may be the best and most important contribution to securing human rights in poor countries[48]. But the emerging differences over values between them may not be good for China's relations with the developing world in the long term. China will have to deal with opposition parties, nascent civil societies, and other new political actors in multiple African and Asian countries.

The World Bank and the International Monetary Fund's ideologically driven economic policies such as privatization and liberalization have been not so successful. Many African countries have resisted the West's combination of aid and political conditions. Nevertheless, these countries will find that China cannot be used as an excuse when they don't fully implement Western programs because China still provides smaller amounts of development assistance. As leaders in Beijing have repeatedly said, China is still a developing country; African countries have to continue to depend on development assistance from the West.

In short, the West's criticism of China's value-neutrality in the developing world is weakening China's political influence in these countries. The emerging values gap between China and its strategic partners in Asia and Africa have constituted another challenge to China's soft power. China is conducting its "development diplomacy" in Asia and Africa, and it has provided many economic benefits to these countries. But China should not neglect the importance of values in managing its relations with the developing world. If China not only delivers economic growth, quality cheap products, and infrastructure, but also assists in governance at various levels, those in the West who criticize China's role in the world will lose ground.

CONCLUSIONS

China's development dilemma leads to its soft power dilemma. There is a real imperative to fully develop China's soft power potential. Negative developments within China are harmful to its lure to the outside world. The country is now the world's factory but few countries want to emulate the high environmental and human costs of this model. It is impossible to have a soft power surplus as the country lacks the intellectual infrastructure. The stability of China's foreign relations, especially China's relations with the United States and Asia, are maintained only by economic common interests. China exports few ideas and values to the world; its values gap with the world is widening rather than shrinking.

China needs to revise its development strategy to focus on making itself a world-class soft power. The country has an abundance of creative and inspirational ideas for human and social development, so to increase its soft power, China needs to make the following changes. First, it needs to pursue real "scientific development," which can help solve China's soft power dilemma by alleviating China's crises (for example, the environmental degradation). Second, China must seek an effective and pragmatic path to reform its political system in order to further empower its people. Third, China needs to narrow its widening values gap with the world; otherwise, a genuine "Beijing Consensus will be impossible. Finally, China should use the achievements of its "scientific development" to demonstrate that it is not an "authoritarian modernity"[49] but rather a growing democratic society.

NOTES

1. Heribert Dieter, "Healthy Competition," *Development and Cooperation* 48, no. 6 (2007): www.inwent.org/ez/articles/055144/index.en.shtml.

2. China's official translation of "fa zhan shi ying daoli" is "development is a fundamental or absolute principle."

3. Paul Wolfowitz, "China has valuable lessons for sub-Saharan Africa," *Financial Times,* October 30, 2006.

4. See Barry V Sautman, "Friends and Interests: China's Distinctive Links with Africa," Hong Kong: Center on China's Transnational Relations, *Working Paper*, no 12 (2006): 14.

5. Joshua Cooper Ramo, *The Beijing Consensus* (London: The Foreign Policy Centre, 2004), 3–5.

6. Zhang Weiwei, "The allure of the Chinese model," *International Herald Tribune*, November 1, 2006.

7. Robert Gabriel Mugabe, "State of the Nation Address," House of Assembly, Harare, December 6, 2005, www.zimfa.gov.zw/speeches/president/pres0024.htm

8. Heather Sidiropoulos, "China and Africa: Into Africa," *The World Today* 62, no. 10 (2006).

9. Sautman, "*Friends and Interests*," 14.

10. *NEPAD Brainstorming Concept Documen*t, (Midrand, Johannesburg: South Africa, 2005), p. 2.

11. *Declaration of the Beijing Summit of the Forum on China-Africa Cooperation*, (Beijing: November 2006.)

12. The US government hosted "historic meeting" the "Major Economies Meeting on Energy Security and Climate Change" in Washington DC in late days of September 2007.

13. Ken DeWoskin, "The 'Made in China' Stigma Shock," *Far Easter Economic Review*, September 2007, 10.

14. William H. Overholt, "China and Globalization," Statement before the U.S.-China Economic and Security Review Commission, May 19, 2005.

15. DeWoskin, "*Made in China,*" 12.

16. Ian Taylor, "China's Oil Diplomacy in Africa," *International Affairs* 82, no. 5 (2006): 954.

17. Zhang, *"The Allure of the Chinese Model."*

18. Denis M. Tull, "China's Engagement in Africa: Scope, Significance and Consequences," *Journal of Modern African Studies* (2006): 44.

19. F. Petiteville, "Exporting 'Values'? EU External Cooperation As a 'Soft Diplomacy'," in *Understanding the European Union's External Relations*, eds. Michèle Knodt and Sebastian Princen (New York: Routledge, 2003).

20. *See* "Washington Consensus," *Wikipedia,*October 28, 2008, en.wikipedia.org/wiki/Washington_Consensus. (accessed October 31, 2008)

21. Tull, "*China's Engagement in Africa,*" 476.

22. Petiteville, "*Exporting Values,*" 128.

23. Financial Times, "Chinese Model is No Panacea for Africa," February 6, 2007.

24. Yu Keping, "Dialogue on 'Beijing Consensus' and 'the China Model'," *People's Website*, October 26, 2005.

25. Huang Ping, "'China Model'" or 'Chinese Experience'," *People's Daily* Website, October 26, 2005.

26. Daniel Twining, "Asia's challenge to China", London: *Financial Times*, September 25, 2007

27. Fareed Zakaria coined his term "illiberal democracy." *See* Fareed Zakaria, "The Rise of Illiberal Democracy," *Foreign Affairs* (November/December): 1997.

28. Gideon Rachman, "Illiberal Capitalism: Russia and China Chart Their Own Course," *Financial Times*, January 8, 2008.

29. Financial Times, "Chinese Model is no panacea for Africa."

30. Zhang, "*The Allure of the Chinese Model.*"

31. "Declaration of the Beijing Summit of the Forum on China-Africa Cooperation", (Beijing: November 5, 2006).

32. Ibid.

33. Peter Brookes, "Back to the Maoist Future: China's African Ambitions," *The Weekly Standard*, April 17, 2006.

34. Overholt, "*China and Globalization.*"

35. Overholt, "*China and Globalization.*"

36. Ian Taylor, *NEPAD: Towards Africa's Development or Another False Start*? (Boulder, CO.: Lynne Rienner, 2005), 94.

37. Taylor, "*NEPAD,*" 75.

38. Sautman, "*Friends and Interests,*" 20.

39. Chris Alden, "China in Africa," *Survival* 47, no. 3 (Autumn 2005): 157–8.

40. Alden, *"China in Africa."*

41. The ASEAN Charter, Preamble, 2007.

42. The ASEAN Charter, Preamble, 2007.

43. White House, "President Bush Attends APEC Business Summit," September 7, 2007, www.whitehouse.gov/news/releases/2007/09/20070907.html. (accessed October 31, 2008).

44. The Joint Declaration of the ASEAN-EU Commemorative Summit, (Singapore, November 22, 2007).

45. George Yeo, "Statement by ASEAN Chair Singapore's Minister for Foreign Affairs," New York, September 27, 2007, www.aseansec.org/20974.htm.

46. Twining, "*America's Grand Design in Asia,*" 86.

47. China signed ASEAN's Treaty of Amity and Cooperation (TAC) in Phnom Penh in 2003. This was the first non-ASEAN country signature.

48. Dieter, "*Healthy Competition.*"

49. Daniel Twining, "Asia's Challenge to China," *Financial Times*, September.25, 2007.

Chapter Eight

China's Cultural Exports and its Growing Cultural Power in the World

Xiaogang Deng and Lening Zhang

In the past three decades, China's economic performance has captured the attention of the world. Although cheap Chinese products have deluged world markets, little attention has been paid to China's sustained efforts in exporting and exercising its cultural power. Current discussion of the cultural dimension of China's soft power has been predominantly focused on the Confucius Institutes and the growing popularity of learning the Chinese language.[1] Few studies discuss China's overall efforts in cultural export and its drive to become a major world cultural power.

One potential source of soft power is a nation's culture, which may appeal to other countries. However, not all aspects of a culture produce soft power; indeed, some cultural practices actually harm a nation's soft power if the foreign audience finds them unappealing. That is why all nations attempt to display the good aspects of their culture. Also, a state's international cultural policy could be coercive and heavy handed. The recent China-South Korean dispute about the cultural and historical heritage of Koguryo is a good example. Only a non-coercive approach to international cultural relations contributes to soft power. Compared to economic and military power, it is much cheaper and more effective to use various cultural means to achieve one's political objectives. This is particularly the case if one considers international image and reputation as part of a state's national interests and goals.

In this chapter, we examine various resources in Chinese culture to evaluate China's growing ambition to become a major world cultural power. In the first section, we analyze China's envisioned grand program to boost its cultural influence in the world. In the next two sections, we assess whether China is becoming a major world power in cultural production by examining its cultural trade and the promotion of its media in the world. In the final section, we explore China's cultural influence in Africa and Latin America. Contrary to the common perception that China has very limited cultural power that insignificantly affects world opinions, we argue that China's intentions go beyond becoming simply an economic superpower. As the significance of Chinese economic power continues to grow, China also wants to become a major world cultural power.[2] There is some evidence that China may have more cultural power than people ordinarily think.

CHINA'S NEW AMBITION TO BECOME A MAJOR CULTURAL POWER

China's current aspiration and drive to be a major world power is significantly shaped by its "superiority-inferiority complex."[3] Although China has a glorious past and a very rich cultural heritage, its modern history since 1840 has been marked by a series of humiliating defeats in various wars, invasions by Western powers, unequal treaties, internal wars, and socio-political chaos. All these failures and humiliations have been deeply ingrained in the Chinese mentality.

After the establishment of the People's Republic in 1949, China had few diplomatic connections with the outside world. China's international isolation from 1949–1971 may have also contributed to such a superiority-inferiority mentality. In the minds of the Chinese, "Beijing was treated by the Western world largely as an 'international outlaw'."[4] With limited political and economic resources, China had to rely on informal channels of communication ranging from trade exhibitions, cultural shows, and overseas Chinese connections to build up social and economic foundations for subsequent diplomatic recognition.[5]

China started its economic reform in 1978 and since then its economy has taken off. It gradually increased its world status from an international outlaw to a major economic and political power. As China's economy grew at an exponential rate, its self-confidence gradually increased. Now, for the first time in modern history, Chinese leaders see that China has an opportunity to catch up with the Western powers and to revisit China's glorious past to become a major world power.[6]

Cultural exports have been perceived as having critical functions for China's emerging cultural power in the world. First, they can satisfy China's desire to be a major world cultural power in addition to their economic and political influence. China feels that its current status in cultural exports does not adequately match its economic power in the world. Moreover, a superpower should also influence the world through its cultural products, as clearly seen in U.S. cultural domination.[7] Cultural exports can help "promote Chinese culture abroad and enhance our country's cultural soft power and meet the urgent need to increase China's comprehensive power in the world."[8]

Second, cultural exports can enhance China's cultural security and counterbalance America's influence. According to Zhao Qizheng, the former Director of the State Council Information Office, China should rejuvenate its culture to enhance its cultural security: only "when we have cultural security . . . [can] we discuss the security of our value orientation and the security of our ideology."[9]

Third, cultural exports may help China take a larger share of the world cultural market. Juxin Wang argues that China has rich cultural resources and that cultural exports can contribute to the promotion of Chinese culture in the world. Cultural exports can draw the world's attention to Chinese culture and meet the increasing demand for its cultural products. He maintains that people around the world are not only interested in the economic indicators of China's development but also show "strong interests in the cultural environment that has contributed to China's development, and they want to know China and its history and culture. Thus, there is a vast market demand for Chinese culture in the world."[10]

At the same time, some Western countries are beginning to perceive China as a security threat and strong competitor that may be harmful to their own economic prosperity. Some scholars argue that China's "siege mentality" and "national humiliation mentality" will not easily disappear among Chinese elites.[11] The Chinese believe that their national image is negatively portrayed and even demonized by the Western media.[12] Various accusations about violations of human rights, intellectual property rights, and trade rules reflect "Westerners' hostilities, biases, and misunderstandings."[13] According to the official Chinese rebuttal, the real goal of these accusations is to prevent China from becoming a true world power. The Chinese feel that their voices cannot be heard in the world because of the domination of the Western media. If China wants to be a major world power, it has to develop its cultural power and make itself heard in the international arena.

According to Zhao Qizheng, China has a serious deficit in cultural trade and concerted efforts should be made to redress this imbalance. China's cultural deficit indicates that China does not have much power in the international arena. "China cannot become a cultural superpower until China has a sufficient market share in the world's culture market. Only when China becomes a cultural superpower, is it possible for China to be a world superpower."[14] Zhao further argues:

> if China can only export TV receivers but not attractive TV programs, it means that China cannot export its own ideas and we will become "a hardware factory."

> China must develop a strategy for its national cultural advancement. Cultural export and the media's role in international communications should be an important part of our national plan.[15]

China also feels the urgent need to increase its power in various forms of media. Liu Changle, a television executive, argues that although the Chinese constitute twenty percent of the world's population, eighty percent of world media is dominated by the Western English media:

> On one hand, the English media shapes how the audience views the world in its daily coverage. On the other hand, how the English media selects and reports major world events directly affects how the audience perceives and evaluates these events. . . . Non-Western media, including the Chinese media, is excluded from the mainstream of the world and we are in a very weak position.[16]

Recognizing its weak position as a cultural power, the Chinese government recently unveiled a strategic five-year cultural development plan to boost China's cultural exports and promote Chinese culture abroad.[17] The plan recognizes that culture plays a crucial role in international competition and is an important factor in assessing a country's comprehensive power and competitiveness. "Cultural power has increasingly become an important yardstick to measure a nation's comprehensive power. On the international stage, China not only needs strength in economy, science, technology, and defense, but also cultural strength to be ahead of international competition."[18] It emphasizes that China should substantially increase its efforts to expand its channels of cross-cultural exchanges, promote Chinese media abroad, and increase the competitiveness and influence of Chinese cultural products. The plan also stresses the importance of actively promoting Chinese culture in the world. As Liu Yunshan, the former head of the Publicity Department of the Communist Party of China (CPC) Central Committee recently pointed out, "The first two decades of this century are a critical strategic period for China's cultural development, and we should seize this opportunity to greatly improve the country's cultural 'soft power.'"[19] It is clear that China intends to become a major cultural superpower commensurate to its growing economic power.

CHINA'S CULTURAL EXPORTS AND CULTURAL POWER

It is a well-known fact that China has become a world power in producing cheap products such as clothing, shoes, electronic equipment, and toys. However, little is known about China's vigorous marketing of its cultural exports and its overall status in the global cultural trade. The current literature also does not adequately address the role of the media in China's overall cultural promotion and its determination to be a major cultural power. It is critically important to evaluate these issues because it can help us assess China's cultural resources and their role in the application of Beijing's soft power.

Sources of Data to Assess China's Cultural Exports

Conceptually, cultural power can be measured quantitatively through nation-states' custom records of import and export in cultural products. Those nations that export more cultural products than import them can be seen to have higher cultural power. Rapid globalization may also substantially reduce the costs of cross-border trade and make cultural products more readily available. However, it is difficult to operationalize foreign trade in cultural products because cultural products that are intangible intellectual assets (such as music or a novel) cannot be easily measured in terms of sales. Moreover, there is a substantial variation in the definition of cultural products in different countries.[20] For instance, a video game may be defined as a toy or a cultural product depending on the country. Furthermore, lack of reliable and valid data that can capture cross-country cultural trade has constrained researchers' evaluation of nation-states' cultural power.

For the past twenty years, the United Nation Education, Science, and Cultural Organization (UNESCO) has worked diligently to develop more reliable measures of cultural exports that can capture the flow of cultural products both in volume and content. Currently, the UNESCO's report on International Flows of Selected Cultural Goods and Services is the only available data that can comprehensively capture cross-cultural trade. In its latest report, it develops a new method to distinguish between content products and those products that make possible their creation, production, and distribution. Although the data have some limitations, it is all that is available to comprehensively assess China's overall cultural trade in the world market.[21]

Another possible source is statistics from the Chinese government. However, Chinese Custom's product classification system is quite different from the definitions of the Ministry of Culture and the Ministry of Commerce and this complicates a comprehensive evaluation. Chinese statistics usually do not include information about the content of cultural products. Thus we can only use data from Chinese documents in international trade to assess China's cultural power in the publication area.

One observation is that the evaluation of China's cultural exports can be elusive, depending on what you look at. UNESCO and Chinese government sources do not cover the same aspects and sometimes contradict each other. The UNESCO reports include more information on cultural production (equipment and supplies such as blank CDs or DVDs) instead of the creative side and overall cultural influence. Some discrepancies are therefore expected to result from the limited available data. However, we think that the UNESCO data are more complete and consistent across different regions of the world.

In our discussion below, we will first present UNESCO's report on cultural exports and then discuss China's import and export data in printed media and audiovisual media. Based on these data, one may get two entirely different pictures of China's cultural exports in the world.

China's Cultural Exports

According to the UNESCO Institute for Statistic's 2005 report "International Flows of Selected Cultural Goods and Services 1994–2003," China ranked fourth in the world in terms of export revenues of cultural goods and services. China's total cultural export revenue was $5.27 billion in 2002 and only the United Kingdom (U.K.), United States (U.S.), and Germany had higher numbers of cultural exports than China. The UNESCO report was based on each country's import and export data from 1994 to 2002 in the following areas: 1) heritage goods, including collections and collectors' pieces or antiques of over 100 years old; 2) books, including printed books, brochures, children's pictures, drawings, or coloring books; 3) newspapers and periodicals; 4) other printed matter such as maps, postcards, and pictures and designs; 5) recorded media, including gramophone records, audio compact discs, magnetic tapes, and other recorded media for sound; 6) visual arts, including paintings sculptures, statuettes, lithographs, etc.; 7) audiovisual media, including video games with a TV receiver, photographs, and movies; 8) equipment and support material, including musical instruments, sound player/recorders, recorded sound media, television and radio receivers, etc.

The report indicated that China's export in cultural products has developed at a fast pace. For instance, China only had a 8.3 percent share ($636 million) of the U.S. cultural product market in 1994 but its share increased to 30.8 percent ($4.2 billion) in 2003. Some of China's cultural and creative products were in the top-ranking categories: China is 1) number one in audio-visual media, which is one of the fastest growing cultural products in the world; 2) number two in visual arts; and 3) number seven in export of books and other printed matter.[22]

Overall, the report shows that China is a major exporter of cultural products and has a positive trade balance. Previous studies have paid scant attention to China's cultural production capability in enhancing its attractiveness.

As discussed earlier, data from UNESCO are more comprehensive and cover a wider range of cultural areas both in content and culturally related products or services. It is a valuable source of data and makes cross-country comparisons possible although its ability to capture the complexity of cultural exports is limited.

China's Publication Trade

Publication is a crucial component of cultural production, so it is important to review China's status in the publication trade when assessing its cultural power. If a country exports more cultural products such as books, newspapers, and periodicals than it imports, it has a positive trade balance and thus has more cultural power in the world. Table 8.1 shows that China has a significant cultural imbalance in the publication business. For instance, it exported $36.3 million worth of books in 2006 while importing $180 million. Similarly, China exported only $2.8 million worth of audio and video products while it imported $30.8 million. The import-to-export ratio for audio and

Table 8.1. Imports and Exports in China's Publication Industry[24]

	Total # of Export Books, periodicals & newspapers (Total Value in U.S. dollars)	*Total # of Import Books, periodicals & newspapers (Total Value in U.S. dollars)*	*Total # of Export Audio, Video & Electronic Publications (Total Value in U.S. dollars)*	*Total # of Import Audio, Video & Electronic Publications (Total Value in U.S. dollars)*
1998	5.199mln ($14.81mln)	2.50mln ($49.75mln)	68,460 ($0.323mln)	0.442mln ($3.02mln)
1999	4.839mln ($15.89mln)	.2.57mln ($56.56mln)	0.2169mln ($0.482mln)	0.505mln ($3.59mln)
2000	5.90mln ($16.72mln)	14.13mln ($57.92mln)	0.354mln ($0.595mln)	1.17mln ($5.02mln)
2001	6.05mln ($17.64mln)	16.82mln ($69.04mln)	0.457mln ($0.769mln)	0.947mln ($10.72mln)
2002	6.20mln ($17.41mln)	14.18mln ($94.87mln)	0.885mln ($2.17mln)	0.830mln ($12.23mln)
2003	7.66mln ($23.30mln)	18.77mln ($146.08mln)	1.33 mln ($1.39mln)	1.4mln ($22.73mln)
2004	7.68mln ($25.46mln)	19.74mln ($162.54mln)	1.28mln $2.20mln	0.633mln ($21.36mln)
2005	7.32mln ($32.87mln)	14.29mln ($164.18mln)	0.752mln ($2.11mln)	0.149mln ($19.33mln)
2006	10.07mln ($36.31mln)	23.95mon ($180.9mln)	1.05mln ($2.85mln)	0.178mln ($30.79mln)

video products is thus 10.8, suggesting that China has a significant cultural trade deficit in this market.[23]

In the publication trade, copyrighted products also reflect a country's cultural power in marketing its products abroad. Those countries that export more copyrighted books or titles are likely to have more influence in the world. China has suffered a large cultural deficit in its copyright trade. For instance, China imported 12,386 copyrighted products in 2006 while it only exported 2,057.[24] The Chinese government has been aware of the cultural deficit in the publication business, especially its deficit in copyright trade. According to a report by China Book International, the deficit does not match China's economic position in the world and Chinese publishers must work hard to promote Chinese culture and help the outside world develop a positive image of China. The report argues that it is critically important for China to promote its culture abroad through publication because

> export of culture is of great significance to protecting, developing and enhancing a nation's influence in the world as well as to the building of the nation's image. . . . The China Book International program we are now carrying is part of this cultural promotion. Having Chinese books exported to the outside world is a national strategy as well as a challenge that Chinese publishers face in their journey to the international market.[25]

The content of China's publication exports primarily focuses on language, culture, and education.[26] In 2005, exports surged significantly partly due to a worldwide "fever" for the Chinese language. But fads can end as quickly as they start. In recent years, international customers increasingly are interested in philosophy, social sciences, traditional medicine, and children's books. However, buyers are predominantly from China's traditional markets in Hong Kong and Southeast Asia.[27]

The report recognizes that major barriers are the difficulty of the Chinese language for foreign readers and translation.[28] The Chinese government sponsors the China Book International Program to sell its products of printed media abroad. For the first time in Chinese history, China has developed its specific long-term strategic five-year plan for cultural development (the cultural development used to be embedded in the social development plan). Chinese leaders have realized the critical role of culture in boosting the country's overall power. Funding for translation is one of the major national projects included in the five-year plan. China has set aside a special state budget to cover translation costs and to encourage foreign publishers to translate and publish Chinese books in the world. The program formally started in 2006. The Information Office of the State Council signed contracts with more than ten foreign publishers in seven countries to promote 170 books on China in

2005. The total funding was about RMB 3 million in 2005. China spent more than RMB 10 million to fund 210 projects with fifty foreign publishers in nineteen countries in 2006.[29]

According to the UNESCO report, China is a major player in the publication business, ranking seventh in the world.[30] However, this assertion is contradicted by the data cited above. Two major factors may contribute to the observed differences. First, Chinese official statistics are still a reflection of a state-planned economy. Its data is primarily comprised of major state-owned publication firms while many foreign-owned or private publication firms do not have to report their trade figures to the state authority directly. Second, Chinese publication export data only reflect books or products that are indeed produced by the major state-owned firms and do not count value-added or outsourcing products by foreign publication firms. The UNESCO data reflect outsourcing in publication trade that is not accounted for in the Chinese statistics.

China's International Television and Radio Industries

Similar to the Chinese publication industry, all media in China have the designated function of supporting, promoting, and serving the Communist Party and the government as their "mouthpiece" for propaganda.[31] Chinese TV and radio are under the dual control of the State Administration for Radio, Film and Television (SARFT) and the Publicity Department of the Chinese Communist Party. Administratively, the SARFT has direct control. For instance, China Central Television's (CCTV) or China Radio International's annual budget allocations have to go through the SARFT. The SARFT is also in charge of the technical and operational aspects of the media industry. The Publicity Department makes sure that the media is accurately presenting the Party's policies and is not distorting the Party's positive image in the minds of the people. Internationally, Chinese media has to keep in line with Chinese foreign policy and promote China's image abroad, which is considered an important part of public diplomacy.[32]

CCTV has about 1.88 billion viewers at home, covering 95.9 percent of the population in China. Because it's under the direct control of SARFT, CCTV is able to monopolize the media market and reduce potential competition.[33] It has three international channels specifically for foreign audiences. CCTV's programs are transmitted via satellite twenty-four hours a day, seven days per week, and can be viewed in more than 100 countries in the world. It claims to have more than 65 million viewers outside China at the end of 2006.[34] In 1992, CCTV-4 became the first international channel; it primarily targets overseas Chinese and those who understand Chinese. It has about 15 million viewers worldwide. CCTV-9, the first English international channel, was launched in September 2000 and its target audience is the non-Chinese. It has nearly 50 million subscribers worldwide. In 2004, CCTV started its first Spanish and French channel, CCTV-E & F, with more than 2 million viewers in the world in 2006.[35] However, there are no independent sources to verify whether China's official estimates are accurate. Although it is very expensive to broadcast its programs all over the world twenty-four hours a day, China offers these channels free of charge.

CCTV has made headway into the United States, and has become its largest overseas market with over 10 million viewers for CCTV-9 and 800,000 for CCTV-E & F.[36] China considers entering the US market as a major media event. There are more than 6 million ethnic Chinese in the United States but the TV market is fragmented. Chinese language TV stations have been dominated by Taiwan and Hong Kong programs produced by immigrants. Sometimes these programs report events from a Taiwanese perspective and their view on China may not be as positive as what China would like to see. With three CCTV TV channels in the United States, China expects that it can counter-balance Taiwan's influence and affect public opinion. According to China's Radio and Television Yearbook, CCTV's entrance "has changed the landscape of the U.S. TV market where Taiwan has a strong presence and our voice is weak."[37] CCTV also helps China's "One China" foreign policy to counter-balance Taiwan's influence in the US.

CCTV's presence in the U.S. market also indirectly affects the Chinese TV market by providing low cost or no cost news programs and TV series.[38] As Chinese immigrants have increased rapidly, local Chinese TV stations emerged in the late 1990s (in Houston, New York, or Washington, DC, for example) and the local Chinese prefer to watch TV programs that they are familiar with. These TV stations usually cover happenings in their respective local areas then use low-cost CCTV news and series to attract a large audience.[39]

For the international radio and TV industries, China also has its own promotion plan as part of the national five-year plan. The main purpose of the promotion project is to

> get China's voice heard in every part of the world. Within five years (2001–2006), our country's radio, TV, film industries should have a major development or breakthrough in reaching out to viewers or listeners in every country in the world, especially in North American and Western Europe, and let these audience have a better understanding of the 'real China.' Efforts should be made to let foreign audience know China's position and perspective on all major international issues. In the next ten years our radio, film and TV industries should be strong enough to compete with major Western media companies.[40]

The ultimate goal for the media industry is to

> have Chinese voices heard in any location where major Western media outlets are able to present their audio and visual images, and let our radio, TV programs and films have significant international impacts, and substantially improve the current unfavorable situation that Western media is strong but Chinese media is weak in the international media arena[41] (the State Administration of Radio, Film, and TV, 2001).

China's video and audio exports are also developing rapidly. In 2003, China produced 456 million audio and video products.[42] It exported about RMB 100 million worth of video and audio materials in 2003. The primary markets are North America, Southeast Asia, Hong Kong and Taiwan. Some firms have established an overseas market and rental network in America, Canada and Europe. In 2004, Chinese-produced movies had RMB 110 million in foreign box office revenues, which was fifty percent higher than in 2003.[43]

In summary, China's active promotion of its media abroad is an important part of its cultural promotion plan to exert greater influence beyond its borders and speak to the world with its own cultural voice. It reflects its concerted efforts to export Chinese-related content to the outside world and influence how overseas audiences think about China. Although at present its influences may be limited to the Chinese living abroad, its impacts cannot be underestimated. It could potentially help China achieve its political and diplomatic goals indirectly as more overseas Chinese integrate into host countries and participate in the democratic process. China's growing influence in the U.S. media market, especially among ethnic Chinese, is a good example.

REGIONAL DISTRIBUTION OF CHINESE CULTURAL INFLUENCE

China's traditional sphere of influence is in Asia but as the Chinese economy grows, it needs more resources from other parts of the world. Its foreign policy objectives have also changed, focusing more on Africa and Latin America. According to Li (1998)[44], China's foreign policy in the developing world has several major objectives: 1) systematically bring together support from the Third World countries, 2) promote economic cooperation, 3) counter Taiwan's diplomatic efforts to gain formal recognition from a small number of countries that still maintain formal ties with Taiwan, and 4) minimize direct confrontation with the West and emphasize cooperation to achieve a win-win scenario. Under this policy, China has increased its diplomatic, economic, and cultural efforts to court African and Latin American countries.

China's Cultural Power in Africa

China's use of soft power in Africa is not something new; China has a long history of engagement with the region. In the 1950s and 1960s, China was internationally isolated and had few diplomatic relations with the major Western countries, so China had to shore up its alliances in Africa. China supported African nations' independence efforts and encouraged them to break away from the yoke of Western colonial rulers.[45] China's anti-colonialist foreign policy helped it reshape the geopolitical landscape in the region and cultivate friendly relationships with African countries[46] However, from the late 1970s to 1980s, China focused more on its internal development and its activities in Africa became relatively dormant. According to two U.S. observers, China's influence in Africa was relatively limited and its aid programs were hardly significant in the 1980s and early 1990s. Its major goal at the time was to defend its "One China" policy.[47]

China's "continued strong economic growth, a more sophisticated generation of Chinese leaders, better scholarship in China on Africa, and a domestic population more confident in China as a global actor, have encouraged Beijing to take a more proactive approach to foreign affairs."[48] From the Chinese point of view, as its economy developed rapidly in the 1990s, it faced increased protectionism from Western countries. In 1991, China started its strategic drive to diversify its foreign trade market to reduce the risk of anti-dumping legislation. At the same time, China's demand for energy became increasingly insatiable, forcing it to look for energy in Africa and Latin America. Africa's share of trade with China increased from 2.1 percent ($10. 8 billion) in 2001 to 2.8 percent ($39.71 billion) in 2005.[49]

In addition to economic assistance and debt relief, educational and cultural exchanges are also part of China's effort to strengthen its influence in Africa. Chinese culture is quite different from the many indigenous cultures on the African continent. The economic resources of African countries also limit what cultural products they can purchase from China. Instead, China's efforts now focus on two major areas: training future generations of African leaders and cross-cultural promotions.

China has educational exchange agreements with fifty African nations. When international students receive their education in China, they also have full exposure to Chinese culture and political ideas. In 2000, there were 1,388 African college students in Chinese universities, a figure that increased to 3,737 in 2006.[50] From 1950 to 2005, China provided 19,000 scholarships to African students. Twenty percent of China's scholarships were granted to African students in 2005, although they only constituted less than three percent of the total foreign student population. Many students become very successful and some of them have become national leaders in their own countries. African students often use their Chinese language skills and social connections to establish their own businesses, which contribute to the rapid development of Sino-African trade. "Many African students consider China as their second home," according to Mr. Cui, President of China Language and Culture University that has trained more than 4,000 African students over the years.[51] Learning Chinese has become a fad in Africa. China established its first Confucius Institute at the University of Nairobi in 2005.[52]

China has been extraordinarily active in cross-cultural exchanges across the continent, especially in the past decade. In recent years, more than 100 performing arts troupes have taken trips to Africa.[53] China's National Ballet, the National Ballet of China, the China Oriental Song & Dance Ensemble, the China Acrobatic Troupe, the Wuhan Acrobatic Troupe, the Dalian Art Ensemble, and the Sin Kiang Song & Dance Ensemble, along with thousands of artists, actors, singers and other entertainers, have visited African countries.[54] China and African nations have also held hundreds of art exhibitions of different sizes throughout Africa and in China. "China held the Chinese Painting and Sculpture Exhibition in Egypt, the Chinese Watercolor Exhibition in Zimbabwe and Tunis, the Chinese Arts and Crafts Exhibition in Benin, and the Chinese Contemporary Oil Painting Exhibition in South Africa. Meanwhile, African countries held many exhibitions in China."[55]

China's presence in Africa has shaped the geopolitical alliance in the region and the African nations have been China's powerful allies in world politics. With the help of the African countries, China has defeated Taiwan's fourteen attempts to reenter the UN in the past twenty years. They have also supported China to defeat the United States and the other Western countries' eleven attempts to criticize China's human rights records over the years.[56] "At every turn, these African nations have supported Beijing's efforts to sideline the attempts to redress abuses throughout China and Africa."[57] China obtained substantial votes from African countries in the decision to award China the right to hold the 2008 Olympic Games, the 2010 World Trade Show, and to select Chen Feng Fuzhen from Hong Kong as the Head of the World Health Organization.[58]

China's Presence in Latin America

Historically, China has had weak ties with Latin America due to the geographical distance between the two continents. However, in the past five years, China has increased its presence in the region. In 2001 and 2004, two Chinese presidents (Jiang Zeming and Hu Jintao) visited the region. The region has become increasingly important for China's ever-expanding appetite for energy and raw materials such as oil, copper, iron, soybeans, etc.[59] In 2000, China's total trade in the area was $12.6 billion and this increased to

$72.2 billion in 2006.[60] Latin America is one of the few regions in the world that has a positive trade balance with China. While the United States and other Western countries have decreased investment in the area, China has stepped up its investment. In 2005, China's total expenditure in the region was about $11.5 billion. Economically, China is attractive to many countries in Latin America because of its vast market for raw materials and its remarkable purchasing power.

Since Chinese culture is distinctively different from South American cultures, China's attractiveness mainly lies in its unique developmental model for the region. The Chinese model is characterized by heavily handed state intervention in the economy, preoccupation with political stability instead of individual freedom, massive media control, and greater reliance on a strong government to guide the development process.[61] The Chinese model provides a seemingly viable alternative to the Washington Consensus—a free market economy with democratic institutions. Many countries in the region are frustrated with the developmental model of the United States, and how the International Monetary Fund has tried to sell it.[62] The economic rise of China has made many people in the region, including political leaders, reconsider their own political and economic developmental models. China's experience is particularly attractive to those newly elected presidents in Bolivia, Brazil, and Venezuela.[63] In 2005, after Evo Morales was elected as Bolivia's president, he immediately visited Beijing and skipped the United States. This may have strategic implications for the United States since the region, "once firmly in the United States sphere of influence, is slowly but surely drifting East."[64] An influential regional political commentator claimed that the year of 2005 would go down in history as "the year in which the United States lost much of its once almighty influence in Latin America, and [China] began to play a modest but rapidly growing role in hemispheric affairs."[65]

China's cultural ties with the region are relatively weak but it has worked very hard to promote its culture though various cultural exchanges. Cubans now can watch Chinese TV series through CCTV-E & F.[66] China's cultural promotion activities have been very active. In the first eight months of 2007 alone, there were more than thirty cross-cultural activities in the region.[67] For instance, people in Guyana, Mexico, Panama, and Surinam saw Chinese acrobatic shows by three groups of Chinese art performers. There were several cultural and art exhibitions such as Chinese Paintings, Chinese Design, China's Historical and Ethnic Clothing and Decorations Shows in Mexico, Chile, Argentina, Brazil and other countries. China's cultural promotion activities are widespread in the region.

At the same time, China also systematically promotes its culture through the teaching of the Chinese language and the Confucius Institutes in the region. In 2005, China sent sixteen Chinese language teachers to Argentina to cope with its rising demand.[68] There were about 2,000 students who studied Chinese in Argentina in 2005. In 2005, former Chinese Vice President Zeng Qinghong visited Mexico and signed a cultural and educational agreement, promising to provide thirty-two scholarships for Mexican students. In 2006, China established its first Confucius Institute in Mexico. The Chinese language has been taught at about twenty Mexican colleges. The number of students who majored in Chinese has exceeded 1,000 and Chinese teachers are needed by many Mexican colleges. Brazil, Argentina, Peru and Chile are also observing an increasing popularity in the learning of the Chinese language.[69]

DISCUSSION AND CONCLUSION

With the ever-increasing role of China in the international political economy, Chinese leaders see a historical opportunity to revitalize their county's glorious past and foster a renaissance of its rich culture. Apparently, China is not satisfied simply being an economic superpower—it would like to project its power into the cultural sphere as well. China's sense of cultural superiority and repeated humiliations between 1840 and 1949 have significantly shaped China's national aspiration to achieve world superpower status. Chinese elites believe that it is China's 5,000-year old continuous civilization and unique cultural heritage that have motivated them to get what they have achieved so far. Of course, Chinese leaders would like people to believe that their "great leadership" and the socialist system contributed to their success. Chinese leaders have been obsessed with the notion of comprehensive power that usually includes a nation's economic, military, and cultural power.[70]

Currently, China's cultural power is not on par with its economic and political clout in the world. However, it is commonly acknowledged that China has the many cultural resources to become a major world power. The results of our study show that China is indeed a major cultural exporter: the fourth largest cultural exporter in the world in 2002, as shown in the UNESCO report. China seems to be realizing gradually that the best way to promote its culture is through either marketing or economics.[71] Its television network has made major inroads into all the continents of the world and now attracts more than 65 million viewers outside China. Its international radio network is broadcast 1,035 hours per day in forty-three foreign languages all over the world to disseminate China's policies and present China's positive image to the world.[72] It claims to be the most comprehensive and far-reaching radio network in the world.

Although China's publication trade is not as strong as its overall cultural export, China has developed a strategic plan to promote all forms of media and become a major contender in the world media market. Currently, China's media power cannot compete with that of the United States, but it may still have its own market niche (specialty TV programs) tailored specifically to its East Asian neighbors, who tend to be China's traditional sphere of influence, and 30 million overseas Chinese whose background makes them more receptive to the Chinese media. Furthermore, Chinese media has the potential to become more competitive in reporting internal events or major world events when the Western media may have an obvious bias; however, only if the Chinese government can relax its obsessive control. It may be too early to predict how successful China's long-term plan for cultural development will be. However, there are clear signs that China is working very hard to project its cultural power beyond its traditional sphere of cultural influence. It has reached out in Africa, Latin America, Europe and North America, and has become a powerful competitor in multiple forms of communication. With the growing role of the Chinese media supported and controlled by the state, China's alternative developmental model can be attractive to some developing nations through the power of example.

Of course, any scholar of Chinese studies cannot miss China's active promotion of the Chinese language and the rapid expansion of the Confucius Institutes into every continent of the world. The global demand for Chinese language skills has prompted more than 40 million people all over the world to study Chinese. Chinese universities have also increased their appeal to international students. There are more than 1.04 million international students who have studied or are studying in China.[73]

NOTES

1. Ding Sheng and Robert Saunders, "Talking Up China: An Analysis of China's Rising Cultural Power and Global Promotion of the Chinese Language," East Asia 23, no 2 (Summer 2006): 3–33; Joshua Kurlantzick, *Charm Offensive: How China's Soft Power Is Transforming the World.* (New Haven, CT: Yale University Press, 2007).

2. Huang Yanzhong and Sheng Ding, "Dragon's Underbelly: An Analysis of China's Soft Power." *East Asia* 23, no. 4 (Winter 2006): 22–44.

3. Wang Jisi, "What China Needs in the World and From the United States," in *China's March on the 21st Century: A Report of the Aspen Strategy Group*, eds. Kurt M. Campbell and Willow Darsie (Washington, D.C.: Aspen Institute, 2007), 86.; Ding and Saunders, "*Talking Up China.*"; Alan Hunter, "China: Soft Power and Cultural Influence," Coventry University, UK: Centre for Peace and Reconciliation

Studies, 2006, www.ipra2006.com/papers/CRPBC/ChinaSoftPowerAndCulturalInfluence.doc (accessed October 9, 2007).

4. Wang, "*What China Needs in the World*," 85.

5. Chen Hao-su, "On Civil Diplomacy." *The Chinese People's Association for Friendship with Foreign Countries*, 2004, www.cpaffc.org.cn/llts/detail.php?id=177 (accessed August 17, 2007).

6. Zhao Qizheng, "How China Becomes a Major World Power: Four Major Elements," *Wenhui Daily*, March 15, 2006, www.zsr.cc/ExpertHome/ExpertAttention/200603/12959.html (accessed September 1, 2007).

7. Xu Suqin, "Rejuvenation of Chinese Culture and Enhance Our Soft Power," *Jinyang Network*, August 22, 2007, //www.ycwb.com/myjjb/200708/22/content_1592212.htm (accessed September 15, 2007).

8. Wang Juxin, "Theoretical Consideration for Promoting Chinese Cultural Abroad," *Provost Office of Shandong Provincial School of the Communist Party*, November 26, 2007, www.sddx.gov.cn/001/001016/001016007/2401215257846.htm (accessed December 16, 2007).

9. Xu, "*Rejuvenation of Chinese Culture*."

10. Wang, "*Theoretical Consideration for Promoting Chinese Culture Abroad*."

11. Wang, "*What China Needs in the World*," 86.

12. Zhao, "*How China Becomes and Major World Power*."

13. Wang, "*What China Needs in the World*," 86.

14. *See* Xu, "*Rejuvenation of Chinese Culture*."

15. Zhao, "*How China Becomes a Major World Power*."

16. Liu Changle, "Have Chinese Media's Voices Heard in the World," Director of Phoenix Television (Speech at the Advanced Forum of the Chinese Media Development, 2005), academic.mediachina.net/academic_zjlt_lw_view.jsp?id=4528 (accessed August 31, 2007).

17. The State Council of the People's Republic of China, "Outline of the National Plan for Cultural Development During the Period of the Eleventh Five-Year Plan." *The State Council Gazette*, 2006, www.gov.cn/gongbao/content/2006/content_431834.htm (accessed December 20, 2007).

18. The State Council of the People's Republic of China, "*Outline of the National Plan for Cultural Development*."

19. "Senior Official Stresses China's Need for Developing "Soft Power," *Xinhua News Network English*, April 7, 2007, english.sina.com/china/1/2007/0407/108862.html (accessed August 20, 2007).

20. For a more detailed discussion, see UNESCO Institute for Statistics, 2005.

21. UNESCO Institute for Statistics, "The International Flows of Selected Cultural Goods and Services, 1994–2003." (Montreal: UNESCO Institute for Statistics, 2005).

22. UNESCO Institute for Statistics, "*The International Flows of Selected Cultural Goods and Services*."

23. "Basic Facts about China's News and Publication Business in 2006," *China News & Publication*, June 26, 2007, book.sina.com.cn/news/v/2007-06-26/2037216665.shtml (accessed December 20, 2007).

24. Chinapublish.com, "Annual Status of Publication," 1998-2007, www.csc.edu.cn/gb/ readarticle/readarticle.asp?articleid=2560 (accessed December 22, 2007). *Note:* There are some inconsistencies in trade figures provided by different Chinese sources and sometimes the same state agency provides different figures. We consulted with the officials in the State Bureau of News and Publications. In their view the online data from Chinapublish.com may be more reliable because it actively reflects recent changes.

25. "Basic Facts about China's News and Publication Business in 2006," *China News & Publication*, June 26, 2007, book.sina.com.cn/news/v/2007-06-26/2037216665.shtml (accessed December 20, 2007).

26. China Book International, "Promotion of Chinese Publications Overseas Needs a Boom of Translation Industry." *China Book International Report*, August 8, 2007, www.cbi.gov.cn/en/info/infodetail.jsp?ID=1873 (accessed September 10, 2007).

27. "Digital Technology Helped China's Export of Books in 2006." *Publishing Business Weekly*, September 12, 2007, www.chinabookinternational.cn/cn/info/info-detail.jsp?ID=2334 (accessed December 15, 2007).

28. "*Digital Technology Helped China's Export of Books*."

29. China Book International, "*Promotion of Chinese Publications*."

30. Li Yuejin, "Fully Implement the Chinese Book Promotion Abroad Plan," *China Book Reading Newspaper*, April 25, 2007, www.gmw.cn/content/2007-04/25/content_600252.htm (accessed December 20, 2007).

31. UNESCO Institute for Statistics, "*The International Flows of Selected Cultural Goods and Services*."

32. Edward Davis, ed. *Encyclopedia of Contemporary Chinese Culture* (London and New York: Rutledge Taylor & Francis Group, 2005).; Zhao Yuezhi, *Media, Market and Democracy in China: Between the Party Line and the Bottom Line* (Chicago: University of Illinois Press, 1998).

33. Chen, "*On Civil Diplomacy*."

34. Yuezhi Zhao. 1998. Media, Market and Democracy in China: Between the Party Line and the Bottom Line. Chicago: University of Illinois Press.

35. Editorial Committee of China Radio and Television Yearbook, *China Radio and Television Yearbook* (Beijing: Radio and Television Yearbook Press, 2006).

36. Editorial Committee of China Radio and Television Yearbook, "*China Radio and Television Yearbook*."

37. Editorial Committee of China Radio and Television Yearbook, "*China Radio and Television Yearbook*."

38. Editorial Committee of China Radio and Television Yearbook, "*China Radio and Television Yearbook*."

39. Shun Feng, "General Introduction of Chinese Language Media in US," March 5, 2006, column.bokee.com/125167.html (accessed September 8, 2007).

40. Shun, "*General Introduction of Chinese Language Media*."

41. The State Administration of Radio, Film, and TV, "The State Administration of Radio, Film, and TV's Implementation Guidelines for the Promotion of Chinese Media Abroad Project." *The State Administration of Radio, Film, and TV's Document*

1494, December 24, 2001, www.chinalawedu.com/news/1200/22598/22619/22876/2006/3/cd96314749413600228-0.htm (accessed August 31, 2007).

42. The State Administration of Radio, Film and TV, "*Implementation Guidelines*."

43. Northern Media Studies, "China's TV and Film Markets Reflect the Spiritual Ethos of the Era," *Northern Media* 2006, yule.sohu.com/20060817/n244856276.shtml (accessed December 15, 2007).

44. Northern Media Studies, "*China's TV and Film Markets*."

45. He Li. 1998. "Economic Policy." *Problems of Post-Communism* Mar/Apr98, Vol. 45, Issue 2.

46. An Yong-yu, "Great Success of Fifty Years' Sino-African Mutual Benefit Cooperation," *Foreign Affairs Review*: *The Academic Journal of the Institute of Diplomacy of People's Republic of China* 1(2007): 10–14.

47. Li Xiguang, "China's Charming Offensive in Africa," (Speech delivered at the 56th General Assembly of the International Press Institute which by the Executive Dean of The School of Journalism and Communication, Tsinghua University, Istanbul, May 15, 2007). www.media.tsinghua.edu.cn/data/2007/0521/article_522.html (accessed September 8, 2007).

48. Joshua Eisenman and Joshua Kurlantzick, "China's Africa Strategy" *Current History* (May, 2006): 219–224. www.carnegieendowment.org/files/Africa.pdf (accessed September 5, 2007).

49. Eisenman and Kurlantzick, "*China's Africa Strategy*," p. 219.

50. "Brief Introduction to China's Foreign Trade During the Tenth Five Year Plan Period, 2001–2005," *Department of Foreign Trade, the Ministry of Commerce of People's Republic of China*, 2006, wms.mofcom.gov.cn/aarticle/xxfb/200601/20060101322709.html (accessed August 12, 2007).

51. "2006 A Historical Record Setting Year for International Students in China," *China International Studies Network* 2007,www.csc.edu.cn/gb/readarticle/readarticle.asp?articleid=2560 (accessed September 10, 2007).

52. Cui Xiliang, "From the Bottom of Their Hears: African Students Call China Their Second Home," *People's Daily*, October 7, 2006.

53. "First Confucius Institute for Africa officially launched in Nairobi," *Xinhua News Network*, December 20, 2005.

54. Zhang Xiaolan, "Cultural Exchange Promotes Sino-African Friendly Relationship," *People's Daily*, August 8, 2006, 7.

55. An, "*Great Success of Fifty Years*."; Lan Qing, "Sino-African Cultural Exchange Increased: 'Little Red Flower Performance Group' Promotes Chinese Culture in the Chinese New Year," *China Culture*, March 19, 2007, 8.; Zhang, "*Cultural Exchange*."

56. Lan, "*Sino-African Cultural Exchange*"; Zhang, "*Cultural Exchange*."

57. An, "*Great Success of Fifty Years*."

58. Eisenman and Kurlantzick, "*China's Africa Strategy*," p. 220.

59. An, "*Great Success of Fifty Years*."

60. Mark P. Sullivan and Kerry Dumbaugh, "China's Growing Interest in Latin America," *Chinaelection.org* 2004. *Also available in* Congressional Research Service

Report RL32804 www.chinaelections.org/en/readnews.asp?newsid=%7BBEF2823E-5C4D-4E98-A32DD46FC9938EDF%7D&classid=83&classname=Sino-Latin%20Am.%20Alliance (accessed August 30, 2007).

61. Li He, "China's Growing Interest in Latin America and Its Implications," *Journal of Strategic Studies* 38, no. 4–5 (2007): 833–62.

62. Kurlantzick, "*Charm Offensive*."

63. Ana Margheritis, "The Neoliberal Turn in Latin America: the Cycle of Ideas and the Search for an Alternative," *Latin American Perspectives* 34, no. 3(2007): 25–48.

64. Li, "*China's Growing Interest in Latin America*."

65. Marcelo Ballve, "Latin American Sees China in Its Future," *National Catholic Reporter*, January 13, 2006.

66. Ballve, "*Latin America Sees China in Its Future*."

67. Li, "*China's Growing Interest in Latin America*."

68. China-Latin America Economic and Trade Network, "Cross-cultural Exchange Activities in Latin America," 2007. The network is under the supervision of China Economic and Social Development Association and Sino-Latin America Economic and Technological Committee. www.china-latin.com/servlet/Node?Node=25665&Language=1&Pos=25&Listing=6002 (accessed September 16, 2007).

69. Li Xiaohua, "Confucius Institutes Taking Chinese to the World," 2007, www.china.org.cn/english/education/204196.htm (accessed September 1, 2007).

70. Li, "*Confucius Institutes*."

71. Andrew Scobell, "China's Soft Sell: Is the World Buying?" *China Brief* 7, no. 2 (2007): jamestown.org/publications_details.php?article_id=2371836&issue_id=3983&volume_id=422 (accessed September 10, 2007).

72. Gary Rawnsely, "A Survey Of China's Public Diplomacy," Center on Public Diplomacy, The University of Southern California, May 2, 2007, uscpublicdiplomacy.com/index.php/newsroom/pdblog_detail/070502_a_survey_of_chinas_public_diplomacy/ (accessed September 10, 2007).

73. The State Administration of Radio, Film, and Television, *China Radio and TV Yearbook* (China Radio and TV Yearbook Press, 2006).

74. China Ministry of Education. 2007. 1.04 million was calculated from two sources. From 1950–2005 the total number of international students came to China was 884,315 based on China Ministry of Education's website listed below: www.gov.cn/jrzg/2007-05/28/ content_628456.htm (11/20/2007). And in 2006 the number was 162,695 from the following source: www.moe.edu.cn/edoas/website18/33/info20133.htm (accessed on 11/20/2007).

Acknowledgement:

The authors would like to express their appreciation for Dr. He Li's assistance in writing the Latin American section of this chapter.

Part III

SOFT POWER AND CHINA'S INTERNATIONAL POLITICS

Chapter Nine

China's Soft Power in Africa

Joshua Kurlantzick*

When President Hu Jintao embarked upon his first trip to Africa, in 2004, China's image on the continent seemed at its zenith. Flush with the romance of a first date, African states enthused over China's new interest.[1] China had been inking deal after deal on the continent, as many African nations eagerly attracted Chinese investment and China became Africa's third-largest trading partner: a $2.5 billion stake in one of Nigeria's offshore petroleum fields; a $1.5 billion pact to upgrade Ethiopia's telecommunications system; investments in Angola that eventually made that country the largest source of Chinese oil imports.[2] China also was winning striking diplomatic victories. In 2005, Senegal, a leader of francophone Africa, and a country courted assiduously by Taipei, switched relations from Taiwan to China. Not long afterwards, oil-rich Chad switched diplomatic relations as well. Across Africa, Hu received the type of welcome and access once reserved for American or French leaders, and many African media outlets contrasted the Chinese leader's trip with the fact that George W. Bush rarely devoted much attention to the continent.

In 2007, Hu Jintao took another, twelve-day tour of Africa, following on the heels of visits by Wen Jiabao and many other senior Chinese officials. This time, however, Hu faced a more mixed reaction. In Zambia, local leaders welcomed Hu almost like a royal, and Hu announced that China would build an economic cooperation zone in Zambia that would attract some $800 million worth of investments. Former Zambian president Kenneth Kaunda personally received Hu, Chinese in Zambia flocked to the airport to greet Hu,

* Portions of this chapter are adapted from Joshua Kurlantzick, "Beijing Envy," *The London Review of Books*, July 5, 2007 and from Joshua Kurlantzick, *Charm Offensive: How China's Soft Power is Transforming the World* (New Haven: Yale University Press, 2007).

and the Chinese president delivered his usual well-scripted speech, telling his audience, "China is happy to have Zambia as a good friend, good partner, and a good brother."[3] But some average Zambians responded far differently. Two years earlier, accidents at a Chinese-owned copper mine in Zambia had killed fifty-one Zambians. Zambian protestors gathered the following year to demand better safety conditions and higher salaries at the copper mines, since their bosses paid them below the Zambian minimum wage, roughly thirty-five pounds per month.[4] Armed with tree trunks, the protestors marched to the company's gates, but no supervisors came to negotiate. The opposite: guards opened fire on the protestors, nearly killing several more workers. Anti-China demonstrators then took to the streets of Lusaka, Zambia's capital, where they targeted Chinese-owned businesses and rallied outside the Chinese embassy.[5]

Now, with China's president arriving in Zambia, protestors had their perfect target. Hu had planned to visit Zambia's copper-producing region, where he would highlight China's largesse by laying the cornerstone at a new stadium financed by Beijing. At the last moment, Hu's advisors probably realized he might face massive anti-China rallies in the copper heartland. Hu cancelled his trip to the copper belt.[6] Yet Hu faced one popular protest after another in other parts of the continent. In South Africa, the local press blasted the labour policies of Chinese firms investing abroad. In Namibia, Hu faced similar criticisms.

This dichotomy in African reactions to Hu on these two visits was striking. Over the past decade, China has transformed its interactions with Africa. While fifteen years ago China had more limited relations with the continent, it has become one of the most important foreign partners for many African nations. Much of these gains are due to Chinese soft power—to China's aid, investment, and diplomacy in Africa, and particularly to its training programs for African opinion leaders, many of whom come to China and return home amazed by China's growth rates and seeking to emulate China's model of development.

In the short term, these soft power strategies have helped China build strong relationships across Africa without yet engendering as much concern about China's rising power as is evident in Europe, Asia, or North America. Yet at the same time, as evidence by Hu's most recent visit, as China's influence grows it is causing grave concerns among African civil society, trade unions, and some political leaders. Whether Beijing can respond to these concerns in a manner suitable to the local environment, which in much of Africa means a freer climate for media, unions, and political parties than in China itself, will determine whether Beijing can consolidate its ties to the continent.

SOFT POWER THEORY

When Joseph Nye coined the phrase soft power, he originally intended a relatively limited definition of the term. To Nye, soft power originally meant an ability by a certain state to get other nations to do what it wanted by attraction rather than coercion, payments, or force. Other countries, Nye said, would go along with this state because of the appeal of its culture, ideas, ideology, and overall public image. Nye specifically ruled out what he viewed as coercive political, military, and economic tools, including aid, formal diplomacy, investment, sanctions, political pressure, and, of course, military force.[7]

Yet in the period since 1990, when Nye first coined the term, soft power has taken on a broader, more fluid, meaning. In part, this is because scholars and officials have begun to realize that drawing distinctions between hard and soft power can be difficult, especially in real world case studies.[8] As Mingjiang Li notes in the introduction, Nye himself also has realized how the unwise usage of hard power, such as the U.S. invasion of Iraq, can sharply diminish a nation's soft power.

China in particular poses a challenge to Nye's traditional definition of soft power. Many Chinese scholars and officials themselves, as chapter two describes, view China's soft power more broadly than Nye did, and simply use the term to mean all power outside of the military and security sphere, including tools Nye considered coercive, like aid and investment. Chinese officials, including Hu Jintao, also clearly have embraced the idea of soft power, and it has become central to their discourse about China's role in the world.

Mingjiang Li probably comes the closest to summarizing the idea of soft power enunciated by Chinese officials to this author. In the author's experience, these Chinese officials' idea of soft power goes far beyond the ideational sources of soft power, in which China is clearly limited. To many Chinese officials, soft power is, as Mingjiang defines, the soft use of power—using power judiciously, wisely, and prudently, and engaging and accommodating other nations. And as we will see, despite some scholars' claims that China has gained little from this soft use of power, in Africa it has had significant policy implications, producing many favourable outcomes for China, one of the key definitions of successful wielding of soft power. However, unlike in other parts of the world, where one aspect of China's soft power may be assuring other nations that they do not need to balance against China, in Africa there is little of this "assurance" element of soft power referred to by Yong Deng in his chapter. As Yongjin Zhang asks in his chapter, does China's soft power matter? In Africa, where China has no hard power, and where China's ideational leadership in combating poverty is impressive, China's soft power clearly does.

ORIGINS OF CHINA'S MODERN DAY ENGAGEMENT WITH AFRICA

The People's Republic of China has had substantial relations with sub-Saharan Africa since at least the early 1950s. In the 1950s and 1960s, China looked to Africa primarily as a place to spread communism, a centre of the global revolutionary struggle. By portraying African struggles against colonialism or, later, against ruling governments, as Maoist revolutionary battles, China also tried to show that Mao Zedong Thought had a global reach.[9] Chinese media published reports of African insurgents studying Mao's theories, and many African revolutionaries did base their strategies on Mao's successes. China also utilized the Bandung Asian-African Conference to demonstrate its shared history of predation by colonial powers and to portray itself as the ideological leader of the developing world. At Bandung, China also enunciated its adherence to "non-interference" in other nations' affairs, a policy that would continue up to the present day. At the time, China also provided some limited material support to African rebel groups. At one point, it supported the Marxist African National Congress in its struggle against apartheid rule. It funded leftist rebels in Zaire (today's Congo), and it used the Chinese embassy in Tanzania to support rebels in other African nations. These longstanding ties would help China reestablish its Africa relationships in the 2000s, since Beijing enjoyed the trust of older African revolutionary leaders like Robert Mugabe, Kenneth Kaunda, and many others.

Beijing also contributed significantly to new infrastructure development and to agricultural production across the continent. In its aid, China focused on large, high-prestige projects like the Tanzam Railway, which linked Zambia to Tanzania. As Deborah Brautigam notes in her study of Chinese assistance to Africa, during the 1970s, Beijing also launched agricultural aid projects in Liberia, the Gambia, and Sierra Leone, though this aid had little sustainable impact.[10]

By the early 1980s, as China's internal revolutionary struggle diminished, and Deng Xiaoping focused on China's opening and reform, Beijing largely withdrew from its ties to Africa. Though as Brautigam notes, senior Chinese leaders continued to make visits to Africa, China's aid initiatives to the continent dwindled and it occupied a lower priority among Chinese strategic thinkers; major projects like the Tanzam Railway fell into disrepair.[11] Anti-African protests in China in the late 1980s, most notably a series of attacks on Africans in Nanjing—really protests against reform and opening—further soured relations between China and Africa.[12] At the same time, in the 1980s and 1990s Africa itself struggled through famines, the last gasps of authoritarian rule in many nations, and economic declines caused by a collapse in commodity prices and years of failed structural adjustment programs promoted by international financial institutions. Not for nothing were the 1980s called Africa's "lost decade": By the turn of this century, many African nations had barely grown since independence. Between 1960 and 2001, for example, Nigeria grew by an average of 0.2 percent annually, while Ghana's economy shrunk by 0.1 percent over that time period.[13]

Over the past decade, however, China has reengaged with Africa. China's renewed ties with the continent are merely part of Beijing's broader soft power initiative around the world. Deng Xiaoping's leadership circle had emphasized rebuilding China's own economy: China should "keep a low profile and never take the lead" on global issues, Deng warned—Beijing wasn't strong enough to expose itself to a world leadership role. Today both the Chinese leadership and many Chinese elites have become convinced that China, a rising power, should play a larger role in the world. Over the past decade, China's breakneck economic growth fostered greater confidence within the Chinese public, and intellectuals began calling for China to take a larger role in global affairs. Reflecting these sentiments, this winter Jia Qingguo, a leading international affairs scholar in Beijing, told the *New York Times,* "Like it or not, China's rise is becoming a reality."[14]

Meanwhile, China's leadership also was becoming more confident and sophisticated in global affairs. H. Lyman Miller and Liu Xiaohong produced one of the most comprehensive recent assessments of the Chinese leadership. As they found, of the twenty-four officials who became full or alternate members of the Politburo at the Fifteenth National Congress in September 1997, only six had served in the Party leadership before 1992, and most were ten years younger than the men they'd replaced. Many of these new leaders hailed from China's urbane eastern provinces, which had benefited the most from economic reforms, and which were most open to external influence. In contrast to older leaders, they had completed undergraduate and even graduate studies. They had studied outside China, often in Western nations. But these leaders also had seen how, after the Tiananmen crisis, Western nations had shunned China. Several leading African nations supported China after Tiananmen, and Chinese leaders apparently recognized that Beijing could not rely on the US, but must develop its relations with developing Asia, Africa, and Latin America.[15]

With a more sophisticated knowledge of the world, these leaders recognized that China must become a greater international player. China had pressing great power needs—needs for oil, allies, markets, security, and other desires of a major power. Yet the United States had built alliances around the world that could constrain China one day, if Washington chose to contain Beijing the way it had tried to contain Moscow. To break through this American containment, and to gain more allies at bodies like the United Nations Human Rights Commission, Beijing would have to rely on developing nations. The Chinese leaders also increasingly understood that as China continued to grow, and opened its borders, it could not avoid the world's problems, like HIV, drug trafficking, and transnational disease.

Beijing would make soft power the centre of its new engagement with the developing world. In part, according to Chinese officials interviewed by the author, this resolve to focus on soft power was strengthened by the wars in Afghanistan and Iraq, which at least initially showcased the overwhelming power and technology of the U.S. military, which seemed to be widening the gap between it and the People's Liberation Army. Africa, in particular, would be a place nearly impossible for China to exert hard power, as the PLA lacked expeditionary capacity, the Chinese navy had limited range, and, after 9/11, the United States sought to increase its military contacts on the continent through the pan-Sahel Initiative, an African counterterrorism-training program, and the Africa Command, a new department within the U.S. military with a responsibility for Africa alone.

In statements and speeches, Chinese leaders began to enunciate a doctrine of "win-win" (*shuang ying*) relations, highlighting that Latin American and African and Asian and Arab nations could benefit from their relationship with China even as China benefits from its relationship with them. Win-win relations also revolved around noninterference, particularly relevant in an African context where leaders had witnessed decades of intervention by Western powers. In fact, while the ideational aspect of China's soft power may be less relevant in other parts of the world, such as Southeast Asia, in Africa it is clearly relevant. In one major address given in 2005, entitled "An Open Mind for Win-Win Cooperation," Hu Jintao announced, "Dialogue and consultation . . . is an important avenue to win-win cooperation . . . [China] will only [promote] peace, stability, and prosperity."[16] "The aim of Sino-African cooperation is mutual benefit . . . it is particularly conducive for the development of African countries," echoed assistant Foreign Minister He Yafei, in a speech marking Prime Minister Wen Jiabao's 2006 tour of Africa.[17] Beginning in the late 1990s, China also enunciated what a "new security concept," in which it emphasized that Beijing, and other nations, could guarantee their own security by working more closely with multilateral institutions and building mutual trust.[18]

Africa would prove especially important to China. Africa contained large, undeveloped oil and gas deposits, in nations like Angola, Sudan, and Chad. Countries like the Democratic Republic of the Congo and Zambia also were major copper producers, and other African nations were important sources of other metals, as well as timber. Along with Central America and the South Pacific, Africa also was a battleground with Taiwan, which as recently as 1997 still had eight diplomatic allies on the continent. Compared to developed markets in the West and developed Asia, Africa also contained many untapped markets avoided by Western multinationals because of high levels of political risk. As Chinese companies began going global—in the late 1990s, the central government designated favoured firms as part of the *zou chuqu* "going out" strategy—they would look to these African markets for initial opportunities, since African nations like Sierra Leone or Mozambique had little Western investment, and often were less competitive than the domestic Chinese market itself.[19]

Finally, and perhaps most important, many African nations had far less experience with China than countries in Asia, and so had less inherent fear of Chinese security and economic competition. In fact, after years of slow growth following Western-oriented economic reforms, many African states were looking for a new model of development, and a major-power-partner that would treat Africa as a top priority. The ideational aspect of China's soft power would then be relevant, even if China did not explicitly suggest the ideational aspect of its model. After all, a decade of African democratisation during the 1990s also ironically made many African states more amenable to closer ties with Beijing. New, democratically elected African leaders, who enjoyed more popular legitimacy than their authoritarian predecessors, generally felt freer to build relations with a broader range of external actors beyond the traditional Western powers.

CHINA'S TOOLS OF SOFT POWER

As China's international engagement has become more sophisticated, so too it has developed more sophisticated tools of soft power. In Africa, development assistance may be the most important tool. China's total assistance to Africa is difficult to quantify, both because Beijing does not publish thorough, official statistics and because it remains unclear what percentage of China's announced aid actually qualifies as aid under Development Assistance Committee definitions.[20] But it is clear that China has reinvigorated its assistance to Africa. In June 2007, it launched the $5 billion China-Africa

Development Fund, managed by China Development Bank, to support Chinese firms investing in Africa.[21] Over the past seven years, China also has cancelled over $10 billion worth of African debts, and provided some $5.5 billion in aid to the continent, according to the Economist Intelligence Unit.[22] The World Bank estimates that China is now the largest lender to Africa, and at a recent summit in Shanghai, Chinese leaders announced they would offer Africa $20 billion in new financing.

Chinese aid tends to be untied to conditions other than supporting Chinese investment, which makes it popular with African leaders and many African elites, who may support political and economic reform in their countries but do not see tied aid as useful to promoting these goals. China also has taken advantage of African complaints about Western trade barriers to advertise that Beijing has no tariffs on exports from Africa's twenty-five poorest nations.

Since the major international financial institutions stopped funding infrastructure for years, much of China's aid to Africa goes for infrastructure projects like rebuilding the Benguela Railway in Angola and the Nigerian railway system. Yet compared to the 1950s and 1960s, today China's assistance to Africa is more diversified than just focusing on infrastructure. The Chinese government seems to have recognized that it needs to spend aid money on building a broader public appeal in Africa, on improving people-to-people contacts. This is a critical change from the past, when China focused almost exclusively on building relations with African leaders, not African publics. China also has more opportunity to build these people-to-people contacts in Africa than in Southeast Asia, where countries have a much longer experience of interaction with China, and where local ethnic Chinese communities tend to dominate people-to-people interactions with China. Beijing has developed the China Association of Youth Volunteers, a Peace Corps-like program designed to bring young people to countries like Ethiopia on agriculture and language projects. According to the Forum on China-Africa Cooperation's action plan, Beijing also has focused on social needs in Africa, like planning to fund anti-malaria clinics and rural schools. All of these programs help boost China's public appeal.

China, however, rarely coordinates with other donors, which risks duplication and also undermines efforts by other donors to support better governance within African nations. However, there are some signs this may be changing, that China is beginning to learn from other donors. Chinese officials have held meetings with American aid specialists designed to study the U.S. aid program.[23] Chinese aid specialists also have held meetings with officials from the World Bank, the U.S. Ex-Im Bank, the European Bank for Reconstruction and Development, and other major lenders in order to learn about their practices.

Training programs for African opinion leaders are a significant part of China's aid to Africa, and probably a larger component of its aid than in other, more developed regions like Southeast Asia. Again, this demonstrates an understanding by China of the need for building people-to-people contacts, since these opinion leaders will return to Africa and become unofficial ambassadors for closer ties to China. Beginning in 1996, China Foreign Affairs University ran a comprehensive seminar for diplomats from Africa and other regions entitled "Understanding China Symposium"; the class included lectures on Chinese history, culture, and strategies of development.[24] Other, similar training projects include programs at Zhejiang Normal University for African university presidents, seminars run by the Chinese Ministry of Education on training educational personnel, programs on health education for African officials, and a project to provide some 1,500 scholarships annually for African students to come to China, among many others. Perhaps most notably, China has begun organizing training programs for African media, a critical means of ensuring better press coverage.[25]

The training and visitor programs are supplemented by assistance for Chinese language and studies programs on the African continent, whether at Confucius Institutes or, in some cases, at local secondary schools. There is significant incentive for African students to take these classes: As one report notes, "Recently, Khartoum University had a Chinese speech competition, and a Chinese professor there said '...nearly 100 percent of students who graduate from the department get jobs with Chinese companies'."[26] Though the number of Confucius Institutes in Africa remains relatively small at this point, this is largely because of a lack of resources in African universities to support the Institutes, not because of a lack of Chinese will to establish them.

These training and visitor programs, as well as technical assistance programs, implicitly support probably the most compelling aspect of China's soft power to African elites: Its model of development, the so-called "Beijing Consensus."[27] This model is particularly attractive to authoritarian nations in Africa whose leadership would like to emulate China's high growth rates and lack of political liberalization, but it is also attractive to leaders in democratic African nations, who believe China's combination of protecting certain industries, liberalizing gradually, and maintaining some degree of state intervention in the economy have proven more successful than the neoliberal Washington Consensus. Unsurprisingly, the African Development Bank held its 2007 meeting in Shanghai partly because it wanted many of its officials to study, first-hand, China's model of growth. This despite assurances from Chinese leaders that they have no model to suggest to other countries, and that each nation needs to follow its own development path.

Besides the training and visitor programs, the Chinese government has used other, secondary, tools to build soft power in Africa. It has established closer party-party relations across the continent—the number of African parties visiting China rose from sixteen in 2002 to twenty-four in 2005.[28] It has upgraded its diplomatic corps, although according to Chinese diplomats the diplomatic corps in Africa lags behind that in Southeast Asia or Western nations, partly because most Chinese diplomats cannot bring their families with them to Africa and thus do not view the continent as an attractive posting. Still, high-level diplomacy shows African states that China places a high priority on relations with the continent, and has helped bring new life to African multilateral organizations. Senior Chinese leaders have been making two visits per year to Africa[29], in November 2006 China hosted nearly all the continent's leaders for a major summit in Beijing, and China has established the China-Africa Cooperation Forum to provide a formal site for diplomatic relations with the continent.[30]

China also has dramatically boosted its investment in and trade with Africa, with the investment often supported by favourable loans from China Ex-Im Bank, and with trade balances now in Africa's favour. China has become the continent's third-largest trading partner, and according to the International Monetary Fund, bilateral China-Africa trade has been rising by fifty percent per year. In speeches, Chinese leaders suggest to African nations that Beijing will be a fairer trading partner than Western nations—China will help African countries obtain the technology and skills they need to develop themselves, and to earn some of the wealth that industrialized nations now wield.[31]

Yet it remains unclear whether this new investment and trade actually has helped China's soft power on the continent. Clearly, Chinese demand for resources has boosted Africa's growth, and rescued commodity-dependent economies like Zambia. Compared with the more developed economies of Southeast Asia, where Chinese investment generally has been welcomed, many African states, which have virtually no manufacturing sector, worry that trade links with China will prevent them from ever climbing the value-added ladder. This sentiment is expressed widely. "We are back where we started," Wilfred Collins Wonani, who leads the Chamber of Commerce in Zambia, told the *New York Times*. "Sending raw materials out, bringing cheap manufactured goods in. This isn't progress. It is colonialism."[32] At its most extreme, this sentiment finds voice in populist politicians like Zambia's Michael Sata, who used anti-China sentiment to rally support in the 2006 presidential election, and nearly triumphed in the poll. Large, state-linked Chinese energy and construction companies' habit of relying on imported pools of Chinese labour, kept isolated on company compounds, also does not endear them to local populations. Unused to protests and vibrant civil society, lacking expertise in security, some large Chinese companies have responded poorly to popular demonstrations, as with the protests in Zambia.

Recognizing these concerns, the Ministry of Commerce has announced new regulations designed to push Chinese firms on the continent to act more responsibly, including by hiring local workers.[33] But it has little power to actually enforce these regulations. Beijing also has tried to increase transparency about its policies toward Africa by publishing white papers, such as the comprehensive 2006 paper on China's Africa Policy.

The Chinese government has less control over other aspects of China's soft power in Africa, yet some of these non-governmental elements of soft power actually have significantly boosted China's image in Africa. Since liberalizing restrictions on Chinese outbound travel, Beijing has limited control over where Chinese citizens move for business or tourism. Sensing commercial opportunities, significant communities of small-scale Chinese traders have moved to Africa over the past decade. One paper, by Barry Sautman, suggests there are as many as 100,000 Chinese residents in South Africa alone, while other reports note that there are as many as 750,000 Chinese residents on the continent.[34] They tend to concentrate in large cities, where they work trading clothes, cheap electronics, toys, and other medium-value goods, mostly imported from China.[35] Compared to the large Chinese companies, which tend to segregate their workers from local communities, these small traders mix with African populations, where they have boosted local goodwill, and even study in local schools. To be sure, for some of these migrants, their culture does not mesh well with that of Africans—there is little historic overlap, as compared to Chinese and Southeast Asian or Chinese and Northeast Asian cultures. Still, as Barry Sautman notes in an extended paper, compared to Western expatriates, who live in secure mansions, many of these Chinese traders live a local lifestyle, staying in inexpensive housing and winning credit for their simple style.

Just as important, with their stocks of capital, economic knowledge, and wealth—compared to local populations—many of the Chinese businesspeople offer an image of China as a prosperous nation, a country whose success should be emulated. They also tend to bring cheaper goods than Western peers, thereby helping African consumers spread their budgets wider, and these small traders are willing to launch businesses in countries considered too risky for Western entrepreneurs—Chinese firms are building hotels and shops across Freetown, Sierra Leone, for example.[36] Rising Chinese tourism to Africa—roughly 110,000 Chinese tourists visited in 2005—strengthens this perception of wealthy Chinese, though these numbers are small compared to Chinese tourism to Southeast Asia or Western nations.[37]

DROP CAP: SHORT TERM SUCCESS

Partly because many African nations had limited historical experience with China, Beijing has enjoyed a longer, more favourable honeymoon period in sub-Saharan African than it has in Southeast Asia, Central Asia, or other parts of the developing world. Indeed, since the early 2000s, China's global charm offensive has paid off most handsomely in Africa. In the most recent Pew Global Attitudes survey, some of the warmth toward China in other regions of the world, expressed in previous polls, had faded. "The image of China has slipped significantly among the publics of other major nations," Pew noted. Yet in Africa, Pew did not find such trends. People in nearly all the African nations surveyed by Pew had favourable images of China, with some overwhelmingly favourable—in the Ivory Coast and Mali, over ninety percent of respondents had a positive view.[38]

China is able to utilize this public image for policy gains. Growing warmth toward China makes it easier for Beijing to achieve policy objectives on the continent, since African publics back their leaders' desires for closer ties to China. For example, nations like Senegal have severed ties with Taiwan despite the fact that, in democratic Senegal, one might think switching recognition from democratic Taiwan to authoritarian China could spark local protests. Yet China's image is so favourable in Senegal that the decision engendered little public comment, and today Taiwan has only five formal allies in Africa. China also has become a significant contributor to peacekeeping efforts in Africa, deploying troops to Liberia and Sudan.[39] The fact that these troops served with little public complaint, or even comment, indicated how comfortable Africa had become with China, including with the presence of Chinese troops.

According to many African and Chinese officials, China's popularity also allows it to move rapidly on consolidating oil and gas deals across the continent. Again, both Beijing's claims of noninterference and China's warm public image, which makes its firms less vulnerable to militant attacks, help clinch these petroleum concessions. To take just one example among many new oil deals, in 2006 CNOOC took a forty-five percent interest in a major Nigerian offshore oil field, and China also bought a major stake in Nigeria's Kaduna refinery.[40]

This popularity, of course, makes it easier for Chinese firms to ink deals in other sectors as well, particularly in sectors dominated by African state-linked firms. Chinese telecommunications giant Huawei has sewn up deals in Kenya, Nigeria, and Zimbabwe, while Chinese aerospace Great Wall Industry has won the rights to build and launch a satellite for Nigeria, to take but a few examples out of hundreds of new deals.[41]

The appeal of the China model also appears stronger in Africa than in Southeast Asia, where many nations have successfully followed their own growth strategies. Anecdotal evidence suggests that African opinion leaders who attend China's visitor programs, often concentrated in wealthy Chinese cities, return to the continent impressed with China's staggering growth rates, unknowledgeable about rural poverty in China, and hoping to bring elements of China's economic strategy back to their home countries. They also often note that China is the first developing country to enter the ranks of major economic powers, which gives Beijing great credibility. "You are an example of transformation," Madagascar President Marc Ravalomanana told Chinese leaders during the May 2007 African Development Bank meeting in Shanghai. "We in Africa must learn from your success." The appeal of the China model, of course, depends on China's continuing to post astounding growth rates. Any slippage would cost it dearly in soft power; in the old Soviet Union, when sympathetic foreign visitors actually came to the USSR and saw how poorly its economy was performing, they often became far less enthusiastic about the potential spread of the Soviet model around the world.

LONG TERM QUESTIONS

In the longer term, however, China's soft power in Africa faces significant hurdles. This point has been raised by Zhongying Pang in his chapter, but let me provide a more detailed analysis. First, though African civil society initially welcomed China's new relationship with the continent, especially since other powers like the United States ignored many African needs, as the honeymoon period with China wears off African media and non-governmental organizations will begin to speak out more. This is especially true in southern Africa, which boasts vibrant trade unions, newspapers, and activist groups. Already, non-governmental organizations in southern Africa have begun to express concern that China's growing power in Africa will lead to Beijing exporting its own weaknesses, including poor environmental regulation, low labour standards, and weak corporate governance. Though they often detest the World Bank and other citadels of Western power, many of these activists realize that the conditions lenders propose for African governments do help ensure money goes to social welfare.[42] Consequently, they fear that Chinese assistance could contribute to environmental destruction, poor labour standards, or rampant graft, since China does not coordinate with other donors to make sure aid money was spent wisely and in accordance with international standards. Most traditional donors, after all, had realized that good governance is vital to development. But in Angola, one of the most corrupt nations on earth, a Chinese aid package worth as much as $9 billion allowed the regime to avoid having to deal with the IMF, which would have insisted that aid money actually trickled down to the country's vast underclass.[43] The International Rivers Network, a global environmental group, revealed that Chinese support for the Merowe Dam, a project in Sudan, may have displaced as many as 50,000 people, and the Sudanese government has violently suppressed protests against the project. Justica Ambiental, a Mozambican NGO, travelled to Shanghai to launch similar complaints about a China-backed dam in Mozambique. These complaints travel quickly, picked up in the African media: Unlike in the colonial era, when it would take months for stories of colonial atrocities to make their way to the British press, in the era of the Internet abuses get reported immediately.

At times, these attacks have turned violent. In April 2007, militant group in Ethiopia called the Ogaden National Liberation Front launched an attack on a Chinese oil exploration area in eastern Ethiopia, killing nine Chinese workers and kidnapping seven others. The Front warned Beijing "to refrain from entering into agreements with the Ethiopian government." Militants in the Niger Delta have issued similar warnings, and even kidnapped a group of Chinese labourers in January. In the Nigerian commercial capital of Lagos, police have begun expelling recent Chinese migrants from local markets because Nigerians complained that Chinese goods are undercutting local products.[44] In Zambia, Angola, and other countries, local media now report small-scale incidents of violence against Chinese migrants. The attacks will not push Chinese companies out, of course; after the Ethiopia killing, one leader of Sinopec, the company operating in Ethiopia, told reporters, "There is no way we will withdraw from Africa due to the fear of risk"[45] But they have led the Chinese government to reconsider its responsibilities. The Ministry of Commerce, for example, has passed new laws designed to help protect Chinese workers overseas, and the Ministry of Foreign Affairs has launched a massive campaign to remind Chinese heading abroad to respect local laws.

Some African leaders also have begun to doubt whether China will prove any different type of power than anyone else. Though Chinese officials portray their approach to development as a model more appropriate for Africa than Western models, some African officials have begun to question whether China's model, which depends upon the vast stocks of foreign investment into China, really teaches any lessons for the continent, which struggles to attract significant investment. Sensitive to these concerns, in November 2006 Wen Jiabao told African leaders, "China still hopes to further expand its import from African countries."[46] China also has agreed to quotas on its textile exports to South Africa. What's more, in an era where the U.S. war in Iraq has made China's vow of noninterference seem welcome, some African leaders wonder whether China actually is committed to this policy. In Zambia, the Chinese ambassador in 2006 warned that Beijing might cut off diplomatic ties if voters picked Michael Sata in the presidential poll.[47] The ambassador's comments, which sent shock waves through the local media, hardly seemed like an example of noninterference. Initially, when faced with these types of criticisms, Chinese officials wrote them off to isolated incidents or, in the case of complaints about its policy of noninterference, to concerns raised solely by Western states. But it is African elites themselves who have increasingly voiced doubts about China's relationships on the continent. Darfur is a prime example of this. Over the past decade, when Sudan developed a major oil industry, China's leading oil companies have invested at least $10 billion, making them critical to Sudan's economy; China also sold arms to the Sudanese government and repeatedly blocked any United Nations actions against Khartoum.[48] When reports of mass killing first emerged in Darfur in 2004, some Chinese diplomats wrote them off to hype created by human rights groups and America, which they believe never misses an opportunity to criticize Beijing. But by 2007, it became clear that Darfur was not only a concern of Western human rights groups. African leaders themselves called for solutions to the genocide, and some of these African elites wondered why China, a country that supposedly stood on the side of developing nations, stood by silently as those nations' leaders eliminated their own people. Still, Chinese leaders had difficulty understanding why Beijing would be criticized. "The hat of neocolonialism simply doesn't fit China," Wen Jiabao said at a press conference in 2006.[49]

CONCLUSION

Unlike regions of Asia, where nations have had longer interactions with China, and where there is less appetite for the China model, a critical aspect of Chinese soft power, Africa is fertile territory for growing Chinese influence. What's more, because of the absence of significant Western interests in Africa, China's influence has not provoked as strong a reaction as it has in parts of Asia and Latin America. In part because of Africa's receptiveness, China's public image in Africa remains much more favourable than in other parts of the globe, and China's soft power has yielded some significant policy gains.

But some of this goodwill toward Beijing is merely because China is a relatively new actor in Africa, and thus enjoys a kind of honeymoon period in public opinion. As China's honeymoon in Africa has begun to wane, it will prove a critical test of whether Beijing can adapt its new global diplomacy to address local concerns.

There are some signs of this flexibility. After three years of unflinchingly backing Khartoum, in the spring of 2007 a top Chinese official visited refugee camps and then publicly attempted to push Khartoum to allow in a peacekeeping force. China then named a special envoy to focus on Darfur and agreed to contribute 275 troops to the hybrid African Union-United Nations peacekeeping force in Darfur, even winning praise for its actions from U.S. officials like White House envoy to Sudan Andrew Natsios.[50] "China realizes these countries [like Sudan] are ruining its image, and what China wants is international respect," said one long-time observer of China's Africa policies in Beijing in an interview with the author. In recent months, the Ministry of Foreign Affairs also has begun pushing Chinese diplomats to broaden their circle of contacts beyond simply political elites to include the "African street"—NGOs, media, unions, and other important actors outside of typical leadership circles. This will be a tough task, as the Chinese diplomatic corps has little experience interacting with NGOs, and many Chinese diplomats have ignored African NGOs that are seeking a dialogue with them. Still, if China can prove flexible enough to use its soft power with both African leaders and the African "street," it could truly be ready to challenge the values, ideas, and models of Western actors playing a role on the continent.

NOTES

1. In this chapter, Africa refers only to sub-Saharan Africa.
2. Esther Pan, "China, Africa, and Oil," *Council on Foreign Relations* 2008, www.cfr.org/publication/9557/ (accessed August 1, 2007).
3. Joseph Schatz, "Zambian Hopeful Takes a Swing at China," *Washington Post*, September 25, 2006, 16(A).
4. Yaroslov Trofimov, "New Management: In Africa, China's Expansion Begins to Stir Resentment," *Wall Street Journal*, February 2, 2007, 1(A).
5. David Blair, "Ignored by the Mob," *Daily Telegraph online*, October 2, 2006, blogs.telegraph.co.uk/foreign/davidblair/oct06/mob1.htm (accessed July 20, 2007).
6. Chris McGreal, "Thanks China, Now Go Home: Buy-up of Zambia Revives Old Colonial Fears," *The Guardian*, February 5, 2007, 21.
7. Joseph S. Nye Jr., *Soft Power: The Means to Success in World Politics* (New York: Public Affairs, 2004).
8. Recognizing this blurry line, Nye himself has helped launch an initiative focused on "smart power," and has written approvingly of China's soft power, even though China does not fulfil the original, more limited Nye definition of this power.
9. Bruce Larkin, *China in Africa 1949–1970: The Foreign Policy of the People's Republic of China* (Berkeley: University of California Press, 1971).
10. Deborah Brautigam, *Chinese Aid and African Development: Exporting Green Revolution* (Basingstoke, U.K.: Macmillan Press Ltd, 1998).

11. Deborah Brautigam and Adama Gaye, "Is Chinese Investment Good for Africa?" *Council on Foreign Relations,* 2008, www.cfr.org/publication/12622/is_chinese_investment_good_for_africa.html (accessed May 25, 2007).

12. Guillaume Moumouni, "Domestic Transformations and Change in Sino-African Relations," *Centre on China's Transnational Relations Working Paper* no. 21 (2007).

13. Roberto Zagha and Gobind T. Nankani, "Africa's Growth Tragedy," in *Economic Growth in the 1990s: Learning from a Decade of Reform* (Washington: World Bank Publications, 2005).

14. Joseph Kahn, "China Opens Public Discussion of Its Rising Power," *International Herald Tribune*, December 8, 2006, www.iht.com/articles/2006/12/08/news/china.php (accessed January 2007).

15. H. Lyman Miller and Liu Xiaohong, "The Foreign Policy Outlook of China's Third Generation Elite," in *The Making of Chinese Foreign and Security Policy,* ed. David Lampto (Stanford: Palo Alto, 2001).

16. Hu Jintao, "An Open Mind for Win-Win Cooperation," (speech to APEC Summit 2005, Busan, South Korea, November 2005).

17. Antoaneta Bezlova, "China's Soft Power Diplomacy in Africa," *Asia Times*, 23 June 2006, www.atimes.com/atimes/China/HF23Ad01.html, (accessed January 2007).

18. Yong Deng and Thomas G. Moore, "China Views Globalization: Toward a New Great Power Politics?" *The Washington Quarterly* 27, no. 3 (Summer 2004): 117–136.

19. "China Spreads its Wings: Chinese Companies Go Global," *Accenture Consulting Company* 2005, www.accenture.com/NR/rdonlyres/6A4C9C07-8C84-4287-9417-203DF3E6A3D1/0/Chinaspreadsitswings.pdf (accessed September 20, 2006).; and "*Zhongguo qiye jingwai shangwu tousu fuwu zanxing banfa*" [Chinese enterprise overseas business legal claims procedural law], Regulation 16 (2006).

20. To be considered aid under the DAC definition, according to the DAC's glossary of statistical terms, the assistance must consist of "flows of official financing administered with the promotion of the economic development and welfare of developing countries as the main objective, and which are concessional in character with a grant element of at least 25 percent."

21. Jamil Anderlini, "CDB Seeking a Socialist Market System," *Financial Times*, 25 July 2007, 22.

22. Danna Harman, "China Takes up Civic Work in Africa," *Christian Science Monitor*, 27 June 2007, 1.

23. Michael A. Glosny, "Meeting the Development Challenge in the 21st Century: American and Chinese Perspectives on Foreign Aid," (Conference Report: National Committee on United States-China Relations, December 2005), www.ncuscr.org/Publications/Foreign percent20Aid percent20Report.pdf (accessed January 2007).

24. Li Anshan, "Transformation of China's Policy Toward Africa," *Centre on China's Transnational Relations Working Paper* no. 20 (2006).

25. Drew Thompson, "China's Soft Power in Africa: From the Beijing Consensus to Health Diplomacy," *China Brief* 13 Oct 2005, www.jamestown.org/publications_details.php?volume_id=408&issue_id=3491&article_id=2370717 (accessed January 2006).

26. Preeti Aroon, "Chinese: The Language of Choice for Sudanese Students," *Foreign Policy Passport* June 15, 2007, blog.foreignpolicy.com/node/5121 (accessed August 2007).

27. Barry Sautmam, "Friends and Interests: China's Distinctive Links with Africa," *Centre on China's Transnational Relations Working Paper* no. 12 (2006).

28. Li, "*Transformation of China's Policy Towards Africa.*"

29. George Bush, by contrast, has not visited the continent during his second term.

30. For more on the summit, see english.focacsummit.org/.; *also see* Joshua Eisenman, "China's Post Cold War Strategy in Africa," in *China and the Developing World*, eds. Joshua Eisenman, Eric Heginbotham and Derek Mitchell (Armonk, NY.: ME Sharpe, 2007)

31. Sautmam, "*Friends and Interests*."

32. Howard W. French and Lydia Polgreen, "China's Trade with Africa Carries a Price Tag," *New York Times*, August 21, 2007, 1.

33. Bates Gill and James Reilly, "The Tenuous Hold of China Inc. in Africa," *The Washington Quarterly* 30, no. 3 (Summer 2007): 37–52.

34. French and Polgreen, "*China's Trade with Africa.*"

35. Alec Russell, "Small Businesses from China Follow in the Footsteps of Giants," *Financial Times*, August 28, 2007, 6.

36. John Donnelly, "China Scooping up Deals in Africa as US Firms Hesitate," *Boston Globe*, Dec 24, 2005.

37. Elling N. Tjønneland, "China in Africa. Implications for Norwegian Foreign and Development Policies," CMI Report, 2006, www.cmi.no/publications/publication/?2438=china-in-africa-implications-for-norwegian, accessed Aug 2007.

38. Pew Global Attitudes Project, "Global Unease With Major World Powers," (June 2007).

39. Su Qiang and Le Tian, "Peacekeeping—a Rising Role for China's PLA," *China Daily* July 24, 2007, www.chinadaily.com.cn/china/2007-07/24/content_5442172.htm (accessed Aug 2007).

40. "China, Nigeria to Ink Oil Deal," *China Daily*, April 24, 2006.

41. Bright B. Simons, Evans Lartey and Franklin Cudjoe, "China Draws Africa into its Orbit," *Asia Times*, March 30, 2007, www.atimes.com/atimes/China_Business/IC31Cb03.html (accessed August 2007).

42. *See, for example*, Firoze Manji and Stephen Marks, eds. *African Perspectives on China in Africa* (Oxford: Fahamu, 2007).

43. Paul Hare, "China in Angola: An Emerging Energy Partnership," *China Brief*, November 8, 2006, jamestown.org/publications_details.php?volume_id=415&issue_id=3918&article_id=2371629 (accessed January 2007).

44. Laurie Goering, "China's Investment, Clout in Africa Cause Concern," *Chicago Tribune*, February 19, 2006, 11.

45. Howard French, "Letter from Ethiopia: China's Risky Venture into Resource-Rich Africa," *The New York Times*, 2 May 2007.

46. "China-Africa Trade Expected to Top $100 Billion by 2010," *Xinhua*, November 4, 2006.

47. Schatz, *"Zambian Hopeful Takes a Swing at China."*

48. Erica Downs, "The Fact and Fiction of Sino-African Energy Relations," *China Security* 3 no. 3 (Summer 2007): 42–68.

49. Chris Zambelis, "Public Diplomacy in Sino-Egyptian Relations," *China Brief,* April 5 2007, www.jamestown.org/terrorism/news/uploads/cb_007_007a.pdf (accessed August 2007).

50. Downs, "*The Fact and Fiction of Sino-African Energy Relations*," 42–68.

Chapter Ten

China's Warming Relations with South Korea and Australia

Zhiqun Zhu

China's rise as an economic, military, and political power at the end of the twentieth century and the beginning of the twenty-first century has been met with mixed reactions from the international community. While most of China's Asian neighbors and many developing countries in other regions seem to welcome China's steady growth and see it as an opportunity, a few countries, such as the United States and Japan, are more cautious. They question China's intentions as its power, especially its military strength, continues to expand. The Republic of Korea (ROK or South Korea) and Australia, two key allies of the United States, seem not to be as concerned. In fact, relations between China and these two countries have developed rapidly in the past decade or so.

This chapter will explore the reasons why South Korea and Australia hold a more benign view of China than the United States. In addition to promoting robust trade relations, how is China enhancing its influence in the ROK and Australia? Are there any differences and similarities in China's relations with the two countries? Are there any limits to China's "soft power" in the ROK and Australia? The answers to these questions will help explain why and how China is expanding its soft power in Australia and South Korea, and how effective China's new diplomatic strategy is. I argue that China's soft power approach to South Korea and Australia has played a significant role in cementing bilateral relations. Without the play of soft power, China's relationship with the two countries could have been more strained.

PARADIGM SHIFT IN CHINESE FOREIGN POLICY

Since the beginning of the twenty-first century, China has emphasized the peaceful development of its economy and military, which, according to Chinese officials, poses no threat to other nations. China claims that its growth is good not only for itself but also for the world. China is attempting to substantiate this claim by pursuing a "soft" approach in its foreign relations. It is enhancing its soft power by promoting the Chinese language and culture at leading universities in many countries and by presenting an image of itself as a peaceful rising power. Meanwhile, China has increased the number of overseas students coming to its universities, from about 8,000 two decades ago to about 120,000 today.[1] In addition to satisfying China's key economic and security interests, projecting its influence or soft power around the world has become a new objective of Chinese foreign policy.

At the beginning of the reform era, China's prevailing strategy was *yin jinlai* or "bringing in." China enthusiastically attracted foreign direct investment, particularly investment from expatriate Chinese. It established four Special Economic Zones in the south near Hong Kong, Taiwan, and Southeast Asia where the majority of the Chinese diaspora live. However, since the late 1990s, especially after it became a member of the World Trade Organization in 2001, China has been more deeply integrated into the global economy. The strategy in the twenty-first century has become *zou chuqu* or "going out." China has been actively seeking oil and other energy deals around the world, and Chinese companies have started to invest overseas, including purchasing foreign assets. Backed up by a foreign exchange reserve of about $2 trillion, China is now confidently going global. According to China scholar Harry Harding, China is now in a position to make major investments in the United States. Those investments include strategic and iconic ones, such as oil and a well-known American automobile brand.[2]

Indeed, along with the country's growing political and economic power, Chinese foreign policy is undergoing a paradigm shift. As Wu Jianmin, a senior diplomat and former President of the China Foreign Affairs University has observed, China is moving from "responsive diplomacy" (*fanying shi waijiao*) to "proactive diplomacy" (*zhudong shi waijiao*).[3] "The nail that sticks out will get pounded down," the late Deng Xiaoping admonished, meaning that China needed to focus on domestic growth and should keep a low profile and never take the lead in international affairs. Not anymore. The Hu Jintao leadership seems to be walking a different path: take the lead when necessary. The new policy thinking is also reflected in President Hu's theory of the "Three Harmonies" (*San He*), which includes seeking peace (*heping*) in the world, reconciliation (*hejie*) with Taiwan, and harmony (*hexie*) in Chinese society.

Since the beginning of the twenty-first century, China has demonstrated leadership in several international arenas. In 2003, China initiated the Six-Party Talks over North Korea's nuclear program, which involved the United States, Japan, South Korea, North Korea, and Russia. Through several rounds of tough negotiations, the six nations finally reached an agreement in Beijing in February 2007 to dismantle North Korea's nuclear program, the process of which started in July 2007. The Shanghai Cooperation Organization is another multilateral venue where China has demonstrated leadership.

According to Shi Yinhong, a professor of international relations at Renmin University of China, China's peaceful rise is all about its projection of soft power. A peaceful rise relies primarily on non-coercive use of resources. These include economic power, foreign trade, diplomatic and cultural power, esteem from successful national development, and simple persuasion. A peaceful rise is also nonviolent, gradual, and beneficial to all parties. It may meet strong resistance but generates results are a "win for all."[4]

The proposed establishment of 500 Confucius Institutes around the world, together with Chinese trade and investment, has become an important component of China's new diplomacy that emphasizes soft power. China has become more self-confident and aspires to be an active member in the international political economy. Its soft power diplomacy is now more sophisticated and comprehensive and includes, for example, engaging in high-level visits, promoting economic interdependence, highlighting the expected benefits from China's prosperity, expanding cultural and social exchanges, and presenting a peaceful and non-threatening new image around the world. The PRC's close relations with South Korea and Australia must be understood in the context of China's growing power and its more sophisticated new diplomacy or soft power approach.

CHINA'S STRATEGIES FOR RELATIONS WITH SOUTH KOREA

The speed with which China and South Korea developed their close partnership has few precedents in bilateral relations. The two countries established diplomatic relations on August 24, 1992. In only sixteen years after this normalization of relations, South Korea's economic and cultural relationship with China surpassed that with its long-time ally, the United States. This has come as a surprise to South Korea's older generation, who fought against the Chinese People's Liberation Army in the Korean War. "Establishing diplomatic ties then was a shock to the world, and such a leap in the relationship between the two in all aspects is once again shocking the world," Kim Ha-joong, South Korea's ambassador to Beijing, commented in an interview.[5]

It takes two to tango. Both the PRC and the ROK have a strong desire to maintain close ties in today's changing international political economy. Both have worked hard to strengthen bilateral relations and enhance their images in recent years. In the following section, we will focus on the Chinese strategies.

Holding Frequent High-Level Meetings to Consolidate Ties

A solid political relationship is the foundation for expanding ties in other areas, and the frequency of high-level visits is a barometer for bilateral relations in international politics. Whenever the PRC leadership realizes the importance of China's relations with another country, it takes the initiative and makes an extra effort to strengthen ties with that particular country. The ROK, due to its close economic, geopolitical, and cultural linkages to China, is certainly one of China's foreign policy priorities.

Visits at the highest level have been frequent in recent years. For example, after President Roh Moo-hyun took office in 2003, he paid two official visits to China. Notably, during his first visit in July 2003, only about five months after his inauguration, the bilateral relation was officially redefined and upgraded from "cooperative partnership" (*hezuo huoban guanxi*) to "comprehensive cooperative partnership" (*quanmian hezuo huoban guanxi*). Chinese President Hu Jintao paid a state visit to South Korea and attended the APEC summit meeting in Busan in November 2005. Prime Minister Wen Jiabao visited South Korea in April 2007, and his predecessor Zhu Rongji went in October 2000. Significantly, during Prime Minister Wen's visit, the two sides agreed to set up military hotlines between their navies and air forces and conduct joint search-and-rescue operations in the Yellow Sea for humanitarian purposes.

There have been other high-level visits between the two sides in recent years. For example, Jia Qinglin, chairman of the National Committee of the Chinese People's Political Consultative Conference (CPPCC), paid an official goodwill visit to the ROK in August 2004. Prime Minister of the ROK Lee Hae-chan visited China in June 2005. Aside from this frequent exchange of the highest-level visitors, leaders and officials from the two countries also meet regularly at the sidelines of international conferences, such as the ASEAN regional security and economic conferences and APEC summit and ministerial meetings.

To a large extent, South Korea's post-1997 growth was boosted by rapid economic integration with China. In his visit to Seoul shortly after the financial crisis in 1997, then Chinese Vice President Hu Jintao confirmed to the South Korean government that China would not devalue the *yuan*, which proved vital to the economic stability and prosperity in Asia. Hu also announced the Chinese government's decision to allow its citizens to travel to Korea as tourists, thereby helping South Korea's economic recovery.[6]

Regular summit meetings have yielded some South Korean policies deemed favorable to China. President Roh, for example, has attempted to strengthen security relations with China. In a meeting with Chinese Defense Minister Cao Gangchuan in April 2006, President Roh suggested that the two countries further cooperate on security affairs. President Roh's policy of balancing between the United States and China was interpreted by some as a change of the status quo that benefits China at the expense of South Korea's alliance with the United States.[7]

The complex Northeast Asian security challenge binds the two countries together. Both South Korea and China fear a sudden collapse of North Korea, which will create an enormous economic and social burden and potential military clashes.[8] Still haunted by the bitter memory of over two million casualties during the internecine Korean War, South Korea has a tremendous stake in preventing another outbreak of hostilities on the Korean Peninsula. China's leadership role in the Six-Party Talks is timely and crucial. China's efforts to engage North Korea and to help resolve the nuclear dilemma peacefully are much in the interests of South Korea.

Broadening Cultural, Educational, and Social Exchanges

A bilateral relationship only promoted by top leaders without the participation and support of the public cannot be maintained. Realizing this, China has tried hard to promote and expand exchanges between the two societies.

Korea and China have strong cultural and historical bonds. Confucianism is well respected in Korean culture and society. Throughout history, Korean scholars have built many schools to study Confucianism. Toson Sowon (*Taoshan Shuyuan*) in Andong, Korea is one such well-preserved Confucian academies established by Korean scholars in the sixteenth century. In fact, current Chinese efforts to promote its culture abroad began with the establishment of the world's first Confucius Institute in Seoul, Korea on November 21, 2004.

China welcomes South Korean students and many Chinese schools have established scholarships for these students. The number of Korean students in China reached 54,000 by the end of 2006, accounting for thirty-eight percent of the total number of foreign students in China that year.[9] The student exchange goes both ways: out of the 32,557 foreign students studying at South Korean colleges and universities in 2006, 61.7 percent were from the Chinese mainland.[10]

The growing bilateral trade between China and South Korea makes it easier for these visiting Korean students to find employment when they return home. Indeed, an increasing number of South Koreans are making a living in China: as many as 400,000 of them now live permanently in China. About 800 weekly flights connect South Korea's six major cities with some thirty Chinese cities, while the number between South Korea and the United States is only about 200.[11]

The year 2007 marked the fiftieth anniversary of the establishment of diplomatic relations between China and South Korea, and the two countries held various activities to celebrate the "Korea-China Friendship Year." Both countries promoted tourism as part of the anniversary celebration. Over 1.5 million Chinese tourists were expected to travel to South Korea in 2007.[12] Korean tourism authorities predict that the Chinese would replace the Japanese as the largest foreign tourist group in Korea by 2015.[13] South Korea has in turn been the fast-growing foreign country that sends its tourists to China since 1992. By 2005, it had become the largest market for China, with a quarter of Korean tourists (about 4 million people) coming to China.[14] According to the Tourism Bureau of Shandong Province, the birthplace of Confucius, Shandong alone currently receives one million South Koreans a year. It planned to take advantage of the Beijing Olympics to attract two million South Koreans and to send one million tourists of its own to South Korea in 2008.[15]

South Korea currently is experiencing a Chinese language boom as well. In the 1960s, only two South Korean universities had Chinese language departments, graduating about forty or fifty students a year. Today, 131 universities and colleges in South Korea have Chinese language departments, graduating over 3,000 students a year.[16]

Public opinion polls show that these changes are resulting in a growing number of Koreans having a favorable view of China. In an early 2006 *Korea Times* poll of 1,000 South Koreans aged between eighteen and twenty-three, almost forty percent said China should be South Korea's top diplomatic priority, while only eighteen percent opted for either the United States or North Korea.[17] These developments have led some American observers to worry that the Chinese influence over South Korean policy is likely to rise in the future, at the expense of the United States.[18]

Deepening Economic Cooperation

The two economies are highly complementary. South Korea generally considers China's development to be a great opportunity, not a threat. South Korea has become China's third largest trading partner, just after the United States and Japan, while China replaced the United States and became the ROK's largest trading partner in 2004. When the two countries established diplomatic relations in 1992, their bilateral trade volume was less than $5 billion. In 2005, the bilateral trade volume first broke the $100 billion benchmark and reached $134.3 billion in 2006. It surpassed $150 billion in 2007 and is expected to reach $200 billion in 2010.[19] Besides, China is also the biggest importer of South Korean products. Since 2002, China has been South Korea's top investment destination.

By the end of 2006, South Korea had set up more than 30,000 enterprises in China, with an accumulated investment of $35 billion. Meanwhile, more and more Chinese enterprises choose to invest in South Korea.[20] Currently, the two countries are studying establishing a free trade area (FTA). The rapid economic growth in the two countries has not only created an abundant material basis for their exports, but also enlarged their markets. South Korea's acknowledgment of China's market economy provides the necessary atmosphere for trade and economic development of the two countries.

POTENTIAL PROBLEMS IN CHINA-SOUTH KOREA RELATIONS

Though it is true that political, economic, and cultural relations between China and South Korea are strong, China's "charm" in South Korea has also been tainted by several problems. China-South Korea bilateral relations are warm at the highest level, but ordinary Koreans and Chinese have mixed feelings, and sometimes even negative ones, toward each other. The biggest challenge for both countries is to sustain the close relationship by properly handling these issues.

Historical and Other Disputes

China and South Korea have enjoyed a shared history and cultural and economic exchanges for thousands of years. In recent years, historical and territorial issues such as the kingdom of Goguryeo (Koguryo) have aroused emotions by both sides, especially among academics. At its peak (37 BC to 668 AD), the territory of Goguryeo extended to today's Manchuria. Some South Korean scholars argue that the reinterpretation of Goguryeo ownership by China's "Northeast Project" (*Dongbei Gongcheng*) has played a key role in eroding the positive view of China in South Korea.[21] A South Korean scholar states that Koreans now question whether China is a responsible power in East Asia and that more Koreans are accepting the "China threat" argument because of the project.[22] Some worry that the Northeast Project may annihilate China's diplomatic accomplishments over South Korea with one stroke.

Such nationalistic clashes were also shown plainly during the 2002 World Cup and the 2007 Winter Asian Games. Chinese media and Internet users' denouncements of Korea and the Korean soccer team during the World Cup period triggered harsh reactions from South Korea.[23] On January 31, 2007, when being awarded medals in Changchun during the Asian Games, Korean female short-track speed skaters held up signs reading "Mt. Baekdu is our territory." They were expressing many South Koreans' unpleasant feelings toward China, which claims Mt. Baekdu (*Changbai* in Chinese) a part of its territory.[24]

Fortunately, the two governments seem to be trying to dampen the tensions. In an interview with South Korean journalists, Chinese Premier Wen Jiabao stated that there were "no territorial issues between China and South Korea."[25] Wen called on both sides to properly handle issues relating to the Koguryo kingdom. He suggested that while doing research on ethnic movements and territorial changes, the two sides should stick to the principle of separating research from politics and reality from history, and avoid any negative impact on bilateral relations.

In addition to Koguryo, the two countries have been embroiled in other disputes. For example, a South Korean freighter sunk after colliding with a larger Chinese vessel off China's east coast in early 2007, killing all sixteen crewmen on board. The Chinese authorities reported the incident to the Korean Embassy in Beijing almost twenty-one hours after it occurred. Unsatisfied with China's handling of this and other incidents, some Koreans asked a fundamental question: "What sort of a neighbor is China for us?"[26] Issues like these may become obstacles to furthering bilateral relations.

Taiwan and North Korea

Taiwan and North Korea are core national interest issues for China and South Korea, respectively. Taiwan has become a destabilizing factor in Northeast Asia in recent years. While almost every country prefers the status quo across the Taiwan Strait, former President Chen Shui-bian's pro-independence government in Taipei had been challenging it.

In his *America's Coming War with China,* Ted Galen Carpenter of the Cato Institute described an interesting scenario in a hypothetical cross-Taiwan Strait war in 2013. "The South Korean foreign ministry issued a statement emphasizing that its mutual security treaty with the United States did not cover contingencies in the Taiwan Strait. Seoul reiterated its adherence to a one-China policy and admonished Taipei to stop provoking a crisis with the PRC."[27] Perhaps it is true that South Korea is less willing to get dragged into a Taiwan Strait conflict than Japan or even Australia. But exactly what

South Korea would do in such an unpredictable conflict is unknown. Even if South Korea just plays a passive role, such as allowing U.S. troops in Korea to move to the Taiwan Strait, its normal relations with China would be difficult to maintain.

Although there are no official ties between Seoul and Taipei, relations at the non-governmental level have been very dynamic. In both Taiwan and South Korea, there are politicians who argue that the two should form a democratic alliance and reestablish official relations, in spite of the PRC's strong opposition. Similar to China's relations with other powers, the Taiwan factor, if mishandled, has the potential to jeopardize PRC-ROK relations.

While the PRC and the ROK share similar concerns over North Korea's nuclear program and fear a sudden collapse of the North Korean regime, the two countries may not necessarily see eye to eye regarding the future of the Korean peninsula. There is little agreement about when and how Korea should be unified or, perhaps more importantly, what the future relationship should be between a unified Korea and both the United States and Japan. China may, for example, demand a strategic demilitarized buffer with a unified Korea as well as forbidding U.S. troops north of the current Demilitarized Zone.[28]

In addition, South Koreans are not happy with the Chinese government's handling of North Koreans fleeing to China in recent years. For example, on October 9, 2007, Chinese police entered a South Korean international school in Beijing to arrest four people believed to be North Korean refugees. The police were allegedly to have pinned the arms of two South Korean consuls behind their backs, creating a diplomatic incident between the two countries. Refusing to recognize their refugee status, China routinely considers these people "economic migrants" and has sent those fleeing North Korea back home, though it has also allowed most of the North Koreans who take refugee at diplomatic missions to leave China for a third country. South Korea and China's different, even conflicting, interests on these vital issues may hamper their cooperation in the future.

Leadership and Policy Changes

South Korea held a presidential election in December 2007 and Lee Myung-bak, former mayor of Seoul and CEO of Hyundai Motor Company, was elected ROK president. It is not guaranteed that former President Roh's "balancing" and China-friendly policy will be carried on by the new administration. During his campaign, Lee, who represented the more conservative Grand National Party, called for stronger relations with traditional ally the United States and a more critical stance on North Korea. According to some analysts, Lee Myung-bak has insisted on more reciprocity and much better terms than his predecessor in dealing with North Korea.[29]

Although Lee's election is unlikely to lead to an about face in Seoul's engagement policy with Pyongyang as long as the North follows through with its denuclearization pledge, some fine-tuning of existing ROK policies will almost certainly happen. Lee told U.S. President George W. Bush in a phone conversation shortly after the election that he intended to strengthen South Korea's alliance with the United States. At his first news conference as President-elect, he again said he would get tough with North Korea: "I assure you that there will be a change from the past government's practice of avoiding criticism of North Korea and unilaterally flattering it," and "the North's human rights issue is something we cannot avoid in this regard, and North Korea should know it."[30] Seoul's new approach is expected to improve relations with the United States and Japan, which had sometimes been critical of Mr. Roh's conciliatory "sunshine policy" toward North Korea.

In terms of economic ties, some Koreans have already expressed concerns about South Korea's over-dependence on the Chinese market. A 2004 *Chosun Ilbo* editorial called on the Korean government and business to develop a counter-plan to "strengthen the economic system by dispersing the market and production."[31] Meanwhile, some officials, such as the ROK's ambassador to Israel Shin Kak-soo, argue that "Seoul should fully capitalize on its alliance with Washington in solving problems that Beijing's rise may bring forth."[32] It remains to be seen how the new South Korean administration will handle the delicate balance of ROK-China-U.S. trilateral relations.

CHINA'S STRATEGIES FOR RELATIONS WITH AUSTRALIA

China's growing influence in Australia can be gauged from the fact that during the 2007 APEC summit, New South Wales, the state where the conference was held, planned only one formal state dinner—for the Chinese delegation. New South Wales Premier Morris Iemma, who hosted the dinner that was attended by three former Australian prime ministers and other distinguished guests, remarked that "Australia views China's achievements with admiration and satisfaction, not simply because we rejoice in the prosperity of a friend."[33]

China surpassed the United States as Australia's biggest source of imports in 2006. In 2007 it eclipsed Japan as Australia's biggest trading partner, according to Australian Trade Minister Warren Truss.[34] The growing trade between Australia and China is due to Australia's voracious demand for Chinese manufactured imports and China's demand for Australia's mineral and other exports. Australia is where forty percent of the global reserves of uranium are located. The bilateral agreement that allows China to import uranium from Australia speaks volumes about the close relationship between the two countries. Australia is the world's biggest wool exporter and China is its biggest customer, buying $1.3 billion worth, or more than sixty percent of its total clip each year.[35] Two-way trade, excluding Hong Kong's trade with Australia, was expected to top $50 billion in 2007 and continue to grow in the future. In September 2007, the two countries signed a $35 billion (U.S. $28.8 billion) agreement for Woodside Petroleum Ltd to export liquefied natural gas to China.[36] Like South Korea, Australia has recognized China's market economy status and is negotiating a free trade agreement with China. Like most of China's neighbors, Australia is focused on China's growth, anticipating the economic benefits in trade and investment it will bring about. China's growing appetite for energy and other natural resources is feeding an economic boom in Australia and, like other countries in the Asia-Pacific region, Australia wants China's growth to continue without disruption by conflicts over Taiwan.[37]

In March 2006, the United States launched a political forum for security dialogue with Australia and Japan in a bid to checkmate China in the Asia Pacific region. Interestingly, Australia was the only country among the three that had explicitly stated that the talks were not aimed at containing China.[38] Barely a month later, on April 3, 2006, Australian Prime Minister John Howard and his visiting Chinese counterpart Wen Jiabao oversaw the signing of a bilateral nuclear energy deal. This was not only a triumph of China's diplomacy but also demonstrated Australia's increasing autonomy with regard to the United States. In September 2007, Prime Minister Howard announced that Australia would begin security talks with China in 2008, a move regarded as an effort to ease concerns in Beijing about the trilateral security talks between the United States, Japan, and Australia.[39]

Geopolitically, Australia increasingly considers itself an Asian nation, though it has traditionally maintained close ties with Great Britain, the United States, and other Western powers. When meeting with visiting Chinese premier Wen Jiabao, Prime Minister Howard said that the relationship with China is one of Australia's most important foreign relationships. Australia very much welcomes China's development and appreciates its positive role in international and regional affairs. It sees China's rapid development as beneficial for the world at large and disagrees with China containment policies.[40] Similar to South Korea, Australia's strong desire to maintain good ties with China and China's increasingly sophisticated diplomacy make it possible for the countries to enjoy friendly relations. China's strategies to enhance its image and strengthen its relations with Australia include the following initiatives.

Promoting Cultural and Educational Exchanges

On May 20, 2005, the Confucius Academy, the first Confucius school in Australia, was officially launched at the University of Western Australia (UWA) in Perth. Present at the ceremony was a high-level Chinese delegation led by Redi, Vice Chairman of the Standing Committee of National People's Congress. The selection of UWA as the site of the Confucius Institute was significant, since the last six Australian ambassadors to China have all come from Western Australia with five graduating from UWA.[41] The establishment of the Confucius Institute helps promote a greater awareness and understanding of China and Chinese language and culture in the broader West Australian community—particularly in the government, business, education, and industry sectors. Two more Confucius Institutes were set up at the University of Adelaide and the University of Melbourne shortly afterwards.

In 1999, Australia was one of the first Western countries (along with New Zealand) to be granted Approved Destination Status (ADS) by China. In 2005 alone, 285,000 Chinese tourists visited Australia, an increase of 13.4 percent from the previous year. This is forecast to grow by 15.7 percent to 1.2 million tourists by 2015.[42] China has become the country with the fastest growth in the number of tourists visiting Australia.[43] In 2007, nearly 100,000 Chinese students were studying in Australia, making China the largest source of overseas enrollment. Tighter U.S. visa policies and the growing wealth of the Chinese middle class mean that more and more Chinese citizens will go to Australia for study and travel.

Holding Regular High-Level Meetings

This top-down approach is considered to be a favorable strategy by Chinese leaders. President Hu Jintao paid a state visit to Australia in October 2003 and became the first Chinese leader to have been given the honor of addressing the joint sitting of the Australian parliament. Prior to attending the APEC summit in Sydney, President Hu paid another official visit to Australia in September 2007.

Premier Wen Jiabao visited Australia in April 2006. During the visit, he and Prime Minister Howard agreed to establish a mechanism for regular meetings to discuss major issues affecting both countries.[44] Less than three months later, Prime Minister Howard visited China. On June 28, 2006, Premier Wen and Prime Minister Howard jointly attended a ceremony in Shenzhen commemorating the first phase of the Guangdong Dapeng Liquified Natural Gas (LNG).

Other Chinese leaders have traveled to Australia too. For example, Wu Bangguo, Chairman of the National People's Congress, paid an official visit to Australia in May 2005. Leaders of the two countries also meet frequently on the sidelines of international and regional conferences. The China-Australia Agreement on Cooperation in the Peaceful Uses of Nuclear Energy and Agreement on Transfer of Nuclear Material, which came into force in February 2007, is one of the most remarkable outcomes of these high-level meetings.

Reaching Out to the Public

Both President Hu and Premier Wen made public speeches during their visits to Australia in an effort to reach out to the Australian public. They talked about how both countries could benefit from a cooperative relationship and how China is committed to peaceful development. These words and deeds helped create an open, friendly, and peaceful image of China.

During his September 2007 visit to Australia, President Hu Jintao demonstrated his personable side by talking to the Australian public directly. In addition to meeting with Australian officials, he went to Western Australia to meet with executives of Australian enterprises and research institutes, watched a presentation about geological modeling, mining, and exploration, and visited two laboratories.[45] President Hu also visited a sheep farm outside Canberra and drank tea with farmer Ian Cusack and his family, who were very impressed by Hu's charm.[46]

Chinese leaders also seem to understand the importance to cultivating good relations with opposition parties and future leaders. During the same September 2007 visit, President Hu met with Kevin Rudd, the opposition Labor Party head. At the meeting, President Hu invited Rudd and his family to attend the 2008 Beijing Olympics, which Rudd gladly accepted.[47] Rudd was a diplomat in Beijing in the 1980s and speaks fluent Chinese.

In the December 2007 federal elections, the Labor Party defeated the Conservative Party, and Kevin Rudd became the new Australian Prime Minister. China lost no time in cultivating good relations with this first Mandarin-speaking Western leader. Wen Jiabao was one of the first foreign leaders to send congratulatory messages to Rudd. Following his election, Rudd spoke by phone to the leaders of Australia's traditional allies: George W. Bush in Washington and Gordon Brown in London. But Wen Jiabao was the first foreign leader Mr. Rudd spoke with after being sworn in as prime minister.[48]

As another example of how China is displaying its soft power to the Australians, China announced ahead of the 2007 APEC summit that it would lend two giant pandas to the Adelaide Zoo for ten years.[49]

THE LIMITS OF CHINA'S SOFT POWER IN AUSTRALIA

Though China's influence has been growing in Australia, the two sides have substantial differences over certain issues, which may disrupt normal relations.

Human Rights

Close economic, political, and cultural links notwithstanding, Australia does not always kowtow to China. For example, despite warnings from China, both Prime Minister John Howard and opposition Labor Party leader Kevin Rudd met with the Dalai Lama in June 2007. The Australian side emphasized that these meetings were "private" and would not hurt bilateral relations. But China considers such meetings to be interference in its internal affairs, which presents an obstacle in China-Australia relations. At the core of the issue are their different views on human rights.

Even human rights violations by China's neighbors or countries friendly to China may create tensions between China and Australia. During the September 2007 protests and democracy movement in Myanmar, Prime Minister John Howard said his government would press Beijing to urge the junta to end its violent repression. However, China refused to condemn Myanmar's military rulers for the crackdown of the protests, and together with Russia, it contended at the UN that the situation in Myanmar was an internal affair and did not threaten international peace and security. In the future, China may face increasing pressure from the international community, including Australia, to intervene in places where human rights are grossly violated, such as Sudan and Myanmar.

Security Concerns

In early September 2007, Australia, though extremely worried about upsetting Beijing, participated in a joint naval exercise with the United States, Japan, India, and Singapore in the Bay of Bengal. Participants stressed that the exercise in no way threatened a certain growing Asian power to the north, but there was little doubt that such military exercises pointed toward the future geopolitical arrangement in the Asia-Pacific region. As Brahma Chellaney, Professor of Strategic Studies at the Delhi-based Center for Policy Research, commented, some of the countries involved did not want to promote this too much to avoid upsetting China, but at the same time it was a very important reminder to China.[50] Apparently to maintain a delicate balance between China and the United States, Australia invited two Chinese warships to visit Australia at the end of September 2007 for a joint naval exercise involving the

Chinese, Australian, and New Zealand navies in early October. According to Australian Defense Minister Brendan Nelson, more military exercises and cooperation are planned between his country and China.[51]

These balancing efforts notwithstanding, Australia does have security concerns over China's rapid military modernization. Australia's 2007 defense strategy report pointed to the destabilizing effect of China's growing military strength. "The pace and scope of its military modernization, particularly the development of new and disruptive capabilities such as the anti-satellite missile, could create misunderstandings and instability in the region," stated the paper, which was released in early July 2007, coincident with the visit to Sydney of the USS Kitty Hawk.[52] Australia's participation in a four-nation security dialogue, which also includes the United States, Japan, and India, is perceived by some analysts as "encirclement" of China.

South Pacific Islands

China's new diplomacy has extended to small South Pacific island nations. Australia's sphere of influence covers many of these small island nations, especially Melanesia (Papua New Guinea, Solomon Islands, Fiji, Vanuatu). China is moving into the region at a time when many Pacific Island countries, particularly Papua New Guinea and Fiji, have become critical of the Australian government's heavy-handed tactics in the region.

Australia is by far the biggest aid donor in the region with its annual Australian Overseas Development Assistance (ODA) budget to the Pacific standing at $720 million. However, a major part of it in recent years has been earmarked for "strengthening governance and to reduce corruption" in recipient countries. Under these aid schemes, Australia stations bureaucrats, police officers, and financial advisors in strategic departments and law enforcement agencies in the region. In Papua New Guinea and Fiji, this has been greatly resented and seen as an attempt to undermine their sovereignty. In May 2005, a Supreme Court decision in Papua New Guinea deported 800 Australian police officers deployed in the country under the aid program.[53]

China has expanded trade and other relations with Pacific nations lately. Much like China's diplomacy elsewhere, Chinese trade and investment come with no political conditions attached except that recipients must affirm the "one China" policy. This is in sharp contrast to Australia's emphasis on good governance, economic reform, and anti-corruption policies. However, the PRC and Taiwan have been accused of engaging in "checkbook diplomacy" to gain favor with Pacific leaders, which distorts the political process in those countries. China and Australia's different approaches to development and governance may create friction between the two countries in the future.

SIMILARITIES AND DIFFERENCES

Both South Korea and Australia are key allies of the United States, yet they have fostered a strong and close relationship with China. The two sets of bilateral relationships are developing in the broader context of a global and regional power shift. Against the background of the competition between the United States and China, the China-ROK and China-Australia relationships have their limitations. Neither Australia nor South Korea will abandon their crucial alliance with the United States, yet both desire a stable and productive relationship with China. As a result, both Australia and South Korea are adopting a strategy of hedging the power conflict between China and the United States. They are both attempting to maintain a delicate strategic and diplomatic balance in their respective relations with the two great powers. Fortunately, South Korea and Australia are not yet faced with a stark choice between the two powers, though they on occasion have to manage the difficult feat of riding two horses simultaneously.

The two cases also bear other similarities, especially in terms of China's strategies to promote its relations with both countries. These strategies include promoting cultural and educational exchanges (the "bottom up" approach), holding high-level meetings regularly (the "top down" approach), and emphasizing economic cooperation. China is playing its geo-economic cards and emphasizing the softer side of its growing influence in both countries. These efforts have helped China to become a vital partner for both South Korea and Australia. South Korea's expectation of China playing a positive role in resolving the North Korea nuclear crisis also contributes to China's soft power in South Korea. In Australia, the fact that China is not perceived as a direct and tangible threat has provided China with an opportunity to practice soft power. In both cases, the expectation and desire of economically benefiting from China's rapid growth played a very significant role in maintaining good relations with China.

There are differences too, especially in terms of potential obstacles that may hinder further relations. Despite its disclaimer, Australia has become increasingly concerned about China's rising military strength in recent years and has stepped up its security alliances with the United States, Japan, India, and Singapore. This perceived "containment" of China, led by the United States with the participation of Australia, has the potential to disrupt China-Australia relations.

However, China-Australia relations seem to have more potential to improve and expand. For example, current trade volume between the two countries is only about one-third of China-South Korea trade volume. In addition, South Korea and China have historical and other disputes, while Australia and China have neither historical grievances nor conflicts of fundamental interests. Australia is rich in natural resources, and its iron ore, aluminum, grain products, and wool have great market potential in China.

In a 2006 Chicago Council on Global Affairs and Lowy Institute poll, when asked whether they think China will act responsibly in the world, sixty percent of Australians polled reported that they trust China "somewhat" or "a great deal" to act responsibly. In the same poll, when asked about their feelings toward China on a scale from zero (very cold and unfavorable) to 100 (very warm and favorable), China received a mean of sixty-one from Australians and fifty-seven from South Koreans. When asked to rate Chinese and United States influences in Asia on a ten-point scale, with zero meaning not at all influential and ten meaning extremely influential, Australians gave China a 7.5, ahead of America's 6.6.[54] Clearly, most Australians hold a very positive view of China.

South Koreans' positive view of China has declined in recent years due to a combination of factors.[55] But their view of the United States has also declined. This has as much to do with South Korea's recent pursuit of a more independent foreign policy versus any unfavorable policies by China and the United States.

CONCLUSION

China, South Korea, and Australia are good examples of countries with different political systems living together in amity and embarking on mutually beneficial cooperation. China has distinct differences with South Korean and Australian political structures, principles of national governance, and foreign relations, including their alliances with foreign powers. But these discrepancies have not posed obstacles to developing close bilateral relations between China and the two democracies.

China's warming relations with South Korea and Australia are also an embodiment of China's largely successful new diplomacy of the past decade. China's efforts to consolidate relations with these two important nations are consistent with its major foreign policy objectives of building a secure international and regional environment, obtaining energy and other resources for continued domestic growth, and expanding its soft power globally.

Although there are still some "hard" security factors in China's relations with both South Korea and Australia—such as the North Korea issue, China's heavy handed approach toward history, and Australia's lingering mistrust of China—China's soft power diplomacy has been largely successful in strengthening China's relations with both countries. China's growing soft power has also caused South Korea and Australia to pursue a more balanced approach between China and the United States.

How will China's growing ties with South Korea and Australia affect the United States? Are South Korea and Australia true and committed allies of the United States? Maybe so now, but as two Australian commentators have suggested, these alliances will change because of 1) the changing nature of U.S. foreign policy since 9/11, and 2) the rise of China. [56] Generally speaking, South Korea and Australia perceive China's rise differently than the United States. For the United States, China's growth represents the emergence of a potent geopolitical rival. For South Korea and Australia, it is a great opportunity for rewarding relations—an opportunity that has eagerly been seized by both countries. South Korea and Australia have their own set of priorities. At times they may disagree with the United States and adopt policies that seemingly tilt toward China. But China's gain is not necessarily America's loss. China's soft power has its limitations: for one thing, China cannot provide the security guarantees that the United States has to most of the countries in the Asia Pacific. For both South Korea and Australia, the United States remains their most important ally, but China has become an increasingly critical partner in the regional political economy.

To protect their own national interests, South Korea and Australia will continue to attempt to maintain good relations with both the United States and China. However, due to discrepancies in their political systems, differences in their perceptions of history, or the demands of Asian security, neither South Korea nor Australia is likely to form a formal alliance with China. In the foreseeable future, South Korea and Australia will remain inside the U.S.-led security structure in the Asia-Pacific region and, at the same time, will further expand their burgeoning ties with China. Though both South Korea and Australia will refrain from any act that may possibly offend China, they will continue to adopt a strategy of hedging the China-U.S. competition. It is unlikely that China will replace the United States to become their closest ally any time soon. For this reason, there is still much room for China to improve its image and promote its soft power in the Asia-Pacific region.

NOTES

1. Joshua Kurlantzick, "China's Charm Offensive," *Los Angeles Times*, June 23, 2007.

2. Harry Harding et al., "The Gramercy Round: China Goes Global: Implications for the United States," *The National Interest* (September, 2006): 56.

3. Chen Bo, "China's Increasingly Active Diplomatic Stance," *Zhongguo Qingnian Bao*, February 18, 2004.

4. Shi Yinhon, "China's Peaceful Rise Is All About Soft Power," *China Daily*, June 16, 2007.

5. "China Outruns U.S. in S. Korea 15 Years after Normalization of Ties," *Yonhap News*, August 23, 2007.

6. Zhao Quansheng "China and the Korean Peace Process," *The Korean Peace Process and the Four Powers,* eds. Tae-Hwan Kwak and Seung-Ho Joo (Burlington, VT: Ashgate, 2003), 106.

7. Ruediger Frank, "A New Foreign Policy Paradigm: Perspectives on the Role of South Korea as a Balancer," *Policy Forum Online* April 25, 2005, www.nautilus.org/fora/security/0535AFrank.html

8. Shin Kak-Soo, "The Implications of the Rise of China for South Korean Foreign Policy," *Korea and World Affairs* 31, no. 1 (2007): 25.

9. Lie Wei and Zhang Ke, "South Korea Tops the List with Over 50,000 Students in China," *Xinhua,* November 20, 2006.

10. "61.7 percent of S. Korea's Foreign Students from Chinese Mainland," *Zhongguo Wang,* October 25, 2006.

11. "China Outruns U.S. in S. Korea 15 Years after Normalization of Ties," *Yonhap News*, August 23, 2007.

12. Qian Chunxuan, "South Korea Expected to Receive over 1.5 Million Chinese Tourists This Year," *Xinhua News Agency*, July 3, 2007.

13. Zhao Ming, "South Korea No Longer Mistreats Chinese Tourists," *Weekly Chosun*, November 28, 2005.

14. Zhang Youyin, "A Strategic Study on the Market Expansion for South Korean Tourists to China," *Jingji Zongheng*, May 20, 2007.

15. Liu Baosen and Dong Xueqing, "South Korea to Send 2 Million Tourists to Shandong in 2008," *Xinhua,* May 2, 2007.

16. Zhang, "*A Strategic Study.*"

17. Anna Fifield, "US Out of Favor in S. Korea," *Financial Times,* February 24, 2006, 9.

18. Mark E. Manyin, "South Korea-U.S. Economic Relations: Cooperation, Friction, and Future Prospects," *Congressional Research Service,* July 1, 2004, 8.

19. Xu Changwen, "A New Stage: This Year is Likely to See Even Tighter Trade and Economic Ties Between China and South Korea," *Beijing Review,* May 3, 2007.

20. "China Seeks Deeper Economic Ties with S. Korea," *Xinhua*, April 11, 2007.

21. In February 2002, the Center for China's Borderland History and Geography of the Chinese Academy of Social Sciences, together with research institutes from three northeastern provinces, launched the "Northeast Project" (*Dongbei gongcheng*) to study the northeastern borderland's history and current status, with the central government's endorsement. The project concluded that Koguryo was a local regime of China, and thus the history of Koguryo is a part of China's history.

22. Shin Sang-Jin, "China, a Stabilizer or Hegemonic Power?" *Next*, no. 12 (October 2004): 52.

23. It was reported that a female commentator on CCTV-5 shed sorrowful tears when the Korean soccer team beat the Italian team.

24. China designated Mt. Changbai as one of the "Top 10 Mountains of China" in 2004 and is now preparing to register it with UNESCO as a world natural heritage site.

25. "Wen: No Territorial Problems Between China, S Korea," *Xinhua*, April 6, 2007.

26. Kim Tae-Ho, "Impact of Ship Collision on Seoul-Beijing Relations," *Munhwa Ilbo*, May 18, 2007.

27. Ted Galen Carpenter, *America's Coming War with China* (New York: Palgrave Macmillan, 2005), 15.

28. Brue Klingner, Brue, "China Shock for South Korea," *Asia Times online,* September 11, 2004.

29. Ralph A. Cossa, "North-South Summit: Same Bed, Different Dreams," *CSIS*, PacNet 38, (September 29, 2007).

30. Choe Sang-Hun, "Newly Elected South Korean Forecasts Chill with North," *New York Times,* December 21, 2007.

31. Klinger, "*China Shock for South Korea.*"

32. Shin, "*The Implications of the Rise of China,*" 33.

33. Sarah Smiles, 2007. "Ewe Beaut Day for Hu As He Praises Labor PMs," *The Age,* September 6, 2007.

34. "China Will Be Our Top Trade Partner," *The Sydney Morning Herald,* June 14, 2007.

35. James Grubel, "Shear Delight? China's Hu Visits Aussie Sheep Farm," *Reuters India,* September 5, 2007.

36. "Aust, China Sign $36b Gas Deal," *ABC News*, September 6, 2007.

37. Lee Kuan Yew, "China's Soft Power Success," *Forbes,* June18, 2007.

38. Linda Sieg, "Australia Says Not Trying to 'Contain' China," *Reuters India,* June 5, 2007.

39. Peter Smith and Richard McGregor, "China Puts Bush in Summit Shade," *Financial Times,* September 7, 2007.

40. "Premier Wen Jiabao Holds Talks with His Australian Counterpart Howard," *Ministry of Foreign Affairs of the People's Republic of China*, April 4, 2006.

41. "The First Confucius Academy in Australia Established in Western Australian University," *The Office of Chinese Language Council International* (hanban), May 27, 2005.

42. *See Australian Department of Industry, Tourism and Resources website* 2008, www.industry.gov.au (accessed October 9, 2007). Approved Destination Status (ADS) is a bilateral tourism arrangement between the Chinese government and a foreign destination whereby Chinese tourists are permitted to undertake leisure travel in groups to that destination.

43. Zha Peixin, "China-Australia Ties Bring Tangible Benefits," *China Daily*, September 3, 2007.

44. "Premier Wen Jiabao Holds Talks with His Australian Counterpart Howard," *Ministry of Foreign Affairs of the People's Republic of China*, April 4, 2006.

45. "President Hu Visits Australia, Attends APEC Meeting," *Xinhua,* September 4, 2007.

46. Grubel, "Shear Delight?"

47. "Hu Invites Rudd Family to Beijing Olympics," *The Sydney Morning Herald*, September 7, 2007.

48. "Australia to be 'Climate Bridge'," *BBC News*, December 6, 2007.

49. "China Puts Bush in Summit Shade," *Financial Times,* September 7, 2007.

50. "A Gunboat Message to China," *Time,* September 5, 2007.

51. Simon Robinson, "A Gunboat Message to China," *Time,* September 5, 2007.

52. Meraiah Foley, "Australia, US Concerned Over China's Military Buildup, Back Greater Role for Japan," *International Herald Tribune,* July *5, 2007.*

53. Kalinga Seneviratne, "South Pacific: Chinese Relief From Domineering Australia," *Inter Press Service,* April 17, 2006.

54. "Global Views 2006: The United States and the Rise of China and India," *The Chicago Council on Global Affairs* in partnership with *Lowy Institute for International Policy,* 2006.

55. More details can be found in Zhu Zhiqun and Kim Jih-Un, "China's 'Charm Offensive'? Assessment of China's Soft Power in South Korea," (paper presented at the 2007 American Political Science Association Annual Conference: Chicago, Illinois, August 30–September 2, 2007).

56. Owen Harries and Tom Switzer, "US Alliance Will Change," *The Australian,* October 4, 2007.

Chapter Eleven

China's Soft Power and Neoliberal Agenda in Southeast Asia

Ignatius Wibowo

The neoliberal agenda has traditionally been limited to the United Kingdom and the United States. In the 1980s, under the leadership of Margaret Thatcher and Ronald Reagan, both countries implemented an economic policy that was radically different from their previous ones with the aim of invigorating their sluggish economies. Instead of following the prescription of John Maynard Keynes, they chose to adopt the Milton Friedman model, abandoning the state to embrace the market.[1]

Subsequently, more countries in the world followed suit, believing that the "free market" would be the remedy for all their economic problems. In the process, free markets and democracy became inseparable. Wealthy countries throughout the world implemented this model vigorously because it was assumed that a free market could not be compatible with any political system except democracy. Since then, free markets and democracy have been part of the standard discourse of every president and prime minister.[2] This connection has been further strengthened by international organizations such as the International Monetary Fund (IMF), World Bank, and World Trade Organization.[3]

But is the combination of capitalism and democracy the only model of development for all countries in the world? More specifically, is it a model that members of the Association of Southeast Asian Nations (ASEAN) ought to follow? These questions are inevitable since most ASEAN members are developing countries that are in the process of searching for the right development model—despite the imposition of a single model by developed countries and international organizations.

This chapter attempts to show that, despite its popularity, the combined free market and democracy model has been accepted by countries in Southeast Asia only with reluctance and hesitation due to, in part, the rise of China in the past ten years. China has been tremendously successful in its effort to develop its economy not by combining free market economics and democracy, but by separating the two. China has adopted a semi-market system and maintains an illiberal political system. This success story has inevitably attracted the developing countries of the world, especially the countries of Southeast Asia. The more these nations look to the rise of China, the more they become attracted to its model. The attractiveness of China, in turn, has helped it enhance its soft power. China's soft power in Southeast Asia comes from multiple sources, including its culture and its cooperation and participation in ASEAN-related multilateralism. The "Beijing consensus" is not the only decisive factor in influencing the politico-economic development of ASEAN countries, but it is certainly one important factor in shaping their future.

The first part of this chapter presents a historical overview of Southeast Asian countries' attitude toward China, which has evolved from suspicion to a more positive opinion. This is followed by a description of the spread of the Chinese model of development among Southeast Asian countries, which shows how the majority of these countries are converging in their desire to emulate China's success. The fourth section describes the conflict between the two models within international forums, including the ASEAN. The final section of the chapter will conclude with a discussion of the rise of China's "soft power" in Southeast Asia.

ASEAN COUNTRIES IN SEARCH OF A DEVELOPMENT MODEL

Most members of ASEAN, except Singapore, are still struggling to develop their economies. Independence from the colonial powers after World War II has not guaranteed an instant route to prosperity. Most of them have gone through various attempts by trial and error and are still searching for a development model that fits their needs.

From the beginning, the five original members (Indonesia, Thailand, Malaysia, Singapore, and the Philippines) opted for a Western capitalist development model based on private property. These countries pursued different strategies in achieving their development goals, but none of them deviated from the free market system. They also had different degrees of state intervention, but their economies were not centrally planned.[4] Indonesia, Malaysia, the Philippines, Singapore, and Thailand have been committed, since their independence, to develop their economies along free market principles.

Before 1975, Vietnam was divided into North Vietnam and South Vietnam. The former followed the socialist-communist model, whereas the latter followed the capitalist model. After the North Vietnam's victory in 1975, the whole country became communist. Like Vietnam, Laos experimented with both models, supported by two different regimes, but it was only in the early 1970s that the communist model was adopted for the entire country. After the collapse of the Soviet Union in 1991, both Vietnam and Laos decided to reform their economy and adjust their development model. Cambodia, under the rule of King Norodom Sihanouk, first followed the capitalist model. This was interrupted in mid-1970s and replaced by the communist model, but then went back to capitalist model again. Myanmar also walked the capitalist path in the beginning, but shifted, in the early 1960s, to the so-called "Burmese socialist model," a variant of the communist model. Finally, Brunei, a small country at the tip of Borneo Island, has not done any significant experimentation, and has consistently followed only the capitalist model of development.

The "Cold War" between the capitalist and communist powers influenced the adoption of the models by Southeast Asian countries. The region became a battleground between the United States and the Soviet Union over the politics of development. It is no surprise, then, that countries in Southeast Asia also split into two opposing camps: those that formed ASEAN, who adopted the capitalist model despite official pronouncements, and those remained outside ASEAN, who fell under the communist camp.

During much of the Cold War, Mao Zedong wished to be the leader of the socialist movement in the Third World. It was for this reason that China was active in sponsoring communist parties in various capitalistic Southeast Asian countries, including Indonesia, Malaysia, the Philippines, Singapore and Thailand. Under Mao Zedong, China promoted a distinct model of development, in which "people's communes" were meant to be an alternative to the Western model of development. However, to these countries, the "people's communes" were not attractive at all since they ran counter to the tenets of the free market. China itself was still struggling to bring about domestic economic development; indeed, it was still considered a poor country. Chinese sponsorship of revolutionary movements, combined with its status as a poor country, made Indonesia, Malaysia, the Philippines, Singapore, and Thailand look at China with contempt and disdain.

The period of the 1970s through the 1980s was quite confusing in terms of development models. On the one hand, there was a widespread attack on the strategy of import-substitution industrialization (ISI)[5] that to varying degrees was being practiced by developing countries, including those in Southeast Asia. In place of ISI, a strategy of export-oriented industrialization (EOI) was proposed, which gave prominence to free trade. The empirical evidence provided in favor of this model was the high growth of the economies of the "four little dragons": South Korea, Taiwan, Hong Kong and Singapore. On the other hand, there was another school of thought that argued that the success of these "new industrialized countries" (NICS) could not be attributed to free trade or the free market alone, but also to the role of the state. They showed the association between rapid economic growth and pervasive state intervention in Korea, Taiwan, and Singapore. This school was known as the "developmental state" model.[6]

Given these academic debates, Southeast Asian countries were increasingly convinced that the ISI strategy should be replaced by another strategy that combined both free trade and state intervention. It was apparent that they could not simply do away with the state and embrace free markets and free trade. The political reality was simply that the demise of the state would not be tolerated. By coincidence, from 1982 to1986, Southeast Asian countries experienced some external economic shocks: falling oil prices followed by sharp downturns in other commodity prices. Thus, Indonesia, Malaysia, and Thailand created incentives for export-oriented, foreign capital-dependent industrialization.[7]

However, the shift to economic liberalization was not accompanied by political liberalization or democratization. Suharto in Indonesia and Mahathir in Malaysia stopped at economic reform, eliminating the possibility of democratization. Indonesia and Malaysia both retained their authoritarian government that regularly intervened in the economy. Nevertheless democratization did take place in Thailand with the collapse of the military dictatorship in 1986. A year earlier, in 1985, the Philippines saw the dramatic downfall of President Marcos through "People Power," and also started to embark on democratization.

The World Bank as well as the IMF applauded the Southeast Asian countries' moves. In 1993, the World Bank optimistically stated that Thailand, Malaysia, and Indonesia were making rapid progress and that they represented, quite legitimately, the "East Asian Miracle." The World Bank published a special report with the provocative title of *East Asian Miracle: Economic Growth and Public Policy*. However, this report admitted that the "miracle" was the result of a not so absolute adherence to free market principles. In other words, it recognized the practice of an "East Asian developmental state" model.[8]

No ASEAN country at that time sought to emulate the Chinese model of development. For them, the communist model was out of question; hence the capitalist model was the best one available. The promise was clear: development will be accomplished through free markets and democracy. Although China was starting to make an impact on the world economy, Southeast

Asian countries considered it more an exception than the rule. Basically, they believed that China was still searching for the right model and that the path it was currently following was only temporary. In addition, ASEAN countries–in spite of the debate over development models – were committed to a free market-based development strategy.

The Asian financial crisis of 1997 taught all ASEAN members a hard lesson. The value of their currency dropped as a result of the turbulence of the exchange rate, starting in Thailand and then spreading to Malaysia and Indonesia. This situation had a severe impact on business, especially the banking sector, and led to waves of worker layoffs. Eventually, Thailand, Malaysia, and Indonesia were thrown into an even deeper economic crisis.[9] As a matter of fact, all the ASEAN members bore the brunt of the financial crisis; as a result, there was widespread frustration and anger, much of which had anti-Western overtones.[10] Indonesia in particular experienced both an economic and political collapse, which resulted in unprecedented chaos at every level in the country.[11]

In response to the crisis, most of the ASEAN members made various adjustments in their economic and political strategies. The standard prescription came from the IMF and the World Bank, who asked them to implement a "structural adjustment program" (SAP). The root of the financial crisis, they argued, was that the economies of the ASEAN were not liberalized enough and that there was still too much government intervention. Specifically, this meant that ASEAN members had to consistently implement three reforms: deregulation, privatization, and trade liberalization. At the political level, these countries also needed to democratize; although democratization was not part of the SAP package, the pressure to have a democratic system was strong.

Thailand and Indonesia immediately followed the IMF prescriptions and the latter, without hesitation, imposed the infamous "conditionalities" on both countries. Malaysia did not follow their lead but instead adopted the opposite policy of controlling the capital market. Among the ten ASEAN countries, only Indonesia implemented the IMF recipe consistently. After the signing of a "Letter of Intent" with the IMF in late 1997, Indonesia dutifully and faithfully implemented the conditionalities imposed by the IMF. Democratization also took place in 1998 with the fall of Suharto and the emergence of a multi-party system, followed by a general election.[12] Thailand also had to sign "Letters of Intent" with the IMF, which were less stringent than the one signed by Indonesia. The other eight Southeast Asian countries carefully watched these developments and tried to look for an alternative way to overcome the crisis.

It was at this juncture that the search for a new model became urgent. The liberalization of the financial market, they believed, was the main reason for the crisis and this was why they had become easy prey for speculators around the world.

ASEAN LOOKS TOWARD CHINA

China, meanwhile, emerged from the crisis relatively unscathed; indeed, it maintained its high level of economic growth. One of the accepted explanations for this was the fact that China did not carry out financial liberalization as prescribed by the IMF. China "adhered to some of the principles of the original and expanded Washington Consensus, rejected a few and modified others."[13] The absence of financial liberalization, evidently, saved China from the attacks of speculators. China's economy slowed down a little, but it escaped financial collapse like its unfortunate neighbors. China did not even devalue its currency, something that was envied by ASEAN members.

Due to this turn of events, ASEAN members slowly shifted their attention to China. ASEAN had actually been engaging China since the beginning of the 1990s. In 1991, for the first time, China was seated as an observer at the twenty-fortieth ASEAN Ministerial Meeting in Kuala Lumpur, Malaysia. Three years later, letters were exchanged between the Secretary General of ASEAN and Foreign Minister Qian Qichen; ASEAN-China relations were formalised in Bangkok on July 23, 1994. ASEAN accorded full dialogue status to China at the twenty-ninetieth Ministerial Meeting in Jakarta in 1996.

Since then, China-ASEAN relations have taken off. In December 1997, the first ASEAN-China Summit was held in Kuala Lumpur, which saw the signing of a document signaling increased cooperation between ASEAN and China to mark the beginning of the twenty-first century. This was translated into a series of cooperation measures in the economic, political, and cultural spheres. For instance, China agreed to the establishment of the ASEAN-China Cooperation Fund with the purpose of supporting agricultural, information technology, transportation, education, and human resources development. In October 2003, China was accepted as a friend of the ASEAN with the signing of the "Strategic Partnership for Peace and Prosperity" at the ASEAN-China Summit in Bali, which then led to China's signing of the "ASEAN Treaty of Amity and Cooperation." [14]

Among the various treaties China has signed with ASEAN, the two most important were signed in Phnom Penh in 2002: the "Declaration on the Conduct of Parties in South China Sea" and the "Framework Agreement on Comprehensive Economic Cooperation between ASEAN and the People's Republic of China." These two treaties can be viewed as the pillars of the new relationship between China and ASEAN because they cleared away many misunderstandings and prejudices. In the 1990s, China and ASEAN were locked in a dispute over the Spratly Islands, which may have led to a serious armed conflict.[15] China eventually signed an agreement with Malaysia, Vietnam, Philippines, and Brunei, which eased tensions over the territory.[16]

The strained relationship between ASEAN and China was further compounded by the flood of cheap Chinese products into Southeast Asian markets, especially after China joined the WTO in 2001. Numerous small and medium enterprises in the region were reportedly forced to close their doors as they were unable to compete with Chinese products. In response, China took swift action by offering ASEAN a free trade agreement. China also offered an "early harvest" program to be implemented between 2004 and 2006 for the original ASEAN members and until 2010 for new members. The Chinese government unilaterally made the decision in the hope that Southeast Asian countries would not see it as a threat. According to Lu Jianren, China's initiative can be understood as a bid to "quell fears of its rising."[17]

The close relationship between ASEAN and China has substantially increased China's soft power. In forums where ASEAN leaders meet with their counterpart from China, ASEAN leaders consistently speak positively about China and of China's success. Commenting on the meeting between Chinese and ASEAN leaders in October 2006, a journalist correctly noted that "Chinese and Southeast Asian leaders at the China-ASEAN Business and Investment Summit spoke effusively of a relationship based on mutual trust in politics and economic integration."[18] Indeed, ASEAN leaders "take pains to downplay the negative effects of trade with China."[19] This positive atmosphere was not noticeable ten years ago.

Myanmar, Laos, and Cambodia have particularly benefited from their relations with China. As relayed by an eyewitness in 2000, Chinese president Jiang Zemin received a very warm welcome in Laos, where "banners were hung across the capital lauding Jiang, and endless banquets were held in his honour." This scene was repeated in Cambodia where "over 200,000 cheering schoolchildren welcomed Jiang's motorcade." This was in stark contrast to the early 1990s when Cambodia was opposed to China due to its involvement with the Khmer Rouge. Suffering from an embargo by the West, Myanmar is very grateful to China's support, which has translated into multiple economic and political agreements.[20]

Thailand is no exception from this pattern. A long-time British and U.S. ally, Thailand now considers China—along with India—the most important countries for its diplomacy. Although Vietnam and China went to war in 1979, relations have improved remarkably since 1991, when diplomatic relations were restored. This was exemplified in February 2002 when the two countries proposed the "four good themes": good neighbours, good friends, good camaraderie, and good partners. All the countries in the Mekong River basin—Vietnam, Cambodia, Laos, Myanmar, and Thailand—have tremendously benefited from trade with China. Under the framework of the Greater Mekong Sub-Region (GMS) China has agreed to implement a Mekong Basin development program and projects.[21] It is clear that China pays great attention to this region, including providing economic aid, and it is within this area that the soft power of China is most widespread.[22]

Similar trends are evident in maritime Southeast Asia: Malaysia, Singapore, the Philippines, and Indonesia.[23] Malaysia, under Prime Minister Mahathir bin Mohamad, developed a close relationship with China. At both the economic and diplomatic levels, the two countries have consistently been on good terms. Singapore is a "natural" friend of China since the majority of the city-state is of Chinese origin. Although their relations were strained in the 1970s, Singapore–China relations have been reinvigorated since 1990 by an increase of trade and mutual visits of leaders. China and the Philippines, however, have been caught up in a dangerous dispute over Mischief Reef. Fortunately, in the past five years, this relationship has improved, as demonstrated by their many high-level exchanges. The Philippines have also received a grant from China to build a railway, which is vital for its economy.

Historically, the relationship between Indonesia and China has been very difficult, most notably during a thirty-two-year gap in diplomatic relations.[24] Yet in the past eight years, Indonesia and China have developed relations a positive relationship. Visits by leaders of the two countries have become more frequent and trade has increased rapidly. Chinese soft power in Indonesia is most apparent in the area of financial assistance. When the Asian financial crisis hit Indonesia, China took the initiative to extend its assistance. In addition to U.S. $400 million in standby loans as part of an IMF rescue package, China contributed U.S. $200 million in export credit facilities.[25] Chinese assistance kept coming in the following years. Between 1999 and 2003, China provided grants totaling RMB 180 million.[26] Following the tsunami disaster at the end of 2004, China was among the first countries to provide not only financial assistance, but also medical help.[27] (The value of the financial assistance package was not disclosed.) During the visit of President Yudhoyono to Beijing in late July 2005, Indonesia and China signed a series of agreements on grants and loans, and also agreed to work on "technical cooperation." In this agreement, the Chinese government offered RMB 30 million in the form of a grant[28] as well as a loan of U.S. $100 million to finance particular "commercial contracts."[29]

Domestically in Indonesia, the display of Chinese culture, which had been banned for over thirty years, has been revived since the fall of the "Orde Baru" (New Order) in 1998. Chinese characters can now be seen in public places, as well as Chinese dragon dances and other Chinese symbols. Since 2003, the Chinese community in Indonesia has been allowed to celebrate the Lunar New Year openly, without any restrictions, marking a complete reversal of the previous policy. Furthermore, Chinese-Indonesians are no longer afraid to go to temples to pray.

The Chinese-Indonesians, during the Orde Baru era, were not allowed to speak Chinese, or even to learn it. But, after 1998, Chinese language courses both at the university level and non-university level have spread rapidly in big cities. Along with language classes, there has been a proliferation of Chinese language mass media, such as TV news, newspapers, and bulletins. Chinese language courses have received support from the Chinese government. For instance, a group of twenty volunteer Chinese language teachers from Jinan University in Shandong arrived in Indonesia in 2004 to spend a year teaching Mandarin at fifty high schools in nine provinces. This was part of the Chinese Volunteer Program for International CAFL Teachers program, which is supported by the National Office for Teaching Chinese as a Foreign Language and the Chinese Ministry of Education.[30] To further the spread of Chinese language, China has agreed to set up four Confucius Institutes in four Indonesian cities.

There has been no other time in Indonesian history when China and Chinese culture has received such a welcome. There are still problems related to the government's discriminatory practice toward ethic Chinese, but the general mood is positive. The fall of Suharto and the rise of China have both contributed to the emergence of Chinese soft power in Indonesia.

China's soft power is indeed strong among the people of ASEAN. One observer asserts that "Chinese culture, cuisine, calligraphy, cinema, curios, art, acupuncture, herbal, medicine and fashion fads have penetrated into regional culture."[31] He also refers to Chinese films and film stars such as Gong Li and Zhang Ziyi, as well as pop music, which are all very popular amongst Southeast Asian youth. Mainland Chinese consumer brands – such as Hai'er, TCL, and Huawei—are also becoming increasingly popular in the ASEAN region.

ASEAN INTEREST IN THE "BEIJING CONSENSUS"

It was at this critical juncture that countries in Southeast Asia found that they could also learn about strategies for development from China. As presented above, many of them were first fascinated by models of development that came from Western Europe, then those from the Soviet Union, and later those from Japan. The bitter lesson from the Asian financial crisis and China's success story, however, convinced them to turn their eyes to China. The combination of a semi-market economy and illiberal polity that China practices is now considered by many ASEAN countries as the right model to adopt.

Data collected by the Fraser Institute indicate the ten ASEAN members have experienced a gradual change with regard to market freedom. There are five indicators to measure it, but government size is considered the most important one. Government size is calculated from revenues, institutions and staff, expenditures, investments, and subsidies. The report shows that market freedom in most ASEAN countries is decreasing whereas government size has continually increased since 1980.[32] The greater the size of the government, the lower the level of market-oriented economy. This may reflect their distrust of a completely free market – which perhaps can be traced to the 1997 financial crisis—although they do not abandon a market economy entirely.

This is to be compared with data collected by the "Freedom House" in 2000 on the political freedom. The index indicates that most ASEAN countries are "unfree": Myanmar, Vietnam, Laos, Brunei, and Cambodia. Singapore, Malaysia, and Indonesia fall under the category of "partly free." Only the Philippines and Thailand belong to "free country."

From these two sets of data, a pattern emerges: ASEAN members are pursuing a semi-market economy combined with an illiberal polity. At present, some countries of ASEAN are following, to varying degrees, the "Beijing Consensus" by which they practice a semi-market economy combined with an illiberal polity.[33] Table 11.2 shows countries that have adopted the Beijing Consensus. In 2006 Thailand, after having adopted democracy for about

Table 11. 1. ASEAN members and levels of freedom

Southeast Asian Country	*Freedom House Rating (2000)*	*Average Annual GDP Per Capita (1975–2000)*
Un-free countries	(Rating 5.5–7)	
Myanmar	7.7	1.3%
Vietnam	7.7	4.8%
Laos	7.6	3.2%
Brunei	7.5	Unavailable
Cambodia	6.6	1.9%
Partly free countries	(Rating 3–5.5)	
Malaysia	5.5	4.1%
Singapore	5.5	5.2%
Indonesia	4.4	4.4%
Free countries	(Rating 1–2.5)	
Philippines	2.3	0.1%
Thailand	2.3	5.5%

Source: freedomhouse.org, nationmaster.com

Table 11.2. ASEAN members and the "Beijing Consensus"

		Explanation	
Country	*Beijing Consensus?*	*Economy*	*Polity*
Brunei	Yes	Semi-Market	Illiberal
Cambodia	Yes	Semi-Market	Illiberal
Indonesia	No	Semi-Market	Liberal
Laos	Yes	Semi-Market	Illiberal
Malaysia	Yes	Semi-Market	Illiberal
Myanmar	No	Closed Market	Illiberal
Philippines	No	Semi-Market	Liberal
Singapore	Yes	Semi-Market	Illiberal
Thailand	Yes	Semi-Market	Illiberal
Vietnam	Yes	Semi-Market	Illiberal

Source: author constructed from data available at freedomehouse.org and nationmaster.com

eighteen years, slipped back to illiberal polity where the military junta ruled the country again.

Indonesia and the Philippines belong to the group of countries that follow the path of semi-market freedom and democracy. Both countries do not seem interested in the "Beijing Consensus" after having undergone the long experience of living under dictatorships (Suharto and Marcos). Myanmar is at the opposite end of the spectrum; it practices neither democracy nor the Beijing Consensus. It has a closed economy combined with a military regime.

There are, of course, no official statements from these countries about their decisions to follow the Beijing Consensus or not. The attraction to the Chinese model is unconscious – a silent admiration of the spectacular rise of China. Ramo recounts one senior ASEAN economist who asked him: "Why is our experience so different from China's? We are like them. We have low-cost labour. Our political system is strong. What are we doing wrong?" Ramo continued: "The question was a familiar one. All around Asia, and increasingly around the world, you stumble on anecdotes of nations examining China's rise and trying to see what pieces of this miracle they might make manifest in their own land."[34]

Clearly, countries in Southeast Asia and around the world are attracted to the Chinese model of development.[35] They are inspired by China's ability to maintain high economic growth with illiberal politics and, consequently, they try to emulate it. The rise of China has drawn their attention ever since China avoided the Asian financial crisis of 1997 and even more so afterward when it posted double-digit economic growth. In their eyes, China's success story is the result of a certain degree of free markets and a certain degree of free government.

THE CONTEST OF THE TWO MODELS

The United States is, of course, not happy with the situation in ASEAN because of its specific agenda around the world, including Southeast Asia. Since the end of the Cold War, the United States has been aggressively promoting a "free trade" model. According to Hutton, one of the principal aims of the Economic Security Council set up by President Clinton in 1993 was to open up ten countries to U.S. trade and finance. Most of these target countries were the Asian tigers.[36] During his 2000 presidential campaign, George W. Bush consistently promised to "work tirelessly to open up markets all over the world" and "end tariffs and break down barriers everywhere, entirely, so the whole world trades in freedom." Even after 9/11, Bush promised to "ignite a new era of global economic growth through free markets and free trade."[37] Bush argues that "policies that further strengthen market incentives and market institutions are relevant for economies – industrialized countries, emerging markets, and the developing world."[38]

This idea has been further popularized by *New York Times* journalist Thomas Friedman in his book *The Lexus and the Olive Tree*. At present, he states, there are millions of currency traders and CEOs of large multinational corporations that he calls the "Electronic Herd." Their main interest is to find production sites that are the most efficient in the world. In order to succeed in the era of globalization, countries around the world not only have to put on the "Golden Straitjacket" (the free market), but they also have to please the Electronic Herd.

> The Electronic Herd loves the Golden Straitjacket because it embodies all the liberal, free-market rules the herd wants to see in a country. . . . Those countries that put on the Golden Straitjacket are rewarded by the herd with investment capital. Those that don't want to put it on are disciplined by the herd—either by the herd avoiding or withdrawing its money from that country.[39]

The free-trade agenda was not connected to democratization by Clinton and Bush. It was Francis Fukuyama who argued that the "end of history" is marked by a "free market and liberal democracy."[40] Socialism and communism apparently no longer have a place in the future of the world. In his view, the triumph of capitalism cannot be separated from democracy. His book immediately became a best seller. Fukuyama and U.S. Senator Hillary Clinton are both of the opinion that globalization strengthens the existing affinity between democracy and the free market. During her visit to Poland, Clinton insisted that "choosing the path of democracy, free markets, and freedom required a great vision, courage and moral leadership. Ten years ago it was not the obvious choice, nor was it easy. But today in so many of your countries, there is no question that the path of free markets and democracy is the right choice."[41] This campaign of democracy is even more urgent in Third World countries where authoritarian regimes are prevalent. Thomas Friedman underlines this by saying that "the Electronic Herd will intensify pressures for democratization generally, for three very critical reasons – flexibility, legitimacy and sustainability."[42]

The financial crisis of 1997 was the turning point. First, the response of the United States and the IMF to the crisis generated unease, frustration, and anger across Asia. Americans had no interest in the crisis and, at the same time, the IMF's initial response attached stringent conditions. It was no surprise then that at the ASEAN Foreign Ministers' meeting in July 1997, Prime Minister Mahathir of Malaysia said that the West intended to weaken the ASEAN economies by undermining their currencies: "We are told that we must open up, that trade and commerce must be totally free. Free for whom? For rogue speculators? For anarchists wanting to destroy weak countries in their crusade for open societies, to force us to submit to the dictatorship of international manipulators?" For this reason, Malaysia decided on September 2, 1998, not to ask for assistance from the IMF.

Obviously Mahathir echoed the unspoken anger of many ASEAN people who were disappointed by the turn of events. Criticism of the World Bank and the IMF became louder and louder, especially in Thailand, Indonesia, and Malaysia. Indeed, there was a global critical reaction not only to the IMF, but also to the World Bank and the World Trade Organization—the "Seattle War" of 1999 being the most conspicuous example. The discourse against the "Washington Consensus" spread across the world as more and more people joined the World Social Forum that started in 2000 in Porto Allegre, Brazil.[43]

In the end, many people are questioning the validity of the link between free trade and democracy. China, for example, has shown that democracy is not an absolute condition to attain economic prosperity. The proponents of free markets and democracy consistently refer to the U.S. experience just as the opponents point to the Chinese experience. The United States and other developed countries are successful in combining both free markets and democracy, but China is also successful in blending a semi-free market with an illiberal political system. The debate, therefore, is not at a theoretical question, but rather is an empirical one. China has demontstrated that it is now possible to develop an alternative strategy of development using a combination of different concepts.

China has also tried to disseminate the "Chinese model." According to Peerenboom, in 2004 China and the World Bank jointly hosted the Shanghai Global Learning Process. There were at least 1,200 participants from 117 countries who attended the conference to discuss what other countries could learn from China. Slowly, China is developing its soft power through the spread of the "Beijing Consensus." There was no formal announcement when this strategy was adopted, although some Chinese scholars have discussed it.[44] For example, Zhang and Huang came to the conclusion that "it is very crucial for China to develop 'hard power' and 'soft power' at the same time, if China would like to upgrade its international status and developing peace."[45]

Although Peerenboom still puts a question mark on the "Chinese paradigm," he says that disenchanted countries are looking to China for a new model. "Given the many problems confronting developing countries, China may seem to offer a new model for development, albeit one that challenges aspects of the dominant legitimating narrative being exported by Western countries and the international financial institutions they control."[46]

CONCLUSION

In this chapter, I have tried to show how ASEAN members have shifted their development strategy from one based on free markets and democracy to one based on semi-free markets and an illiberal political system. Two factors were predominantly responsible for this shift: (1) the Asian financial crisis and (2) the rise of China. The latter in particular has inspired ASEAN members and has legitimized their economic and political systems. The "Beijing Consensus" has clearly gained ground in Southeast Asia.

Given these changes, it is understandable that China's soft power has spread in the region. It began with China's participation in various multilateral organizations, a move meant to prove that China was not an aggressive rising power. It was then followed by demonstrations of Chinese generosity in providing financial assistance to numerous developing countries.[47] Ramo, who coined the phrase "Beijing Consensus," stated: "many elements of the country's rise have engaged the developing world. Some of that engagement is rooted in China's growing commercial influence, but some of it reflects the appealing spirit of the new Chinese physics."[48]

The rise of China itself has provided a model, which in turn has become a source of its soft power. This has been a more formidable influence than China's participation in multilateral organizations or China's financial aid. Compare this to two similar processes in the past, namely the European ideal of democracy and the Japanese model of development. Both the Europeans and the Japanese have dominated the discussions of political theory and development theory, respectively. But now, the Beijing Consensus will be included in high-level debates, whether one agrees with it or not.

Chinese soft power is growing not only in Southeast Asia but also in Latin America and Africa. "The appealing spirit of the new Chinese physics," as Ramo put it, has traveled across the ocean. People will see that something good is emerging in China. The slogan "peaceful rise" promoted by President Hu Jintao four years ago but derided by many, is gaining credibility today as a result of the increase of China's soft power. This is not to say that problems with China are disappearing. It is in the best interest of China to minimize these potential problems to preserve its recent gains in soft power.

NOTES

1. Daniel Yergin and Joseph Stanislaw, *The Commanding Heights: The Battle for the World Economy* (New York: Touchstone Book, 1998); Will Hutton, "Anthony Giddens and Will Hutton in Conversation," in *Global Capitalism*, ed. Will Hutton and Anthony Giddens (New York: Free Press, 2000).
2. Manfred Steger, *Globalism: Market Ideology Meets Terrorism* (Lanham, Maryland: Roman & Littlefield, 2005).
3. Richard Peet, *Unholy Trinity: The IMF, World Bank and WTO* (London: Zed Books, 2003).
4. Islam and Chowdhury wrote, "In the 1950s and 1960s, many countries in the developing world embraced a development strategy whose key components formed the substance of the so-called dirigiste doctrine." State intervention was acceptable, the most conspicuous one being the strategy of import substitution industrialization. Iyanatul Islam and Anis Chodhury *The Political Economy of East Asia: Post-Crisis Debates* (Oxford: Oxford University Press, 2000), 3.
5. The attack on ISI was initially launched by Ian Little, Tibor Scitovsky and Maurice Scott, *Industry and Trade in Some Developing Countries* (Oxford: Oxford University Press, 1970).; and the Asian Development Bank.
6. Among the proponents of this model are Chalmers Johnson, *MITI and the Japanese Miracle* (Stanford: Stanford University Press, 1982).; Robert Wade, *Governing the Market: Economic Theory and the Role of Government in East Asian Industrialization* (Princeton, NJ: Princeton University Press, 1990).; Alice Amsden, *The Rise of 'The Rest': Challenges to the West from Late-Industrializing Economies* (Oxford: Oxford University Press, 2001).
7. Islam and Chodhury, *The Political Economy of East Asia,* 30.
8. Islam and Chodhury, *The Political Economy of East Asia,* 22–23.
9. Ross Garnaut,"The East Asian Crisis," in *East Asia Crisis: From Being a Miracle to Needing One,* ed. Ross H. McLeod and Ross Garnaut (London: Routledge, 1998), 3–27.
10. Edward J. Lincoln, *East Asian Economic Regionalism* (New York: Council on Foreign Relations, 2004), 148.

11. Ross H. McLeod and Ross Garnaut, eds., *East Asia in Crisis. From Being a Miracle to Needing One* (London: Routledge, 1998).

12. Zainuddin Djafar, *Rethinking the Indonesian Crisis* (Jakarta: Pustaka Jaya, 2006).

13. Randall Peerenboom, *China Modernizes: Threat to the West or Model for the Rest?* (Oxford: Oxford University Press, 2007), 73.

14. For a good review, *see* Ho Khai Leon and Samuel C.Y. Ku, eds., *China and Southeast Asia: Global Challenges and Regional Challenges* (Singapore: ISEAS, 2005).

15. Bob Catley and Makmur Keliat, *The Dispute in the South China Sea* (Aldershot: Ashagate, 1997).

16. Hasjim Djalal, *Preventive Diplomacy in Southeast Asia: Lessons Learned* (Jakarta: The Habibie Center, 2002).

17. Lu Jianren, "China's Economic Growth and Its Impact on the ASEAN Economics," in *Harmony and Development: ASEAN-China Relations*, ed. Lai Hongyi and Lim Tin Seng (Singapore: World Scientific, 2007), 112.

18. Donald Greenlees, "ASEAN Hails the Benefits of Friendship with China," *International Herald Tribune,* November 1, 2006.

19. Joshua Kurlantzick, *Charm Offensive How China's Soft Power Is Transforming the World* (New Haven: Yale University Press, 2007), 4.

20. Joshua Kurlantzick, "China's Chance," *Prospect Magazine* 108 (March 2005): 1.

21. Kao Kim Hourn and Sisowath Doung Chanto, "ASEAN-China Cooperation for Greater Mekong Sub-Region Development," in *ASEAN-China Relations, Realities and Prospects,* ed. Saw Swe-Hock et al. (Singapore: ISEAS, 2005), 316–328.

22. Zhang Haibing, "China's Aid to Southeast Asia," in *ASEAN-China Economic Relations,* ed. Saw Swee-Hock (Singapore: ISEAS, 2007), 261–262.

23. Jüngen Haacke, "The Significance of Beijing's Bilateral Relations," in *China and Southeast Asia,* ed. Ho Khai Leong and Samuel C.Y. Ku (Singapore: ISEAS, 2005), 111–145.

24. David Mozingo, *Chinese Policy Toward Indonesia, 1949–1967* (Ithaca: Cornell University Press, 1976).; Rizal Sukma, *Indonesia and China: The Politics of a Troubled Relationship* (London: Routledge, 1999).

25. Michael Leifer, "Indonesia's Encounter with China and the Dilemmas of Engagement," in *Engaging China: The Management of An Emerging Power*, ed. Alastair Iain Johnston and Robert S. Ross (London and New York: Routledge, 1999), 104.

26. Author's Interview with a staff member of the Chinese Embassy in Jakarta, January 2004.

27. "Indonesia Praises Chinese Aid, Commitment," *China Daily,* January 8, 2005. According to another source, China donated about U.S. $62 million for all countries affected by tsunami. Jim Yardley, "In Multilateral Role, China Tests Its Ability," *International Herald Tribune,* January 4, 2005.

28. *See* the Agreement on Economic and Technical Cooperation Between the Government of the Republic of Indonesia and the Government of the People's Republic of China, July 28, 2005.

29. *See* the General Loan Agreement of U.S. $100 million of Preferential Buyer's Credit from the Government of the People's Republic of China to the Government of the Republic of Indonesia, July 28, 2005.

30. "Ketika Guru Bahasa Mandarin Jadi Duta Bangsa" [When Chinese teacher becomes the ambassador for the nation], *Kompas,* June 23, 2005.

31. Cheow Eric Teo Chu "ASEAN + 3: The Roles of ASEAN and China," in *ASEAN-China Relations, Realities and Prospects, ed.* Saw Swe-Hock et al. (Singapore: ISEAS, 2005), 63.

32. *See* "Economic Freedom of the World Annual Report" *The Fraser Institute of Canada* 2007, www.freetheworld.com/2007/3EFW2007ch3.pdf (accessed January 10, 2009).

33. This concept was created by Joshua C. Ramo in 2004.

34. Joshua C. Ramo, "The Beijing Consensus," (London: Foreign Policy Centre, 2004), 26.

35. I. Wibowo, *Belajar dari Cina* [To learn from China], (Jakarta: Penerbit KOMPAS, 2004).

36. Hutton, "Anthony Giddens and Will Hutton," 41.

37. *Quoted in* Steger, *Globalism,* 57.

38. *Quoted in* Steger, *Globalism,* 58.

39. Thomas Friedman, *The Lexus and the Olive Tree* (London: HarperCollins, 2000), 109–110.

40. Francis Fukuyama, *The End of History and the Last Man* (London: Penguin, 1992).

41. *Quoted in* Steger, *Globalism,* 78.

42. Friedman, *The Lexus and the Olive Tree*, 187.

43. Marlis Glasiuss et al., *Global Civil Society* (Oxford: Oxford University Press, 2002).

44. Peerenboom, *China Modernizes*.

45. Zhang Youwen and Huang Renwei, "Zhong Guo Guoji Diwei Bao Gao" [Report on the international status of China], (Beijing: People Publishing House, 2006), 271.

46. Peerenboom, *China Modernizes*, 19.

47. I. Wibowo, "The Rise Of China's Power: How Hard And How Soft?" (paper presented at the International Conference on Rationalising China's Place in Asia, 1800 to 2005, the National University of Singapore, Singapore, August 3–4, 2006).

48. Ramo, "The Beijing Concensus," 5.

Chapter Twelve

China's Climate Diplomacy and Its Soft Power

Gang Chen

The growth of a state's soft power comes not only from its domestic policies and bilateral relations with foreign nations, but also from its participation in international treaties and agreements. This chapter addresses China's soft power within global institutions by examining the case of China's participation in international negotiations concerning climate change.

Climate change has been an important international issue since the 1980s, when calls for multilateral actions to control and reduce greenhouse gas (GHG) emissions first appeared. Due to its large population, rapid economic growth, and heavy reliance on coal, China has become one of the largest emitters of GHG. It is estimated that its emissions reached 6,100 million tons of CO_2 in 2004, accounting for 12.45 percent of the world's total of 49,000 million tons. China has also played an especially important role in international climate talks as well as the formation of climate institutions.

In this chapter, I first outline some observations regarding the relationship between international institutions and soft power. The next part traces China's participation in negotiations for the United Nations Framework Convention on Climate Change (UNFCCC). I then examine China's role in the talks on the Kyoto Protocol. These two cases clearly demonstrate how China attempted to exercise and cultivate its soft power through various means, such as setting the agenda, gaining diplomatic support from other like-minded states, making proposals to attract others to its side, and creating win-win situations that would benefit all. Meanwhile, its willingness to accept international environmental norms and to support international climate accords also enhanced its soft power and enabled it to gain respect from others. In the third part of the chapter, I analyze the challenges that China faces in post-Kyoto negotiations and some of the major actions that the Chinese government has taken to meet those challenges. I conclude that active participation in international climate negotiations and institutions has been an important part of China's diplomatic activities since the early 1990s and has effectively elevated China's international image and soft power.

INSTITUTIONAL PARTICIPATION ENHANCES SOFT POWER

International Institutions and Soft Power

Voluntary participation in major international institutions and compliance with established rules in the international community are essential for the maintenance of soft power. International institutions are "the rules that govern elements of world politics and the organizations that help implement those rules."[1] Although international society is still described as anarchical, with world politics driven by the traditional exercise of state power, international institutions are increasingly important and no longer marginal. In reality, even the most powerful states are relying increasingly on international institutions—not so much on institutions such as the UN but rather on other organizations and regimes that set rules and standards to govern specific sets of activities.[2] Institutions create the capability for states to cooperate in mutually beneficial ways by reducing the costs of making and enforcing agreements—what economists refer to as "transaction costs."[3] International institutions have become extremely important nowadays when sovereign states are facing more global problems that need joint effort and policy coordination. These urgent problems include terrorism, transnational crimes, global warming, trade protectionism, hot money flow, increasing epidemic diseases, and overuse of common-pool resources. Without the necessary institutions, self-interested sovereign states face the prisoners' dilemma and few states are willing to take voluntary actions for the collective benefit of international society. Certain institutions and rules have to be set up to provide incentives and disincentives for individual states in order to act collectively.

By reducing the uncertainty of enforcing agreements, international institutions help states achieve collective gains.[4] Meanwhile, participating in international institutions requires an acceptance of certain types of commonly recognized norms and rules. Joining the Non-Proliferation Treaty (NPT) or the Convention on Biological Diversity is an indication that a state recognizes and is willing to follow international norms limiting the spread of nuclear weapons or the conservation and sustainable use of biological diversity. Therefore, a state's stances on various kinds of international institutions are extremely important for its soft power expansion because they directly affect its moral attractiveness in the eyes of other states that value cooperation in the frameworks of these institutions.

Participation in international institutions is an important indicator of a state's soft power because it provides the arena for a state to use its power—and other states take notice of how this is done. If a state uses its power resources coercively in international institutions to get what it wants, it is clear display of hard power. Conversely, if a state uses attraction, persuasion, and appeal to achieve its goals, it is essentially using soft power.

Such soft power can be gained through various means. First, a state's participation in multilateral institutions often results in positive responses from the rest of the international community. Non-participation quickly raises concern and suspicion of that state's motives. Joining an international institution is not only a part of a country's foreign policy but it is also an indicator of its political values. Second, if a country's policies and practices abide by commonly recognized international norms that win the support and respect of others, its soft power will be fortified. Moreover, soft power is in play if a country can effectively exercise its influence through non-coercive means, set the agenda in international affairs, have its positions accepted by the majority of other countries, shape other states' preferences, have the ability to offer suggestions to solve problems, delegitimize other countries' positions, and build coalitions. The best scenario for a state's soft power would be a situation in which it can provide international public goods that other states can enjoy freely or at low cost. This is of course not always possible since all states have their own selfish interests. The second best thing a state could do is to create win-win situations.

China's Active Participation in International Institutions

As a permanent member of the UN Security Council, China is a signatory to a large number of international treaties and a member of many influential international organizations. In the field of disarmament and arms control, China has signed almost all the major international accords including the NPT, the Comprehensive Nuclear-Test-Ban Treaty (CTBT), the Convention on the Banning of Chemical Weapons, the Convention on the Banning of Biological Weapons, and the Convention on Certain Conventional Weapons. In the field of environmental protection, China has ratified more than fifty international environmental treaties including the well-known UNFCCC, the Montreal Protocol, the Kyoto Protocol, the Convention on Biological Diversity, the UN Convention to Combat Desertification, the Rotterdam Convention on the Prior Informed Consent Procedure for Certain Hazardous Chemicals and Pesticides in International Trade, and the Stockholm Convention on Persistent Organic Pollutants. Despite its deficient protection of intellectual property rights domestically, China is a member of the World Intellectual

Property Organization, the Berne Convention for the Protection of Literary and Artistic Works, the Madrid Agreement Concerning the International Registration of Marks, the Universal Copyright Convention, and the Agreement on Trade Related Aspects of Intellectual Property Rights administered by the World Trade Organization. Although the United States often attacks China's human rights record, China has ratified more international treaties on human rights protection than the United States. As the world's second largest greenhouse gas emitter, China's participation in the international climate regime and the Kyoto Protocol shows how the country gained its soft power through joining an international institution that seeks a common global goal. It also means that if China fails to make further commitment as expected by the international community in the next round of climate talks, its soft power will probably be weakened.

CHINA'S PERFORMANCE IN UNFCCC NEGOTIATIONS

Global warming, mostly caused by an increase in human activities that generate GHG emissions, is one of the most serious environmental problems confronted by the international community today. Scientists believe that a continual rise in temperature will lead to frequent meteorological disasters, including drought, floods, and tropical storms, as well as rising sea levels that may submerge coastal cities and island states, alter entire ecosystems, nurture the insect pest population, and cause epidemic outbreaks.

An effective negotiation strategy has become extremely important for a sovereign state to protect or promote its national interest in climate negotiations. On the one hand, whether or not a country can successfully utilize its soft power to attract others to its side and maximize diplomatic support is essential for its final gains from long-lasting multilateral negotiations. On the other hand, to what extent the final outcome reflects the basic proposition of a state will enhance its soft power in the eyes of other states.

China's Unity with Developing Countries Enhances Soft Power in Climate Talks

To prevent an ecological catastrophe, the international community started negotiations under the framework of United Nations to draft international treaties restraining GHG emissions in the early 1990s. A milestone in this process was the signing of the UNFCCC at the 1992 Earth Summit in Rio de Janeiro. The UNFCCC, with the anticipation of subsequent agreements establishing more concrete obligations, aimed to protect the world's climate against the effects of anthropogenic GHGs, most notably CO_2, and their adverse climatic warming effects.[5] The parties to the UNFCCC can be roughly categorized into two groups: Annex I lists members of industrialized countries and non-Annex I lists the developing countries. The UNFCCC set basic guidelines for future international climate negotiations, but heated quarrels and sharp divergences still remain among the different parties due to the fear that emission controls will hamper national economic growth and be very costly.

China has taken part in the negotiations for the UNFCCC since its preliminary stages, viewing climate change as a controversial issue that involves North-South equity problems. China believed that developed countries should take responsibility for environmental protection and give developing countries the opportunity to develop as much as the developed countries were able to.[6] As the world's largest developing country and a permanent member of the UN Security Council, China has been playing a leading role among developing countries in steering international climate change negotiations, uniting with other developing countries to form the "bloc of G-77" (the group of seventy-seven developing countries), which comprises about ninety percent of the developing countries that signed the UNFCCC.

China Exercises Soft Power to Set the Agenda in Climate Talks

When the Intergovernmental Negotiating Committee (INC) meetings in preparation for the UNFCCC began, China argued for equity on historical grounds, placing the blame primarily on the North.[7] From June 1991, China aligned itself closely with India and pushed for a fair convention, arguing that the South had a much smaller responsibility than the North, whose high per capita emissions and opulent lifestyle were the primary causes for climate change. As China was the largest greenhouse gas emitter among all developing countries, its officials feared that they might come under undue pressure to reduce emissions immediately.

In February 1991, when formal negotiations on a climate change convention began with the first meeting of the INC in Chantilly, Virginia, a core element of China's negotiating position included an emphasis on the major scientific uncertainties that surrounded the causes of climate change.[8] In February 1995, during the final negotiating session leading up to the Conference of Parties (COP) 1, China again explicitly questioned the scientific conclusions of the Intergovernmental Panel on Climate Change (IPCC) that served as the basis for those arguing for the inadequacy of existing commitments.[9] China's stance echoed that of the United States and was also supported by large developing countries such as India and Brazil. The European Union and some small island countries, however, argued that despite all the scientific uncertainties, the consequences of climate change may be so serious and irreversible that humanity cannot afford to risk inaction. In June 1991, China convened the Ministerial Conference on Environment and Development in Beijing, attended by delegates from over forty developing countries.[10] At its conclusion, a ministerial declaration was unanimously approved that largely reflecting the principles enunciated earlier by China: differentiated responsibilities, obligations and capabilities, state sovereignty and equality, untied aid, and preferential treatment.[11]

In 1992, Chinese Premier Li Peng explained China's views on green issues at the UN Conference on Environment and Development (Earth Summit) in Rio de Janeiro, Brazil. He said "protecting the environment is a common task of humanity, but economically developed nations should take greater responsibilities." He also mentioned safeguarding national sovereignty as a basic principle for international environmental cooperation. China strongly opposed legally binding emission reduction targets for developing countries. It insisted that industrialized countries should transfer advanced, environmentally friendly technologies and offer financial aid to developing countries in fighting against climate change. It advocated the preservation of national sovereignty, claiming that developing countries have the right to develop and should neither be obliged to undertake measures that might impede development nor be subject to conditions being placed on aid or development financing. As early as the 1992 Rio Earth Summit, China and India, speaking on behalf of other developing countries, insisted that developed countries should commit themselves to technology transfer as a requirement for gaining developing countries' support for the proposed agreements on global warming. These stances are consistent with those of other developing countries and are embodied in the UNFCCC. China's adherence to the principle of "common but differentiated responsibilities" won support and praise from developing countries, asserted its legitimacy, and increased its soft power. By consolidating a coalition around itself, China sought to ensure that its interests would be better supported, and that it would gain international prestige by being proactive in environmental protection.[12]

From this stage, we can see that China showed a very effective ability to influence other developing countries and help set the agendas of the climate negotiations. China used its soft power already established among developing countries to form the "bloc of G-77 plus China" in order to magnify their say in the talks. China's success partially comes from soft power that already existed before the start of climate talks: the image of China being a major power, its UN Security Council membership, and the perceived leadership role in championing the interests of the developing world ever since the Mao era. Through giving unselfish material aid to developing countries and political support for independence movements, China succeeded in accumulating huge soft power in the 1970s. China's early reforms and "opening-up" in the 1980s further elevated its appeal among developing countries.

Due to the enormous scientific uncertainties over the climate change issue in the early 1990s, most poverty-stricken developing countries paid more attention to development than environmental issues, and so the principle of fairness raised by China was very attractive in their eyes. Beijing's success in hosting the Ministerial Conference of Developing Countries on Environment and Development in 1991 and the unanimous approval of the Beijing Declaration were apparent evidence of China's ability to unify the stances of developing countries and gain support from them. Hence, it was quite clear that emphasizing the principle of "common but differentiated responsibilities," the Third World's right to develop, and the need for monetary and technological aid from developed countries, China enhanced its soft power among developing countries in the early stages of international climate negotiations.

China Uses the Climate Issue to Regain Soft Power Among Developed Countries

Meanwhile, China adjusted its stance when negotiating with developed countries by showing its respect for international norms of environmental protection and trying to reduce Western countries' hostility toward it after the Tiananmen incident in 1989. China felt diplomatically isolated in the early 1990s, and relations with the United States and European countries deteriorated sharply. Some international aid was suspended or cut off. The climate change issue came into focus at the same time, thereby serving as an ideal tool for China to regain its international position.[13] The UNFCCC negotiations were high profile negotiations, putting China in the spotlight whenever it took the initiative.[14] China was not only one of the first countries to formulate a domestic "Agenda 21" in 1994, mirroring the UN Conference on Environment and Development (UNCED) program on sustainable development, it also passed the Air Pollution Law in 1996, accounting for provisions in the UNFCCC.[15] China thought it would gain international prestige in being proactive in environmental protection cooperation. Though refusing to accept any commitment at first, China and other developing countries agreed finally in the UNFCCC to establish national emissions inventories, report on national programs, and promote cooperation, sustainable development and information exchange.[16] Due to a long-time suspicion that Western countries may shift their own responsibilities and use environmental issues to hamper China's economic rise, China initially opposed a new protocol on the grounds of scientific uncertainty, fearing that giving credit for reduced emissions may lessen developed countries' commitment to emissions abatement. China also opposed "joint implementation" programs, which allow industrialized countries to meet part of their required cuts in GHG emissions by paying for projects that reduce emissions in other industrialized countries. As the international talks proceeded, however, China gradually changed its tough stance on these issues in the following COPs to the UNFCCC, paving the way for the 1997 Kyoto Protocol.

KYOTO PROTOCOL AND CHINA

China's Participation in the Kyoto Protocol: A Diplomatic Success

After years of heated debates, delegates from 149 countries and regions passed the Kyoto Protocol (KP) in Japan in December 1997. The KP is the first international treaty to set detailed, legally binding obligations for industrialized nations to reduce their greenhouse gases. The principle of "common but differentiated responsibilities" advocated by China, India and other developing countries was included in the KP, which stipulated the Clean Development Mechanism (CDM) to encourage developed countries to provide financial and technical assistance to developing countries. Conversely, developing countries have no concrete abatement commitments.

The KP represents a success for China's diplomacy, showing the country's ability to use soft power to formulate international rules serving its own interests. The outcomes of the Kyoto negotiations were conducive to China: no compulsory emission cutting obligations for developing nations and potential economic benefits from the flexible mechanism of the Kyoto Protocol. China certainly does not have enough hard power to coerce other developing countries to support its stance or force developed countries to compromise on the climate issue. Only soft power is effective.

China completed its domestic ratification process in 2002, and appealed to other hesitant parties to ratify the protocol as soon as possible. The KP came into effect in 2005, requiring thirty-eight industrialized countries to reduce their greenhouse gas emissions between 2008 and 2012 by an average of 5.2 percent below 1990 levels. China is not one of the thirty-eight countries named, and it is not required to reduce greenhouse gas emissions. But it is the world's second largest greenhouse gas emitter after the United States, and has announced its willingness to reduce its emissions on account of the rapid deterioration of its own environment.

China Preserves its Favorable International Image as a "Responsible Power"

In contrast to the United States' withdrawal from the Kyoto Protocol, China's active participation in international treaties on global warming has proven to be a diplomatic success, winning applause from both developing and developed countries. China's cooperation has special importance to the international community because of its large GHG emissions and quickly growing energy consumption. China's active participation in climate change negotiations is closely related to its concern to preserve a favorable international image as a responsible major power. Enhancing China's international image and elevating its international stature are important goals of Chinese foreign policy. China traditionally considers solidarity with developing countries as fundamentally important, and the climate change issue has provided an unprecedented opportunity for China to boost its prestige and shore up support from developing countries as well as enhance its relationship with developed countries.[17]

China's ratification of the Kyoto Protocol shows that it is willing to accept international norms of environmental protection, which have been gradually developed since the 1950s. The logic of collective action prevents sovereign states from making joint efforts to cope with the global warming problem without any new institutions established to provide incentives and disincentives for individual states. As every country will benefit from the public goods of climate change mitigation—no matter if the country controls its own emissions or not—the best way for it to maximize its national interest is to take a "free ride" strategy with no substantive domestic emission cutting that may lead to huge economic costs. Refusing to join international institutions that seek to regulate such negative externalities, therefore, would be regarded by other states as selfish and irresponsible. Its charm and attraction in the international community would definitely be weakened if it refused to shoulder its responsibility for global issues.

The U.S. case was a good example that showed how soft power could be badly impaired by not participating in international climate institutions. In 2001, U.S. President George W. Bush announced that his country would withdraw from the Kyoto Protocol because the deal did not include meaningful participation by key developing countries. The unilateral U.S. action immediately aroused long-lasting global anger and criticism. The IPCC, the United Nations' leading body on global warming, then published its Fourth Assessment Report in 2007, which described the connection between climate change and human activity with a higher degree of certainty. As a result, the

Bush Administration and Australia's Howard faced even greater international pressure for not joining the Kyoto Protocol. Former U.S. Vice President Al Gore, George Bush's rival in the 2000 presidential election, together with the IPCC, won the 2007 Nobel Peace Prize for spreading awareness of man-made climate change and laying the foundations for counteracting it. This was seen as increasing pressure on the Bush Administration and showed that President Bush's approach missed the mark. Australian Prime Minister Kevin Rudd also declared Australia's returning to the Kyoto Protocol immediately after he beat John Howard in the 2007 election. Voluntarily cutting GHG emissions and joining global efforts to mitigate climate change, therefore, have become the mainstream consensus in the international community, even if some suspicions and reluctance lingers. If a sovereign state now evades its responsibility in this area, its soft power would be greatly reduced.

POST-KYOTO NEGOTIATIONS THREATEN CHINA'S SOFT POWER

China's Growing Emissions Come Under International Scrutiny

In 2007, the tenth anniversary of the Kyoto Protocol, the global warming debate became more heated. New reports released by a UN panel described the connection between climate change and human activity with an even high degree of certainty. The Kyoto Protocol, which is scheduled to expire by 2012, cannot meet the demand from the international community for further emission reductions. At the UN climate change summit in Bali, Indonesia in December 2007, a new round of international negotiations formally started over a new accord to replace the Kyoto Protocol. China, whose greenhouse gas emissions have been rising as rapidly as its double-digit economic growth, is now facing more international pressure for stringent emission reduction targets. If China cannot handle this problem effectively in the future talks, its soft power may be weakened and its international image damaged.

In May 2007, more than 400 scientists and experts from about 120 countries attended a major conference held in Bangkok by the IPCC, the United Nations' leading body on global warming. Delegates finalized the third IPCC Working Group report of 2007, laying out an arsenal of anti-warming measures that must be rushed into place to avert a disastrous spike in global temperatures. According to the IPCC report, global GHG emissions increased seventy percent between 1970 and 2004, while global mean surface temperatures have risen by 0.74 °C ± 0.18 °C over the last 100 years (1906–2005). The rate of warming over the last fifty years is increasing, and the IPCC predicted global temperature to rise 1.8 to 4 °C by 2100 even with various kinds of mitigation actions.

China was one of the nations under the most scrutiny at the Bangkok meeting. With carbon dioxide-spewing, coal-fired power plants generating around 70 percent of China's exponentially growing energy needs, the world's most populous nation is now firmly entrenched as one of Earth's most significant climate changers.[18] Without any detailed emission cutting obligations in the Kyoto Protocol, China's GHG emissions have been growing very rapidly due to its heavy reliance on coal and the booming of its nascent auto industry. As a carbon-intensive fuel, coal contains almost twice the amount of carbon per unit of energy compared to natural gas, and about twenty percent more than petroleum. In fact, there are more coal power plants installed in China than in the United States, the UK, and India combined. In Beijing, the number of automobiles doubled in just five years to reach 3 million, with more than 1,000 new private cars hitting the roads every day. In the capital city, transportation already accounts for twenty percent of the total energy consumption, and frequent traffic congestion exacerbates the problem. China's emissions of carbon dioxide climbed approximately nine percent in 2007 to more than 6.2 billion metric tons based on projected fuel consumption figures, after jumping roughly the same amount in 2006 and ten percent in 2005.[19]

At the Bangkok meeting, China was seen by some participants as the "biggest obstacle" in approving the new IPCC report that outlined a specific strategy to charge polluters for their emissions.[20] The report suggested that stabilizing greenhouse gas levels in the atmosphere would require charging polluters up to U.S. $100 per ton of carbon dioxide equivalent by 2030. Although the IPCC reports are not binding agreements, they have become quite powerful in forging international consensus on climate change. During the Bangkok talks, China called for removing a statement that developing countries were responsible for half of the current emissions. The statement was ultimately deleted. China sought more than ten amendments to the draft summary of the IPCC report, saying it would cost more and be much harder to reduce GHG emissions than the report indicated. But the voices of dismay over China's tactics were largely silenced after it agreed to the final report, which emphasized that the world already had the money and technology to fend off the worst impacts of climate change.[21] Beijing-based Greenpeace climate and energy campaigner Li Yan, who attended the Bangkok conference as an observer, said China had appeared to be interested in political issues at the start of the week rather than dealing with the problem, but later became more open, more constructive, and more helpful.[22]

Besides growing GHG emissions, many other worsening environmental problems in China have drawn international attention and threatened the country's image and soft power. Environmental degradation is now so severe in China, with such stark domestic and international repercussions, that it poses not only a major burden on the Chinese people but also an acute challenge to the country's soft power in the long run.

China's Actions to Salvage its Reputation

China has long been fending off an international accord that could force it to cut emissions and scale back its economy. Beijing's fears of being targeted on climate change were heightened by the statement in April 2007 by an official of the International Energy Agency (IEA) that China could soon become the world's largest emitter of greenhouse gases.[23] The Netherlands Environmental Assessment Agency (MNP) even announced that China's 2006 CO_2 emissions have already surpassed those of the United States by eight percent. In 2006, global CO_2 emissions from fossil fuel use increased by about 2.6 percent, which is less than the 3.3 percent increase in 2005. The 2.6 percent increase was mainly due to a 4.5 percent increase in global coal consumption, of which China contributed more than two-thirds. With this, China topped the list of CO_2 emitting countries for the first time. In 2005, CO_2 emissions from China were still two percent below those of the United States.[24]

The growing international pressure on China to protect its environment has made it pay more attention to bilateral and multilateral cooperation on green issues. China plans to join more international environmental agreements to improve its image on ecological protection and enhance its soft power, which may help it better position itself in the forthcoming global climate negotiations.

Multilaterally, China is more willing to accept international agreements that call for voluntary actions rather than those with mandatory emission targets. The former will help China to enhance soft power while not harming its hard power (economic growth). In the recent Asia-Pacific Economic Cooperation (APEC) summit in Sydney in September 2007, both China and the United States accepted a program with non-binding goals on energy efficiency and reforestation. According to the program, APEC members will reduce "energy intensity"—the amount of energy needed to produce a dollar of gross domestic product—by twenty-five percent by 2030. They also pledged to increase forest cover in the region by at least 20 million hectares (50 million acres) by 2020 (APEC, 2007), and establish an Asia-Pacific Network for Energy Technology and Forest Management. This declaration, which does not have any compulsory targets, was criticized by some environmental activists and green NGOs for having no real restrictive effect upon sovereign states' GHG emissions.

In 2005, China joined a collective action with Australia, India, Japan, South Korea, and the United States to establish the Asia-Pacific Partnership on Clean Development and Climate (AP6), which also emphasized energy conservation and technology cooperation instead of setting mandatory emission cuts. The six founding partners have agreed to work together and with private sector partners to meet goals for energy security, national air pollution reduction, and climate change in ways that promote sustainable economic growth and poverty reduction. The AP6 will focus on expanding investment and trade in cleaner energy technologies, goods, and services in key market sectors. It has approved eight public-private sector task forces covering aluminum, buildings and appliances, cement, cleaner use of fossil energy, coal mining, power generation and transmission, renewable energy, distributed generation, and steel.

Once again, China's ability to use its soft power in setting the agenda in international negotiations was manifested. China's long-time attention to technology transfer and sustainable economic growth was reinforced in the AP6 framework. In addition, many of the eight task forces chosen—aluminum, cement, coal mining, power generation, renewable energy and steel—are also major Chinese industries.

The six partner countries of the AP6 represent about half of the world's economy, population and energy use, and produce about sixty-five percent of the world's coal, forty-eight percent of the world's steel, thirty-seven percent of world's aluminum, and sixty-one percent of the world's cement.[25] The United States and Australia, two of its members, have not ratified the Kyoto Protocol. The Asia-Pacific Partnership on Clean Development and Climate is therefore a mechanism for cooperation outside the UNFCCC and Kyoto Protocol. The AP6 is regarded by some observers as a ploy used by these large emitters to fend off international pressure and avoid mandatory emission cutting obligations. The establishment of the AP6 showed that these big powers, including the United States and China, have realized that their international image and soft power might be greatly damaged if they are inactive in the international actions against climate change. The six founding countries warmly welcomed Canada as an official partner in October 2007, during the second AP6 ministerial meeting in New Delhi, India.

In the bilateral context, China pays more attention to its own interests, namely by seeking aid and technological transfer.[26] In the 1990s, Japan's generous environmental assistance to China, including low interest loans for environmental projects and aid to the establishment of the China-Japan Friendship Environmental Protection Center, increased the level of trust between China and Japan.[27]

During Singaporean Senior Minister Goh Chok Tong's meeting with Chinese Premier Wen Jiabao in Beijing in April 2007, Goh proposed jointly developing an "Eco-City" in China. This coincided with Wen's demand for much tougher action domestically to deal with the country's grave environmental problems, and so won Beijing's interest and endorsement in principle. During Chinese Vice Premier Wu Yi's visit to Singapore in July 2007, the Eco-City plan was again emphasized during the bilateral talks and it will hopefully serve as an iconic project for sustainable development that the Chinese leadership is very eager to develop. During Wen's visit to Singapore in November 2007, the two countries signed an agreement to locate the Eco-City Project in Tianjin's Binhai New Area. This scheme will surely promote China's international environmental image, a long-term goal of its diplomacy.

By joining all these multilateral and bilateral green programs, China wishes to lessen international pressure for further emission cut and to improve its image. For this reason, China, for the first time, publicized a lengthy national program in response to global warming on June 4, 2007. The "National Climate Change Program," which took the Chinese government two years to formulate, documents the efforts China has made in tackling climate change, analyzes its future challenges, and describes China's policies and positions on international cooperation. Climate change "is an issue involving both environment and development, but it is ultimately an issue of development," the national program said in its first paragraph. This indicates that China will continue to put economic growth ahead of climate change without committing itself to quantified emission cuts.

However, this does not mean that China's original stance on climate change remains unchanged. Compared with its previous suspicion about the certainty of the global warming trend, the national program uses much stronger language to confirm the trend and describes serious consequences of climate change. In the document, China admits that "annual average air temperature has increased by 0.5 to 0.8 °C during the past 100 years, which was slightly larger than the average global temperature rise." China also now admits that it is facing a potentially devastating impact from climate change, which has become a social and economic problem in the country. The predicted increase in droughts will lead to reductions in agricultural output, while the acceleration of glacial melting on the northwestern Qinghai-Tibet plateau will reduce the water supply to the Yangtze and Yellow Rivers, the two largest in China. China's rising sea level, triggered by global warming, is faster than the global average, and this will threaten China's coastal cities, the nation's economic powerhouses.

The Chinese government has now come to realize that if the worsening environmental problems are not properly addressed, the consequences may be so disastrous as to cancel all benefits from economic development. The government has been especially sensitive to heightened public complaints about the pollution. The number of protests caused by environmental pollution in China has been growing at an annual rate of thirty percent, according to Chinese Vice Premier Zeng Peiyan.[28]

Through publicizing the national program, China wants the international community to know that the Chinese government pays intensive attention to environmental issues. China established the National Leading Group to Address Climate Change in 2007, with Premier Wen Jiabao as the director. China's Foreign Ministry in 2007 also set up a special office to address the climate change issue, with Foreign Minister Yang Jiechi as the head. However, unique national conditions, such its coal-dominated energy infrastructure, still prevent the country from accepting mandatory emission cuts.

Despite its refusal to shoulder its share of emission reductions, China's national program is putting forward some voluntary targets in energy conservation and fuel use that can be converted to a certain amount of emission cutting (see table 12.1). The plan reiterates the goal in China's eleventh Five-Year Program that the country will achieve the target of about twenty percent reduction of energy consumption per unit GDP by 2010. China also said it wants sixteen percent of its energy mix to come from renewable energy by 2020. However, in 2006, China cut energy use per unit of GDP by only 1.23 percent, well below the target for that year of four percent.

Table 12.1. Estimated Emission Reductions From Energy Saving Measures by 2010

Emission Reduction Means	*Estimated Emission Cutting (in millions of tons of CO2 equivalent)*
Developing hydropower stations, especially in western areas	500
Developing nuclear power stations	50
Upgrading technology in thermal power generation	110
Developing coal-bed methane, coal-mine methane industry	200
Developing bio-energy	30
Developing wind, solar, geothermal and tidal energy	60

Source: China's National Climate Change Programme (2007)

The release of the national program came at a calculated time so as to fend off international pressure. On the same day the program was made public, the Ministry of Foreign Affairs announced that President Hu Jintao was expected to discuss China's views and policies on global climate change during his meeting with the G-8 leaders in Germany.

Imbalanced Carbon Trade Income Distribution Poses Threat to China's Soft Power

Another source of international pressure and discontent comes from the imbalanced regional distribution in global carbon trade income. China, India, and other developing countries' persistent diplomatic efforts have helped to shape the current climate regime under the Kyoto Protocol framework into a kind of "Robin Hood" scenario, in which billions of dollars from rich countries are transferring to poor countries to curb the emission of global warming gases.

According to the Clean Development Mechanism, a market-based flexible mechanism introduced by the Kyoto Protocol, affluent regions like Europe, Japan, and Canada that have difficulties meeting even the minimum requirement set by the protocol, can invest in overseas environmental projects in developing countries and then buy the certified emission reductions (CERs) to offset their obligations. China is the biggest beneficiary, receiving three-fifths of the money from international carbon trade in 2006.[29] According to the World Bank, China captured U.S. $3 billion of the U.S. $4.8 billion in subsidies last year for dozens of CDM projects. Of course, China is no longer so poor, with U.S. $1.4 trillion in foreign exchange reserves. However, it only accounted for less than two-fifths of the developing world's fossil fuel consumption, the major source of greenhouse gases.[30]

Together with China, several other large developing countries, including India, Brazil, Mexico, and Argentina, are claiming the bulk of the CDM bonanza. The possible price rise of carbon credits will probably make China's business more lucrative. The supply of credits will be 300 million metric tons short of demand when the Kyoto Protocol expires in 2012.[31] Increased demand has raised the price of the credits by more than seventy percent from February to May 2007: Japan paid as much as $16 per ton of carbon dioxide equivalent, compared with an average price of $10 last year.[32]

Most other developing countries, including many very poor ones that are extremely vulnerable to global warming, have been largely left out of the CDM pie. In 2006, all of Africa only received less than U.S. $150 million from selling carbon credits, or three percent of the global total.[33] The imbalanced regional distribution in carbon trade income as well as China's surging energy consumption and emissions have led to international dissatisfaction about the current climate change regime dominated by the Kyoto Protocol. If the imbalance cannot be changed, China's image and soft power concerning the climate change issue will be damaged even among many developing countries that used to support China's climate stances in the international arena.

CONCLUSION: THE INTERPLAY OF HARD AND SOFT POWER

From this study, we can see that a sovereign state sometimes has to sacrifice some material interests (in this case, economic growth and benefits) to gain soft power (international image related to green issues). According to the IPCC estimation, in 2050, the macroeconomic costs for stabilization between 710 and 445 ppm CO_2 equivalent are between a one percent gain and a 5.5 percent decrease of global GDP.[34]

The United States, fearing that emission cutting obligations would hamper its economic growth, refused to ratify the Kyoto Protocol and thus witnessed its soft power and international reputation greatly damaged. China actually gained both its hard power (via huge economic gains from CDM projects) and soft power through joining the first international cooperation against climate change, but it seems very likely that China now has to make a choice between the two in the next round of international talks. China once gained soft power among African countries by giving them huge material donations during the Cold War, and now it may need to transfer part of the material interest gained in the emission trading to African countries to gain soft power in the combat against climate change.

The next round of international talks kicked off in Indonesia's Bali Island at the end of 2007 to formulate a new pact replacing the Kyoto Protocol, and the international onus as been on China to accept compulsory emission cuts. Environmental activists hope that this time, the United States, the current world's number one greenhouse gas emitter, plus China and India, will all be included in the new treaty with fixed emission quotas or even carbon taxes.

China is in a dilemma. On one hand, it frets about damage to its reputation due to its environmental problems and hopes to utilize international cooperation to solve them; on the other hand, it fears that emission abatement obligations may block its fast economic growth. China's total GDP is still less than one-fourth the size of the United States, but its total emissions have ballooned because of an investment splurge on steel, cement, and aluminum production, all hugely energy-intensive industries, plus reliance on coal to produce power. From China's perspective, the international effort against climate change is a two-edged sword: it can both transfer funds and technology to China or put economic shackles on it if disadvantageous regulations are passed.

Chinese experts argue that if China accepts emission quotas just like those placed upon industrialized nations in the Kyoto Protocol, it will eventually pay much more than it currently gains from CDM projects. The carbon tax, if adopted in the next protocol, is expected to cost Chinese industry billions of dollars or more if China's economy and emissions continue to grow at the current rates.

Whether China can gain more soft power through all these proactive measures to mitigate climate change is yet to be seen. Some countries and international environmental organizations have expressed their disappointment in the goals agreed upon at the 2007 APEC summit in Sydney, claiming that all the targets are still only voluntary. China will definitely face greater challenges to its policy in the coming climate talks. China's economic strength has grown so rapidly in the past decade that it has to shoulder a greater international responsibility. Otherwise, its soft power will probably be damaged if it continues on its present course.

NOTES

1. Robert O. Keohane, "International Institutions: Can Interdependence Work?" *Foreign Policy* 110 (1998): 82.
2. Keohane, "International Institutions," 84.
3. Keohane, "International Institutions," 86.
4. Keohane, "International Institutions," 86.
5. United Nations, *Framework Convention on Climate Change* (1992), Article 2.
6. Yuka Kobayashi, "Navigating Between 'Luxury' and 'Survival' Emissions," in *Global Warming and East Asia: The Domestic and International Politics of Climate Change,* ed. Paul G. Harris (London: Routledge, 2003), 88.
7. Chandrashekhar Dasgupta, "The Climate Change Negotiations," in *Negotiating Climate Change: The Inside Story of the Rio Convention,* ed. Irving Mintzer and J.A. Leonard (Cambridge: Cambridge University Press, 1994), 133.
8. Michael Hatch, "Chinese Politics, Energy Policy, and the International Climate Change Negotiations," in *Global Warming and East Asia: The Domestic and International Politics of Climate Change,* ed. Paul G. Harris (London: Routledge, 2003), 50.
9. Hatch, "Chinese Politics," 52.
10. Hatch, "Chinese Politics," 51.
11. Hatch, "Chinese Politics," 51.

12. "Kobayashi, "Navigating Between 'Luxury' and 'Survival' Emissions," 88.
13. "Kobayashi, "Navigating Between 'Luxury' and 'Survival' Emissions," 91.
14. "Kobayashi, "Navigating Between 'Luxury' and 'Survival' Emissions," 91.
15. "Kobayashi, "Navigating Between 'Luxury' and 'Survival' Emissions," 91.
16. United Nations, *Framework Convention,* Article 4.
17. Zhang Zhihong, "The Forces behind China's Climate Change Policy," in *Global Warming and East Asia: The Domestic and International Politics of Climate Change,* ed. Paul G. Harris (London: Routledge, 2003), 78.
18. Karl Malakunas, "Question Marks over China's Climate Commitment," *AFP News*, May 6, 2007.
19. Rhett A. Butler, "China May Top U.S. in Greenhouse Gas Emissions in 2007," *Mongabay.com*, March 23, 2007, news.mongabay.com/2007/0323-china.html, (accessed January 11, 2009).
20. Alan Zarembo, "China Seen as a Roadblock to U.N. Climate Report," *Los Angeles Times*, May 3, 2007.
21. Malakunas, "Question Marks."
22. Malakunas, "Question Marks."
23. Richard McGregor, "China More Assertive in Climate Talks," *Financial Times,* May 4, 2007.
24. "China Now No. 1 in CO_2 Emissions; USA in Second Position," *Netherlands Environmental Assessment Agency* 2007, www.mnp.nl/en/dossiers/Climatechange/moreinfo/Chinanowno1inCO2emissionsUSAinsecondposition.html (accessed January 11, 2009).
25. David Mulford, "Address Climate Change in Real Terms, Not by Sacrificing Growth," *Embassy of the United States: New Delhi,* India 2007, newdelhi.usembassy.gov/pr061107.html (accessed January 11, 2009).
26. Kobayashi, "Navigating Between 'Luxury' and 'Survival' Emissions," 98.
27. Kobayashi, "Navigating Between 'Luxury' and 'Survival' Emissions," 101.
28. Yao Yi, "Protests Caused by Pollution Grow at Annual Rate of 30 percent," *Fa Zhi Wan Bao*, May 13, 2007, 3.
29. Keith Bradsher, "China Knows Which Way Wind Blows: Country Gets Largest Share of UN Credits to Curb Emissions," *International Herald Tribune*, May 10, 2007. 1–4.
30. Bradsher, "China Knows Which Way Wind Blows," 1.
31. Dinakar Sethuraman, "Carbon-Credit Sales May Double This Year," *Bloomberg News*, May 27, 2007.
32. Sethuraman, "Carbon-Credit Sales."
33. Bradsher, "China Knows Which Way Wind Blows."
34. Intergovernmental Panel on Climate Change, *4th Assessment Report*, (2007), 22.

Part IV

CONCLUSION

Chapter Thirteen

The Prospect of China's Soft Power: How sustainable?

Suisheng Zhao

As China's status rises on the global stage, its soft power has increasingly become a subject of scholarly scrutiny in recent years. While most analysts agree that China is not in a position to employ its military might against Washington, they are not quite sure about China's soft power challenge to the United States. One book among the growing body of works on China's increasing soft power is titled *Charm Offensive* and has the alarmist subtitle *How China's Soft Power Is Transforming the World.* China is portrayed as extremely skillful and effective in the fields of public diplomacy and the global battle for hearts and minds—effective enough to seriously challenge the United States in selected regions of the world as American soft power is waning in the aftermath of the invasion and occupation of Iraq, among other factors.[1] Indeed, China has moved quickly and made self-conscious efforts to mobilize its soft power resources to promote its interests and cultivate its influence as a rising power.

The future growth of China's soft power, however, is seriously restrained by the fact that pragmatic political values behind China's rapid economic growth are attractive mostly to authoritarian elites. In addition, China's view of a world order derived from either the old Sinocentric hierarchy or the realist tradition with an emphasis on absolute national sovereignty is hardly compatible with evolving transnational norms. In spite of its initial success, China's current approach to soft power lacks a contemporary moral appeal and therefore is hardly sustainable in the competition with the United States to inspire the vision of building a free and prosperous world.

CHINA'S SOFT POWER POTENTIAL

Soft power is one indispensable component of national power and tangible military and economic power alone is no longer sufficient for a nation to project its might in international affairs. With the diminishing possibility of major wars in the post-imperial era, competition in soft power has become more and more important in international relations. National governments need to use intangible soft power along with hard power to gain influence in the global stage. As Nye suggests, "in a global information age, soft sources of power such as culture, political values, and diplomacy are part of what makes a great power. Success depends not only on whose army wins, but also on whose story wins."[2] While Nye has urged the U.S. government to use soft power to complement its hard power, especially in the wake of the September 11 attacks, the Bush administration ignored his advice and relied mostly on U.S. military might in its war on terrorism. As a result, the U.S. international image has suffered in recent years.

Beijing Embraces Soft Power

In contrast to the U.S. approach, "the concept of soft-power advocacy has made a strong impression in China."[3] Chinese leaders have moved quickly to grasp the distinction between hard power and soft power and begun to make efforts to increase China's soft power while building its hard power to enhance China's global influence. One scholar surveyed a Chinese academic journal database and revealed that the phrase "soft power" first appeared around 1997 and has become a popular phrase since 2001.[4] China has readily embraced the concept of soft power not only because it is compatible with many aspects of Chinese traditional and strategic thinking but more importantly because the concept offers a ready solution to ease the anxieties around the world about China's rise.

In its strategy of "peaceful development," China has already emphasized building comprehensive national power, which includes soft as well as hard power. Together with the development of its coercive power, it is not difficult for China to become sensitive to mobilizing its soft power resources, which would be less alarming and thus more acceptable to other countries in the world. The timing cannot be better for Beijing to mobilize its soft power resources because China has achieved robust economic growth in recent decades and has not involved itself in any major war. In the meantime, the United States' Iraq misadventure has tarnished the international image of the world's sole superpower and the Bush administration's unilateralism has led to the decline of U.S. moral leadership in the world.

As a result, whereas the United States has been busy reacting to international crises and terrorism, the Chinese government has taken active steps to enhance its soft power influence in many parts of the world. One study of China's soft power by two Western scholars reveals that (1) China has been trying to promote its traditional culture as a world culture; (2) China's successful economic development model has been sold to many countries as a preferable choice for their own modernization drives; and (3) China has sought to play a more active and responsible role in international affairs.[5] One *People's Daily* report confirms this observation, claiming that Chinese culture is quite attractive to foreigners and China's tradition of treasuring peace is widely appreciated. China has attempted to put forward the idea of taking a peaceful development road and building a harmonious society. These ideas are very inspiring to the international community and help resolve doubts and fears about China's rapid development.[6]

Chinese leaders clearly see the effectiveness of culture as a soft power resource. A *China Daily* report states that "China hopes to dissolve the misconception of its development as the 'China threat' by making its traditional value systems known to the world."[7] Mobilizing cultural resources, Beijing has established Confucius Institutes all over the world to promote the Chinese language, culture, and business environment. More than one hundred of these institutes have already been established around the world, in such places as Thailand, Japan, Australia, Sweden, and the United States. One *Asian Times* report suggests that the choice of the name is instructive, since for years the Chinese Communist Party (CCP) asserted that Confucianism had held back China's development. In recent years, however, Confucianism has undergone a kind of political resurrection in China and now has a non-threatening connotation.[8]

Meanwhile, the country has been working to present its culture to the world by staging heritage exhibitions and art performances abroad. Wan Yiping, president of the Sino-American Education Consortium, claims that "these endeavors illustrate our aspiration to present a true peace-loving China to the world."[9] In addition, the Chinese government has made great efforts to increase the enrollment of foreign students and the number of foreign tourists in China. A Chinese government scholarship has been established to fund foreign students to enroll in Chinese universities for year-long studies.

Promoting China's traditional culture abroad, Chinese leaders have pleasantly discovered that as the United States fails to sell its liberal model of development to Third World countries, China's rapid economic growth makes it an alternative model of development for many developing countries by default. A Chinese analyst cites the Chinese-African summit that gathered more than forty African heads of states in Beijing in the Fall of 2006 as an example and suggests that "many of the African leaders coming here for the Chinese-African summit meeting are attracted not only by opportunities for aid and trade, but also by the Chinese model of development."[10] According to him, the paramount task for most developing countries is how to eradicate poverty, a root cause of conflicts and various forms of extremism. What they usually need is not a liberal democratic government, but a good government capable of fighting poverty and delivering basic services and security. So long as the American model remains unable to deliver the desired outcome, as shown so clearly in failures from Haiti to the Philippines to Iraq, the Chinese model will become more appealing to the world's poor. He concludes that in terms of eradicating poverty and helping the poor and the marginalized, the Chinese model, however imperfect, has worked far more effectively than what can be called the American model, as represented by the IMF-designed Structural Adjustment Program (SAP) for sub-Saharan Africa and the "shock therapy" for Russia.[11] To a certain extent, this Chinese analyst is correct. Even Joseph Nye admits that although China remains authoritarian, the success of its political economy in tripling gross domestic product over the past three decades has made it attractive to many developing countries. In parts of Asia, Africa, and Latin America, the so-called "Beijing Consensus" of combining authoritarian government with a market economy has become more popular than the previously dominant "Washington Consensus" of market economy and democratic government. China has reinforced this attraction by providing developing countries with economic aid and access to its growing market.[12]

On the diplomatic front, China has proposed a value-free concept of a "world of harmony"—the peaceful coexistence of diverse countries. The concept has two major points: one is to respect and tolerate different ideologies and social systems, and the second is to emphasize consultation among all countries involved, not unilateralism driven by hegemonic ambitions (i.e., the American strategy).[13] The *People's Daily* reported that President Hu Jintao has paid friendly visits to many countries and put forward the idea of building a harmonious world.[14] A Western observer noticed that "China's diplomats and politicians are in charm-offensive mode wherever they speak and travel to these days, reading from pre-written scripts that China is striving for the establishment of a harmonious and peaceful international society."[15]

In light of the concept of a world of harmony, China has advocated non-intervention in the affairs of other countries and is careful not to make its trade, investment, and other aspects of its foreign relations conditional on how well its counterparts live up to political, environmental, or labor standards. China's diplomacy has been particularly successful in the Asia-Pacific region after it abandoned ideology as the policy guide and developed friendly relations with neighboring countries regardless of their ideological tendencies and political systems (*buyi yishi xingtai he shehui zhidu lun qingsu*).[16] Lee Kuan Yew, a state leader in Singapore, writes that "China has been courting its neighbors, and although the Chinese did not coin the phrase 'soft power,' they have exercised it with consummate skill."[17] China has launched this charm offensive in order to settle territorial disputes with its neighbors, take a lead in setting up the Shanghai Cooperation Organization, and join a variety of regional organizations. Nye commends that "this new diplomacy helps to alleviate fears and reduces the likelihood of other countries allying to balance a rising power."[18]

SHORT-TERM SUCCESS, LONG-TERM UNCERTAINTY

Mobilizing its considerable soft power resources, China's influence and image has been enhanced on the global stage in recent years. In an interview, Nye recognized China's increasing attractiveness to other countries when he said, "I think it is a wise policy for China to increase its soft power. China's successful economy makes it attractive, and Chinese traditional culture is attractive. And China has pursued a series of policies which have been attractive to other countries." The fact that a lot of people are learning the Chinese language around the world "helps to expand China's soft power."[19] Polls taken by the Program on International Policy Attitudes and the BBC show that the majority of people in most countries today consider China to be a more positive influence and less of a threat to international peace than the United States. Such sentiments are particularly strong in the developing world.[20] It is from this perspective that one Western observer suggested that "the Iraq war isn't over, but one thing's already clear: China won. As the U.S. model has become tarnished, China's has gained new luster. As the United States has been bleeding popularity and influence around the world, China has been gaining both."[21]

In spite of its initial success, China's exercise of its soft power in the current form is seriously flawed. One study lists an imbalance of resources, legitimacy concerns of its diplomacy, and lack of a coherent agenda as three major factors hindering its efforts to project its soft power effectively.[22] Another study points to a blind spot in China's exercise of soft power as "the absence of Chinese non-governmental organizations (NGOs) on the international stage, which deprives China of a crucial soft power tool, hampers its public diplomacy, weakens the credibility of the messages it seeks to send out, and reduces the amount of feedback."[23] Still another study suggests two major factors that have constrained Beijing's ability to project its soft power. One is the gap between an increasingly cosmopolitan and confident foreign policy and a closed and rigid domestic political system. The other is the constant tension between its multiple foreign policy objectives and the still nascent soft power resources. This study concludes that "soft power remains Beijing's underbelly and China still has a long way to go to become a true global power."[24]

While all these factors are important, the most important flaw is the lack of contemporary moral appeals in relation to China's pragmatic approach to exercising soft power. In a comparison of Chinese discourse of soft power with Nye's discussion of American soft power, one scholar finds that "the American appeal to the world emphasizes the contemporary culture and the political model whereas China's attraction to the world focuses on traditional culture and economic model."[25] The different emphases reflect the different approaches to exercising soft power between China and the United States. China's pragmatic emphasis on its traditional culture and current economic growth may be a convenient way to achieve short-term success but it may be difficult to sustain in the longer term and ultimately win the soft power competition with the United States. The flaws of China's soft power are best illustrated by China's evolving view of the world order and the pragmatism behind its development model.

THE CHINESE WORLD ORDER: STUCK IN ABSOLUTE SOVEREIGNTY

In response to "China fever" in the West in recent years, one Western scholar raised a controversial question: Are Westerners ready to adjust to Chinese civilization's reemergence as one of the main sources of global order?[26] He could not give a definite answer to this question, but one may find some important clues by looking at the evolving Chinese view of the world order in the context of China's entry into the modern international system.

World order is used descriptively by scholars as "an aggregate conception of dominant values, norms, and structures as well as of established patterns of actors' behavior that give shape and substance to international society at any given time."[27] The modern international order began to acquire its present shape and definition more than three centuries ago with the emergence of the nation-state system in Europe.[28] The principle of state sovereignty provided the general framework from which specific state practices on war, peace, commerce, and political competition evolved.[29]

Sinocentrism and the Traditional Chinese World Order

World order meant very different things to the Chinese prior to the coming of the Western powers in the nineteenth century. A China-centered world order existed in East Asia for thousands of years: the "Sinocentric hierarchy."[30] An Asian empire with one of the longest continuous civilizations in the world, China was a proud and strong continental power overshadowing other nations in the region. Its bureaucratic organization was strong, use of its language had spread, and Confucianism, along with other traditional philosophies, gained prominence and influence. It had not only an advanced civilization but also a self-sufficient agricultural economy. As a result, China held a different world outlook from the West, maintaining ethnocentric foreign relations for centuries. There were no concepts such as the nation-state and state sovereignty in the traditional Chinese mindset. Imperial China considered other countries its cultural inferiors; they were expected to appear in the Chinese capital, make obeisance to the emperor, and present tribute. China's relations with the surrounding areas and with non-Chinese peoples generally were colored by the concept of Sinocentrism and an assumption of Chinese superiority.

Such Sinocentrism and the Chinese world order were unusual and maintained for centuries by the strength of Chinese civilization and its military force. Most of the societies in East Asia, especially in Northeast Asia, developed within Chinese cultural boundaries. They were strongly influenced by the civilization of ancient China, including the Chinese ideographic writing system, the Confucian classical teachings about family and social order, the official examination system, and the imperial Chinese monarchy and bureaucracy. The strength of Chinese civilization made China "*zhongguo*" (the Middle Kingdom) and "the natural center of the East Asian world."[31] Under the Chinese world order, its relationship with its neighbors was similar to the relationship between an overlord and a vassal. It was manifested in a highly sophisticated tributary system that was, in effect, the only institution for traditional "international" relations in the region before the intrusion of Western powers.[32]

The process through which China was forcibly drawn into the European-dominated international system began with the demise of Sinocentrism and the Chinese world order. The collapse of Sinocentrism was also a process of

> China's struggle to resist aggressive European expansion, to adjust itself to the changing international realities, to meet its problems without totally abandoning its imperial tradition, and finally to accept slowly and gradually, though sometimes reluctantly, some of the European standards, institutions, rules and values.[33]

This process took several centuries. China's defeat in the 1840 Opium War was a heavy blow to the Chinese sense of superiority and led to the collapse of Sinocentrism and the disintegration of the Chinese world order. In the sixty years after its humiliating defeat, the Qing government was forced to sign numerous treaties with foreign powers. This began a transition from the old tributary system to a treaty system. The Chinese empire was forced to enter into "the Eurocentric family of nations."[34] The new treaty system affirmed the principle of diplomatic equality between China and its treaty partners, shattering the fictive remnants of the ancient tributary system. The first decade of the twentieth century was the end of transition from the Chinese world order to a modern nation-state system. China no longer constituted a world unto itself, but was part of the greater world, a unit in the anarchical international system. After the long and sustained resistance of Sinocentrism, the Chinese world order collapsed, giving way to an international order defined by Western powers.

China: An Adamant Defender of National Sovereignty

Because China entered the modern international system of the nation-states under the threat of imperialism to its territorial integrity, it has become a zealous defender of the concept of sovereign rights, an important underpinning of the nation-state system. Embracing the Western concepts of legal equality and territorial sovereignty, the Chinese political elite has moved to vigorously defend Chinese national and territorial sovereignty against foreign invasion.

When China began to accept the idea of equality among nation-states and struggled to defend its sovereignty, however, the non-Western world had come under the domination of imperialist powers that did not treat weak nations as equals. This was a social Darwinian world in the eyes of many Chinese elites. The status of a nation-state was determined by its economic and military strength. China was stagnant and weak and therefore had to fight for a status equal to other nation-states. As a result, the collision between traditional Sinocentrism and the modern nation-state system, as well as the crushing defeats that China suffered in a series of military confrontations with the West, was accompanied by the rise of the modern Chinese nation-state. The wars, unequal treaties, humiliations, and material and territorial losses suffered by the Chinese people during a century of contact with foreign imperialist powers were continuous sources of inspiration to the Chinese zeal of defending its national sovereignty.

Emphasis on territorial sovereignty thus characterized much of China's thinking about international relations in the twentieth century. This zeal has continued into the twenty-first century when many of the originators of that system had begun to move away from strong views on state sovereignty. China's effort to establish diplomatic relations with other countries of the world on a reciprocal basis, and to participate in the UN and other world organizations with the condition of non-interference in domestic affairs, speaks to an insistence on the absolute sovereignty of the nation-state. China's political leaders all share a deep commitment to overcome humiliation, secure redress of past grievances, and achieve a position of equality with all other major powers. That is why a persistent theme of Chinese foreign policy has been to win back the territories lost during the country's time of internal disintegration and external humiliation in the nineteenth and twentieth centuries. China's rise in the twenty-first century has not fundamentally changed this sovereignty-centered perspective on international relations.

The principle of non-interference in internal affairs has for decades been at the core of China's foreign policy. Foreign criticism of China's human rights violations is rejected as unjustifiable interference in the internal affairs of a sovereign state. In the meantime, China has been building friendly relations across the globe with various nations, including those shunned by the United States and other democracies—nations like Venezuela, Iran, Sudan, Burma, Cuba, and Zimbabwe—because of their records of internal human rights violation and other bad governance issues. Beijing's practice is hardly comparable with the evolving norms of a twenty-first century international, globalized system and has been seriously criticized. As a *New York Times* editorial commented, "human rights violations cannot be relegated to untouchable internal affairs. Just as the world has not hesitated, rightly, to lambaste the United States over issues like Guantánamo Bay, it should not be shy about systematic and widespread violations of human rights in China."[35]

China's realist view of nation-state sovereignty, in this case, has often been a liability in its diplomacy and is subject to modification. For example, because of its close relationship with the Sudanese government, which has been accused of committing genocide in Darfur, China has been under heavy international pressure in recent years. The U.S. Congress, Amnesty International, Human Rights Watch, and others even labeled the 2008 Beijing Summer Olympics the "genocide games." Initially, Beijing reacted with fury to the criticism and "interference" in its affairs, but then it reconsidered its strategy of seeing no evil in Darfur and caved in as the "genocide games" label threatened to have a lasting impact on its ability to stage the "best Olympic Games ever." In May 2007 Beijing announced that it was dispatching a 275-strong team of military engineers to Sudan to join a UN peacekeeping mission set to begin operating in Dafur within the year.[36] Beijing's concern about possible embarrassment at the 2008 Olympics is certainly an important factor that led to the change in Beijing's attitudes toward Darfur. Nevertheless, one analysis found that the Darfur crisis coincided with "a fundamental reassessment" of China's entire approach to foreign policy in "addressing such transnational concerns as terrorism, trafficking in arms, drugs and humans, health pandemics and climate change.[37]

These are significant changes. But China needs to do far more to make a thorough transition in its foreign policy. If China cannot complete this transition, the West, on the rise since the fifteenth century and still dominant, will have difficulty accepting the Chinese view of the world order becoming a dominant position. In this case, China will risk a dangerous clash of civilizations with the Western world. This flaw certainly sets a limit to the attractiveness of China's soft power in the twenty-first century.

THE BEIJING CONSENSUS VERSUS THE WASHINGTON CONSENSUS

The "Beijing consensus" is used to describe the model of development that has allowed China to achieve a high level of economic growth without fundamental change in one-party communist rule. In contrast, the "Washington's consensus" demands a free market system going hand in hand with liberal democratic reform.[38] Indeed, China's economic achievements under the leadership of the Communist Party has stood out as one eye-catching exception to the general pattern of modernization in the West and has provided an example for some developing countries to follow. The Chinese model, however, has a clear fault line; that is, it lacks moral appeals because it is guided entirely by pragmatism, which, by definition, is behavior disciplined by neither a set of values nor established principles.

To a great extent, China's economic development path is a modified version of the East Asian model that emerged in several East Asian newly industrialized economies (NIEs) such as Singapore, Hong Kong, Taiwan, and South Korea in the 1970s and 1980s. Industrialization took place in these NIEs when neo-classical economic policy and political authoritarianism coincided with historical opportunities for export-led development. In a modified way, the Beijing Consensus has displayed the following three features.[39]

First, it has been an economic reform and modernization process driven not by any ideological doctrine or principles but economic success-oriented pragmatism. This was vividly expressed in Deng Xiaoping's cat theory: "a cat, whether it is white or black, is a good one as long as it is able to catch mice." Taking a pragmatic and experimental approach, the reform has been piecemeal and gradual. Potential reform programs are adopted and implemented in selected sectors and regions in order to judge their effectiveness and feasibility. Those that succeed can then be adopted on a wider basis, while those that fail can be abandoned or modified. The Chinese leadership has taken on easier and less controversial reforms first with the hope that the success of the initial reforms would create enough political momentum and support to permit the adoption of more complicated and less popular measures later on. Consequently, China's reform-oriented leadership has rejected "shock therapy" and has worked through existing institutions while gradually reforming and reorienting them to serve their modernization goals.

Second, China's economic development has been led by a strong, pro-development state that is capable of shaping national consensus on modernization and ensuring overall political and macroeconomic stability to pursue wide-ranging domestic reforms. The developmental state has emphasized economic growth rather than civil and political rights as an overarching national goal. A certain degree of political stability has been maintained under authoritarian rule as a pre-condition for economic development. As a result, rapid economic growth has occurred under authoritarian Communist Party rule.

Third, China's modernization process has involved "selective learning" from the neo-liberal American model, especially its emphasis on the role of the market, entrepreneurship, globalization, and international trade. What makes the Chinese model unique is that the communist regime has safeguarded its own policy space as to when, where, and how to adopt foreign ideas. In particular, the Chinese state has adopted most of the basic macroeconomic principles of the Washington Consensus for the domestic economy but rejected or modified the neo-liberal aspects that would greatly reduce the role of the state through rapid privatization and democratization. While the state gradually opened the domestic economy to international competition, it has offered some protection to key sectors and some support to infant industries. The state has also been more active in reducing poverty and in ensuring minimal material standards to compete in a more competitive global economy.

Essentially being a pragmatic approach to economic development and political stability, the Beijing Consensus has gained ground mostly among leaders of authoritarian countries and repressive regimes. These authoritarian elites increasingly look to Beijing largely due to the following three developments over the past decade.

The first is China's economic success under the one-party rule. Making economic growth the country's top priority, pragmatic Chinese leaders have demanded that economic success depends on political stability, which can be maintained only by the authoritarian rule of the CCP. In pursuing these policy objectives, China has created the world's fastest-growing economy in recent decades. An OECD country survey praised that

> the pace of economic change in China has been extremely rapid since the start of economic reforms just over twenty-five years ago. Economic growth has averaged 9.5 percent over the past two decades and seems likely to continue at

> that pace for some time. Such an increase in output represents one of the most sustained and rapid economic transformations seen in the world economy in the past fifty years.[40]

China's astonishing economic success is presented as evidence that the Beijing Consensus is a fast track to economic growth without the visible social and political disorder that often comes as a by-product of democratization. As one observer writes,

> Today's China demonstrates that a regime can suppress organized opposition and need not establish its legitimacy through elections. It shows that a ruling party can maintain considerable control over information and the Internet without slowing economic growth. And it indicates that a nation's elite can be bought off with comfortable apartments, the chance to make money, and advances in personal, non-political freedoms (clothes, entertainment, sex, travel abroad).[41]

The second development is the declining attractiveness of the Washington Consensus due to the United States' economic, political and foreign policy failures. Economically, the globalization process has become less favorable to the U.S. economy. As one study puts it, "the country is now so deeply in debt to China and other export economies that its very solvency is put in question. That is hardly an economic model to offer as the shining example of global development."[42] The American model is largely ideology-driven to spread democratization, and so treats sub-Saharan Africa and other less-developed countries as immature societies in which Western institutions will automatically take root. It imposed liberalization before safety nets were set up, privatization before regulatory frameworks were put in place, and democratization before a culture of political tolerance and rule of law was established. The end result has often been discouraging or even devastating.[43] It is not incidental that

> in Latin America, it produced more than one 'lost decade,' on the Pacific Rim it effectively turned a recession (Asian Crash of 1997) into a veritable Great Depression, and in Russia it propelled the best-connected apparatchiks into global capitalist ranks even as it pushed ordinary Russians into penury.[44]

The failure of U.S. foreign policy, symbolized by the war in Iraq, further damaged the Washington Consensus. As one observer points out, U.S. foreign policy has been dominated by a school of thought that emphasizes military power and has tied the spread of democracy to the use of force. This has not only failed but also undermined support for democracy. U.S. attempts to export free markets and political liberty by force have been unable to bring even security, much less prosperity, to Iraq. And they've eroded the appeal and clout of the United States worldwide.[45] It is from this perspective that Joshua Cooper Ramo argued that developing nations were increasingly fed up with the doctrinaire of Washington Consensus and increasingly impressed by a Chinese model that emphasized pragmatism, innovation, social cohesion, and self-determination. It is not difficult for them to discover that only three decades ago, China was as poor as some of the poorest third-world countries. While many of these countries remain poor, China's economy has expanded rapidly. Given the many problems confronting developing countries, China seems to offer a new model on how to fight poverty and ensure good governance, albeit one that challenges the conventional wisdom being exported by Western countries and the international financial institutions they control.

The third development is China's so-called "value-free" diplomacy toward many developing countries. Unlike Western diplomacy that sets moral principles such as good governance, democracy, transparency, rule of law, and respect for human rights as foreign policy objectives, China's diplomacy is not guided by any moral principles. Pursuing economic or strategic interests, China has developed friendly relations with many developing countries without the preconditions that have often been demanded by the Western democracies. For example, in its global search for energy resources, China has pursued deals with countries that are off-limits to Western companies because of sanctions and the threat of bad publicity. Beijing has justified this policy on the grounds that China is applying the so-called principle of non-interference; i.e., a strategy of not bothering authoritarian regimes with Western-style criticism of human-rights violations and political oppression in countries where business can be conducted. As one study of China's projection of soft power among third-world countries indicates, "Offering no-strings-attached financial aid and economic assistance to Africa and to Southeast, South, and Central Asia has become a central part of China's foreign and trade policies." Examples of this "value-free" diplomacy including awarding Zimbabwe's dictator Robert Mugabe an honorary professorship at the China Foreign Affairs University in Beijing in 2005, and signing economic cooperation agreements with Uzbekistan a few days after the country's Interior Ministry fired into a crowd of peaceful demonstrators in May 2005.[46] Given China's rising power status, political leaders in these countries may readily use Beijing as a hedge against American power. As a result, many authoritarian leaders in third-world countries have welcomed the Chinese development model together with its value-free diplomacy as an alternative to the European and U. S. versions of both.

It is against this background that political leaders in developing countries seeking to combine authoritarian rule with an economic miracle have increasingly taken the Beijing Consensus as a successful model of development and international relations. Their attraction to the Beijing model has come almost entirely due to its tangible economic and political aspects rather than its intangible moral appeals. As the idea of a Beijing consensus gained ground, however, Joshua Cooper Ramo returned to the fray with dissonant data. In a pamphlet called *Brand China*, he takes a much less optimistic view of China's image. Using global opinion research conducted by Young and Rubicam, Ramo concludes that China's brand is weak and that the country is not trusted overseas.[47] Citing Ramo's changing view, one Western observer believes that even the more vaunted examples of Chinese soft power can easily be turned on their heads. The Chinese may get on famously with the governments of Sudan and Zimbabwe, but such relationships are only likely to confirm the damaging impression that China is a country that will always put profits above human rights and other moral principles. Seen in this light, "China's growing influence in Africa and even Southeast Asia has little to do with a new Beijing Consensus; it is simply old-fashioned power politics."[48] Joseph Nye, the original theorist of soft power, also argues that while the "Beijing Consensus" is attractive in authoritarian and semi-authoritarian developing countries, it undercuts China's soft power in the West because China suffers from corruption, inequality, and a lack of democracy, human rights and the rule of law."[49] In this case, the United States is better placed to polish up its image than China since it is much easier to change a country's policies than to change its political system.

In addition to its authoritarian nature, the Beijing Consensus has not been effective in dealing with many important dimensions of human development at home and abroad. As one observer writes, "Chinese economic growth, while undeniably impressive, is widely associated in the West with pollution, cheap labor and a threat to jobs."[50] A *New York Times* editorial comments that although the "Chinese miracle" has been the biggest economic story for several years now, a tale of a nation rising from the ashes of a Stalinist command economy to become the world's premier trading partner, China reminds us with distressing regularity that the progress has been selective. It cites the recent reports of slave labor in Chinese factories and the discovery that some of the popular Thomas the Tank Engine toys manufactured in China contain lead in their paint. It also points to the earlier reports about the contaminated dog food, the stubborn support of Sudan for its oil, the regular reports of human rights abuses, the huge economic disparities between city and country, and the controls on the media. According to this editorial, China's unreformed political system fosters corruption and an undue focus on short-term economic gains, which will lead to more internal inequities and injustices and more tainted exports.[51]

From a historical perspective, the current Beijing Consensus is only a transitional model of development. It may go from a "value-free" to a "value-added" model involving the sequencing of economic growth, legal reforms, democratization, and constitutionalism, with different aspects of development being emphasized at different times. This has been demonstrated by the evolution of several East Asian NIEs. After achieving high levels of economic growth, these NIEs have eventually implemented the rule of law and eventually democratize and protect the full range of human rights through some form of constitutionalism.

A study of the China model in comparison with the East Asian model by an American scholar describes a potential transition of the China model along this direction. According to him, although democratization in the sense of freely contested multiple party elections for the highest level of office may be postponed until a relatively high level of wealth is attained, as the economy grows and wealth is generated, the government will invest in human capital and in institutions, including reforms to establish a legal system that meets the basic Fullerian requirements of a procedural or thin rule of law. Over time, as the legal system becomes more efficient, professional, and autonomous, it will come to play a greater role in the economy and society more generally. Constitutionalism begins to emerge during the authoritarian period, including the development of constitutional norms and the strengthening of institutions. Social organizations start to proliferate and civil society begins to develop, albeit often a civil society with a different nature and political orientation than in Western liberal democracies, and with organizations with a political agenda subject to limitations. Citizens will enjoy economic liberties, rising living standards for the vast majority, and some civil and political rights, although with limitations especially on rights that involve political issues and affect the control of the regime. There will be greater protection of civil and political rights after democratization, including rights that involve sensitive political issues, although with ongoing abuses of rights in some cases and with rights frequently given a communitarian or collectivist interpretation rather than a liberal interpretation.[52]

CONCLUSION

China's rise has included both building its tangible economic-military power and intangible political-cultural influence. This was the position that China had enjoyed before a rising Europe began to eclipse it in the eighteenth century. In particular, the Chinese government has become aware of the distinction between the two components of power and become conscious of developing soft power to increase its legitimacy as an emerging great power. It is aware that many countries are anxious about a rising China and if China looks like an attractive and friendly place, these countries might be more relaxed about its growing power. This has been known as China's "charm offensive" for transforming the world and has caused concerns in the United States and elsewhere.

Indeed, China is mobilizing its soft power resources to transform the world. But, as this chapter has argued, it is not yet clear how effective and how far the transformation can go because of the flaws in China's soft power resources. It is true that the decline of the United States' international image since the Iraq War is increasingly evident. It is also true that China's extraordinary rise from poverty to prosperity has served as an inspiration for some third-world countries that are in despair. However, as one Western scholar asserts, "For a rich, free and culturally powerful country such as the United States to lose a soft power contest with China seems all but impossible. It would be like losing a boxing match with a one-armed man."[53] Even Kurlantzick, the author of *China's Charm Offensive*, suggests that America is not to be dismissed even if its soft power is waning. It still offers a set of values, based on the twin attractions of freedom and prosperity, which appeal to average people around the world. China cannot offer a comprehensive, inspiring vision of how to build a free, rights-oriented political system and economy, a vision that remains popular in many parts of the world. And it is America to which countries will turn if China's soft power ceases to appear that soft after all.[54]

Looking at the young people in China's major cities, one observer found that many of them saw that Westernization is China's future. "It gives Chinese students 'face' to speak some English—more 'face' if it is American English. On campus they practice sports popular in the West, and after graduation they would opt preferably for a career in a joint venture where the corporate culture is supposed to be Western—and the pay higher."[55] Just as China's economic and military power is far from matching that of the United States, China's soft power still is not an equal of the United States, particular in terms of its political values and moral appeal.

Of course, this does not mean that the United States can ignore the rise of China's soft power. If the decline of the U.S. global image continues and China eventually moves out of the shadow of its modern history and takes a fundamental turn in its reform toward democratization, as some of East Asian NICs have done, it is not impossible that China will win the soft power contest with the United States. Joseph Nye is correct in saying that "although China is far from America's equal in soft power, it would be foolish to ignore the gains it is making. The declining poll results and Washington's absence at the East Asian Summit are warning lights. It is time for the United States to pay more attention to the balance of soft power in Asia."[56] Views and opinions regarding China's soft power are fairly diverse both within China and in the international arena. This book largely reflects this reality. While not attempting to build a consensus, the chapters taken as a whole do provide a variety of observations of China's soft power. The central theme of this book is that soft power is a useful and important perspective to understand Chinese foreign policy and the future evolution of China's role in international politics.

A few common arguments have emerged. First, it is clear that soft power has become a very popular concept in China, even among political elites and decision-makers. Second, China is seriously contemplating and exploring a soft power strategy as it rises on the international political stage. Third, in the past decade, there have been noticeable elements of soft power in China's diplomatic practice, including softer rhetoric, promotion of Chinese culture abroad, economic diplomacy, and image building. Finally, this book describes some of the limitations of China's soft power. These restraints primarily stem from China's political values and its ongoing transformation.

NOTES

1. Joshua Kurlantzick, *Charm Offensive: How China's Soft Power Is Transforming The World* (New Haven: Yale University Press, 2007).

2. Joseph S. Nye, "The Rise of China's Soft Power," *The Wall Street Journal Asia*, December 29, 2005.

3. He Jingying, "The Charm of China's Soft Power," *People's Daily Online*, March 14, 2006, english.people.com.cn/200603/10/eng20060310_249577.html (accessed January 6, 2009).

4. Hongying Wang and Yeh-Chung Lu, "The Conception of Soft Power and its Policy Implications," *Journal of Contemporary China* 17, no. 56 (August 2008): 426.

5. Bates Gill and Yanzhong Huang, "Sources and Limits of Chinese Soft Power," *Survival* 48, no. 2 (Summer 2006): 17–36.

6. He "The Charm of China's Soft Power."

7. "China Threat" Fear Countered By Culture," *China Daily,* May 29, 2006. news.xinhuanet.com/english/2006-05/29/content_4613721.htm (accessed January 6, 2009).

8. Purnendra Jain and Gerry Groot, "Beijing's 'Soft Power' Offensive," *Asia Times Online*, May 17, 2006, www.atimes.com/atimes/China/HE17Ad01.html (accessed January 6, 2009).

9. *China Daily,* "'China threat' fear countered by culture."

10. Wei-wei Zhang, "The Allure of the Chinese Model," *International Herald Tribune*, November 1, 2006.

11. Zhang, "The Allure of the Chinese Model."

12. Nye, "The Rise of China's Soft Power."

13. Lun Tan, "China's Dream of Harmonious Existence," *China Daily*, November 11, 2005, 4.

14. He "The Charm of China's Soft Power."

15. Alex Berkofsky, "The Hard Facts on Soft Power," *PacNet* 26 (May 31, 2007).

16. Suisheng Zhao, "The Making of China's Periphery Policy," in *Chinese Foreign Policy, Pragmatism and Strategic Behavior*, ed. Zhao Suisheng (Armonk, NY: M. E. Sharpe, 2004), 260.

17. Lee Kuan Yew, "China's Soft-Power Success," *Forbes*, June 18, 2007.

18. Joseph S. Nye, "The Rise of China's Soft Power," *The Wall Street Journal Asia*, December 29, 2005.

19. "China Increasingly Attractive to Others," *Xinhua*, August 8, 2006, www.chinadaily.com.cn/china/2006-08/08/content_659235.htm (accessed January 6, 2009).

20. Joshua Kurlantzick, "Beijing's Big Push," *Newsweek International*, April 9, 2007, www.msnbc.msn.com/id/17886723/site/newsweek/ (accessed January 6, 2009).

21. James Mann, "China's Dangerous Model of Power," *Washington Post*, May 20, 2007.

22. Gill and Huang, "Sources and Limits," 2.

23. Lu Yiyi, "Blind Spots in China's Soft Power," *The Straits Times*, July 15, 2007.

24. Huang Yanzhong and Sheng Ding, "Dragon's Underbelly: An Analysis of China's Soft Power," *East Asia* 23, no. 4 (Winter 2006): 41.

25. Hongying Wang and Yeh-Chung Lu, "The Conception of Soft Power,"

26. David Gosset, "A New World with Chinese Characteristics," *Asian Times Online*, Apr 7, 2006, www.atimes.com/atimes/China/HD07Ad01.html (accessed January 6, 2007).

27. Samuel Kim, "Mainland China and a New World Order," *Issues and Studies* 27, no. 11 (November 1991): 4.

28. There are many studies of the Thirty Years War and the subsequent international system in Europe. See, for example, C. V. Wedgwood, *The Thirty Years War* (London: J. Cape, 1938); Henrik Tikkanen, *The 30 Years' War*, trans.George Blecher and Lone Thygesen-Blecher (Lincoln, NB.: University of Nebraska Press, 1987); Hugh Redwald Trevor-Roper, ed., *The Age of Expansion; Europe and the World, 1559–1660* (New York: McGraw-Hill, 1968); John Baptist Wolf, *The Emergence of the Great Powers, 1685–1715* (New York: Harper, 1951); Herbert Langer, *The Thirty Years' War* (Poole, England: Bandford Press, 1978); and Theodore K. Rabb, ed., *The Thirty Year's War* (New York: University Press of America, 1981). For an excellent brief description of the emergence of the great powers in Europe during this period, *see* Gordon A. Craig and Alexander L. George, *Force and Statecraft* (New York: Oxford University Press, 1983), 3–27.

29. Donald Kagan, *The Outbreak of the Peloponnesian War* (Ithaca, N.Y.: Cornell University Press, 1969), 31–35, 345–56. For a classic work on the nation-state system in the Western tradition, see Hans J. Morgenthau, *Politics Among Nations: The Struggle for Power and Peace* (New York: McGraw-Hill Inc., 1948).

30. Yang Lien-sheng, "Historical Notes on the Chinese World Order," in *The Chinese World Order* ed. John K. Fairbank, (Cambridge: Harvard University Press, 1968), 20.

31. John K. Fairbank, "A Preliminary Framework," in *The Chinese World Order* ed. John K. Fairbank, (Cambridge: Harvard University Press, 1968), 2.

32. A bibliography of some 55 studies of aspects of China's tributary relations was published in J. K. Fairbank and S. Y. Teng's, "On the Ch'ing Tributary System," *Harvard Journal of Asiatic Studies* 6, no. 4 (June 1941): 135–148.

33. Zhang Yongjin, *China in the International System, 1918–20, The Middle Kingdom at the Periphery* (New York: St. Martin's Press, 1991), 16.

34. John K. Fairbank, "The Early Treaty System in the Chinese World Order," *The Chinese World Order* ed. John K. Fairbank, (Cambridge: Harvard University Press, 1968), 258.

35. Editorial**, "**The China Puzzle**,"** *New York Times*, June 22, 2007.

36. Berkofsky, "The Hard Facts on Soft Power."

37. Gareth Evans and Donald Steinberg, "Signs of Transition," *The Guardian*, June 11, 2007.

38. Joshua Cooper Ramo, *Beijing Consensus: Notes on the New Physics of Chinese Power*, (London: Foreign Policy Center, 2004).

39. The discussion of the features is based on Randy Peerenboom, *China Modernizes: Threat to the West or Model for the Rest?* (Oxford: Oxford University Press, 2007); and Wei-wei Zhang, "The Allure of the Chinese Model," *International Herald Tribune*, November 1, 2006.

40. OECD, "Economic Survey of China 2005: Key challenges for the Chinese economy," www.oecd.org/document/7/0,2340,en_2649_201185_35343687_1_1_1_1,00.html. (accessed January 6, 2009).

41. James Mann, "China's Dangerous Model of Power," *Washington Post*, May 20. 2007.

42. William Thornton, "Sino-Globalization: Politics of the CCP/TNC Symbiosis," *New Political Science* 29, no. 2 (June 2007): 212.

43. Zhang "The Allure of the Chinese Model."

44. Thornton, "Sino-Globalization," 211.

45. Mann, "China's Dangerous Model of Power."

46. Berkofsky, "The Hard Facts on Soft Power."

47. Joshua Cooper Ramo, Brand China, London, UK: The Foreign Policy Center, 2007, pp. 12–19

48. Gideon Rachman, "The Hard Evidence That China's Soft Power Policy is Working," *FT.com,* February 19, 2007.

49. Nye, "The Rise of China's Soft Power."

50. Gideon Rachman, "The hard evidence that China's soft power policy is working," *Financial Times*, February 19, 2007.

51. Editorial, "The China Puzzle," *New York Times*, June 22, 2007.
52. Peerenboom, *China Modernizes*.
53. Rachman, "The Hard Evidence."
54. Kurlantzick, *Charm Offensive*.
55. Gosset, "A New World."
56. Nye, "The Rise of China's Soft Power."

Index

16th Party Congress, of the Chinese Communist Party, 22
17th Party Congress, of the Chinese Communist Party, 23, 58, 68
211 project, 111–113

American soft power, 49, 57, 247, 252. *See also* U.S. soft power
ARF. *See* ASEAN Regional Forum
ASEAN Regional Forum, 52, 54, 67, 72

Beijing Consensus, 2, 6, 13, 15, 26, 29, 51, 57, 69, 70–71, 75, 78, 125, 127, 133, 139, 208, 215–217, 220, 250, 256–257, 260–261. *See also* Chinese model of development or China model
Beijing Olympics, 71, 73, 190, 197, 255
Bush, George W., 2, 5, 68, 92, 137, 165, 194, 197, 218, 233–234, 248

CBMs. See Confidence-Building Measures
CCTV. See China Central Television
Central Foreign Affairs Leadership Group, 1, 23
Charm offensive, 11, 14, 45, 52–53, 83, 103, 115, 176, 247, 251, 262
Chen, Zhili, 114
China Central Television, 51, 151–152, 156
China model, 6, 28, 177, 179, 261
China threat, 9, 31, 38, 55, 59, 66, 76, 96–97, 191, 249
Chinese media, 21, 36, 146, 151, 153, 158, 192
Chinese model of development, 2, 6, 26, 208, 210, 217, 250
Chinese People's Political Consultative Conference, 23, 188
Cold War, 15, 46, 49, 52, 65–66, 76, 89, 95–96, 209, 241
Competition for soft power, 2, 32. *See also* soft power competition
Comprehensive national power, 2, 22, 28, 66, 248
Confidence-Building Measures, 9
Confucius institute, 13–14, 29, 38, 51, 70, 103, 114, 116–117, 156–158, 173, 187, 189, 196, 215, 249
CPPCC. *See* Chinese People's Political Consultative Conference
Cultural hegemony, 4, 33
Cultural power, 4, 14, 29, 33, 73, 143–148, 153, 157–158, 187
Cultural Revolution, 89, 126

Darfur, 179–180, 255
Deng, Xiaoping, 68, 75, 90–91, 93, 97, 109–110, 126, 134, 168–169, 186, 256

Economic assistance, 134, 154, 259

Financial aid, 220, 230, 259
Financial Crisis, 15, 53, 67–69, 77, 98, 116, 137, 211, 214–220
FOCAC. *See* Forum on China-Africa Cooperation Ministerial Conference
Forum on China-Africa Cooperation Ministerial Conference, 135, 172
Four modernizations, 109

Globalization, 3, 13, 25, 32, 70–71, 73–74, 76–78, 92, 135, 147, 218, 257–258
Great power status, 12, 64, 75

Hanban, 70, 117
Harmonious society, 31, 68, 73, 90, 249
Harmonious world, 52, 71, 73, 86, 97, 250
Hu, Jintao, 1,16, 23, 28, 31, 68, 90, 93, 97, 155, 165, 167, 170, 186, 188, 196, 197, 221, 240, 250
Human rights, 49–50, 54, 65, 131–132, 134, 136–138, 145, 155, 179, 194, 198, 228, 255, 259–261

Image of China, 22, 38, 51, 55, 115, 150, 175, 176, 197, 230
Iraq war, 5, 47, 50, 251, 262

Jia, Qinglin, 23, 188
Jiang, Zemin, 93, 97, 110–112, 155, 213

Koguryo, 143, 191–192

Liberal democracy, 6, 133, 218
Liu, Yunshan, 146

Made in China, 130, 135
Mugabe, Robert, 128, 168, 259

National Climate Change Program, 238–239
National Planning Guidelines for Cultural Development, 34
Neo-liberalism, 132, 134
New world order, 75, 92–94
No strings attached, 3, 134. *See also* value-free diplomacy
Non-interference, 134, 137–138, 168, 254–255, 259

Peaceful development, 186, 197, 248–249
Peaceful evolution, 33, 110
Peaceful rise, 24, 31, 56, 64, 71, 76, 83, 187, 221
Political reform, 39, 129
Publicity Department of the Chinese Communist Party, 146, 151

Qian, Qichen, 212, 114

Responsible stakeholder, 46, 74, 77, 95
Rudd, Kevin, 2, 197–198, 234

Scientific development, 129, 139
SCO. *See* Shanghai Cooperation Organization
Shanghai Cooperation Organization, 71, 93, 187, 251
Sinocentrism, 252–254
Six-Party Talks, 54, 71, 93, 189
Soft use of power, 1, 3, 7, 9, 167
Soft power competition, 252
South China Sea, 72, 89–90, 212
State Council Information Office, 29, 34, 145
Strategic partnership, 67, 212
Sun Zi, 87

Tiananmen, 11, 65, 68, 75, 109–110, 126, 169, 231

Traditional Chinese culture, 8, 25–26, 33, 35, 50, 52, 115
Tribute system, 88, 104–105, 253–254

U.S. soft power, 5–6, 9, 57, 68. *See also* American soft power

Value-free diplomacy, 138, 250, 259

Washington Consensus, 26, 57, 69–70, 78, 127, 132, 135, 156, 173, 212, 219, 250, 257–259. *See also* Western model
Wen Jiabao, 94, 165, 170, 178–179, 188, 192, 195–197, 238–239
Western culture, 26, 96
Western model, 131–133, 178, 209
Westernization, 73, 76, 262
Win-win cooperation, 67, 69, 153, 170, 225, 227

Zhao, Qizheng, 34, 145
Zheng, He, 89, 105

List of Contributors

Gang CHEN is Research Fellow at the East Asian Institute, National University of Singapore. He received his Ph.D. in International Relations from China Foreign Affairs University. His research interests include China's domestic politics and foreign policy, international environmental governance and climate change. His papers have appeared in journals such as *The Chinese Journal of International Politics, American Studies Quarterly, Journal of China Foreign Affairs University,* and *the International Forum.* He is the author of *The Kyoto Protocol and International Cooperation on Climate Change* (Beijing: Xinhua Press, 2008).

Jianfeng CHEN is Professor of International Relations and Dean for Academic Affairs at Shanghai University of Political Science and Law. He received his Ph.D. in International Relations from Fudan University. He is the author of *The Study of Party Policies from the Perspectives of Documentary Films* (coauthor, 2008), *Culture and International Order in East Asia and West Europe* (2004), *Contemporary Economics and Politics on the World Stage* (bilingual textbook, 2004), *Theories of Contemporary Western International Relations* (coauthor, 2001), and *International Business Communication* (1996). He has published more than thirty articles in various periodicals in mainland China and Hong Kong.

Xiaohe CHENG is an assistant professor at the School of International Studies, Renmin University of China. He did his undergraduate work at Fudan University and received his Ph.D. degree from Boston University. He worked for China's Institute of Contemporary International Relations in the 1990s. Cheng's research interests include international relations in the Asia-Pacific and China's diplomacy. He is currently working on the book tentatively entitled *The Rise and Fall of China's Alliances.*

Xiaogang DENG is Associate Professor of Sociology in Sociology Department at the University of Massachusetts-Boston. He is the Director of the Criminal Justice Program. He received his Ph.D. in Sociology from the State University of New York-Buffalo in 1994. His teaching areas include statistics, criminology, deterrence, research methods, and deviance. He received a Post-doctoral Research Grant ($30,000) from Chiang Ching-Kuo Foundation for International Scholarly Exchange (U.S.A.) in 2001. His papers have appeared in various sociological or criminological journals on recidivism, criminological theories and comparative criminology.

Yong DENG is a professor of Political Science at the United States Naval Academy at Annapolis, Maryland. His research has been focused on Asian international relations and Chinese foreign policy. Currently he is interested in the domestic origins of China's foreign policy choice. He is the coeditor of two volumes on Chinese foreign policy, *In the Eyes of the Dragon: China Views the World* (1999) and *China Rising: Power and Motivation in Chinese Foreign Policy* (2005). His single authored books are *Promoting Asia-Pacific Economic Cooperation: Perspectives from East Asia* (1997) and *China's Struggle for Status: The Realignment of International Relations* (2008). His other scholarly works have appeared in such journals as *Political Science Quarterly, China Quarterly, Pacific Affairs, Washington Quarterly, Journal of Strategic Studies, Journal of Contemporary China*, and *Harvard China Review.*

Joshua Kurlantzick was previously foreign editor at *The New Republic, a correspondent* for *U.S. News and World Report and The Economist.* He is a visiting scholar in the Carnegie Endowment's China Program. Also a special correspondent for *The New Republic,* a columnist for *Time*, and a senior correspondent for *The American Prospect*, Kurlantzick is assessing China's relationship with the developing world, including Southeast Asia, Africa, and Latin America. Additionally, Kurlantzick is currently a fellow at the USC School of Public Diplomacy and the Pacific Council on International Policy. His new book, *Charm Offensive: How China's Soft Power is Transforming the World* (Yale University Press, 2007) has been nominated for the Council on Foreign Relations' 2008 Arthur Ross Book Award. Kurlantzick's articles have appeared in *The New York Times Magazine*, *The Washington Post*, *Foreign Affairs*, *Harper's*, *The Atlantic Monthly*, *GQ*, *The American Prospect*, *Mother Jones*, *Current History*, and *The Washington Quarterly.*

Mingjiang Li is an Assistant Professor at the S. Rajaratnam School of International Studies, Nanyang Technological University. He was a diplomatic correspond for Xinhua News Agency. His main research interests include the rise of China in the context of East Asian regional relations and Sino-U.S. relations, China's diplomatic history, and domestic sources of China's international strategies. He received his Ph.D. in Political Science from Boston University. He is the editor or coeditor of several books on China's international relations in East Asia. He has published many papers and book chapters on China's domestic politics and foreign policy.

Zhongying PANG is Professor of International Relations at Renmin University of China. He was a senior fellow at the China Institute of International Studies and worked as a diplomat with the Chinese Embassy in Jakarta. He received his B.A. in Economics from Nankai University, his M.A. in Politics from University of Warwick, and his Ph.D. in International Relations from Beijing University. He was a visiting fellow at the Brookings Institution in Washington during 2007–2008. His areas of expertise include global political economy, regional issues, and Chinese foreign policy. His is the author of *Economic Nationalism* (Shandong Renmin Press, 2002), *China and Asia* (Shanghai Academy of Social Sciences Press, 2004), *Global Governance: Chinese Perspectives* (editor, The Peace Books Inc., Hong Kong). His articles have appeared in many Chinese journals and English Periodicals, such as *International Peacekeeping*, and *International Politik.*

Ignatius Wibowo is the Head of the Centre for Chinese Studies, Faculty of Humanities, the University of Indonesia. He received his doctorate degree from the School of Oriental and African Studies, University of London. Among his publications are two books *Negara dan Masyarakat di Cina* [State and Society in China] (2000) and *Belajar dari Cina* [To Learn from China] (2004), and a few edited books on globalization and Chinese Indonesians. He has contributed to international journals and his articles on the Chinese Communist Party can be found as book chapters. In Indonesia he has regularly contributed op-eds on China to various national newspapers. In the past three years, he was interested in research on "China's Rise," especially in Southeast Asia.

Lening ZHANG is Associate Professor of Sociology/Criminal Justice in the Department of Behavioral Sciences, Saint Francis University. He has published about 50 articles and a coedited book, *Crime and Social Control in a Changing China* (Greenwood, 2001). He is a coprincipal investigator of a research project that was funded with a grant of $300,000 by the National Science

Foundation of the United States. The project has successfully collected primary data of criminal victimization from a sample of 2,500 households in China and has been conducting comparative studies of criminal victimization in China and Western countries.

Yongjin ZHANG is Professor of East Asian Studies and Director of Centre for East Asian Studies at the University of Bristol in Britain. He has previously held teaching and research posts at Oxford University, Australian National University, the University of Auckland and the Institute of International Politics in Beijing. Professor Zhang has published in such prestigious journals as Review of International Studies, European Journal of International Relations, The China Journal and Journal of Contemporary China. His most recent publications include 'China and the Emerging Regional Order in the South Pacific' in Australian Journal of International Affairs (2007); 'Politics, Culture and Responsible Scholarship in China—Towards a Culturally Sensitive Analytical Framework' in Asian Perspective (2007); 'Discourses of Security in China—Towards a Critical Turn?' in Anthony Burke and Matt MacDonald, Critical Security in the Asia-Pacific (Manchester University Press, 2007); and 'Understanding Chinese Views of the Emerging Global Order' in Wang Gungwu and Zheng Yongnian, China and the New International Order (Routledge, 2008).

Suisheng ZHAO is Professor and Executive Director of the Center for China-U.S. Cooperation at Graduate School of International Studies, University of Denver. He is the founder and editor of the *Journal of Contemporary China*, a member of the Board of Governors of the U.S. Committee of the Council for Security Cooperation in the Asia Pacific (USCSCAP), a member of National Committee on U.S.-China Relations, and a honorary adjunct professor at Beijing University, Renmin University and Fudan University. He received a Ph.D. degree in Political Science from the University of California-San Diego. He is the author and editor of nine books. His most recent books are: *China and the United States, Cooperation and Competition in Northeast Asia* (Palgrave/Macmillion, 2009), *China-U.S. Relations Transformed: Perspectives and Strategic Interactions* (Routledge, 2008), and *Debating Political Reform in China: Rule of Law versus Democratization* (M. E. Sharpe, 2006). His articles have appeared in *Political Science Quarterly*, *The Wilson Quarterly, Washington Quarterly, International Politik, The China Quarterly, World Affairs*, *Asian Survey*, *Asian Affairs*, *Journal of Democracy, Pacific Affairs,* and elsewhere.

Zhiqun ZHU is currently MacArthur Chair in East Asian Politics and Associate Professor of Political Science and International Relations at Bucknell University in Pennsylvania. He was previously Assistant Professor and then Associate Professor and Chair of International Political Economy and Diplomacy at University of Bridgeport, Connecticut. He received a Ph.D. in Political Science from University of South Carolina in 2003. Professor Zhu's teaching and research interests include international relations theory, East Asian political economy, and Chinese foreign policy. He is the author of *U.S.-China Relations in the 21st Century: Power Transition and Peace* (Routledge, 2006), and is working on a manuscript about China's new diplomacy in the developing world. His research articles have appeared in *Asian Perspective, Global Economic Review, Journal of International and Area Studies, Journal of Asia-Pacific Affairs, Journal of Chinese Political Science,* and *Yale Journal of International Affairs.*